THE FILM
in History

THE FILM
in History

Restaging the Past

———◆———

PIERRE SORLIN

BASIL BLACKWELL · OXFORD

First published 1980 by
Basil Blackwell Publisher
5 Alfred Street
Oxford OX1 4HB England

British Library Cataloguing in Publication Data

    Sorlin, Pierre
    The film in history.
    1. Historical films—Case studies
    2. Birth of a nation
    I. Title
    791.43'7   PN1995.9.H5
    ISBN 0-631-19510-6

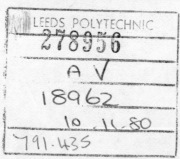
Typeset by Cotswold Typesetting Ltd., Gloucester.
Printed in Great Britain by
Redwood Burn Ltd., Trowbridge & Esher.
Trowbridge & Esher.

Contents

III. THE HISTORY OF YESTERDAY

Foreword

In Michaelmas Term 1976 I was asked to lecture on cinema and history at St Antony's College, Oxford. I had already lectured on the same topic in Cambridge and in London, and I was aware of British work on the subject. I decided therefore to adopt a rather different view.

English scholars, when teaching history, take films into account far more than their French counterparts do. But I think that there is a gap in the otherwise impressive multi-dimensional approach of the British. Academics in Britain have a sound knowledge of 'factual' films – those films which supply information – but they very rarely deal with films based on fiction. Let me take as an example two excellent primers on the subject: D. J. Wenden's *The Birth of the Movies* (London, 1975) and Paul Smith's *The Historian and Film* (London, 1976). Wenden abandons the notion of a conventional 'movie history' and instead places the cinema, as entertainment, in its social and economic context; Paul Smith and his contributors, on the other hand, discuss the problems involved in collecting, restoring, criticising and editing film material. In both works, 'fiction' films receive scant attention: Wenden emphasizes context rather than film, while in the Smith anthology, the lone chapter on fictional film comes from a French writer.

Why are the French more concerned with fiction than the British? With government support, the British documentary film industry has produced literally hundreds of films dealing with various aspects of English life and work. France has produced relatively few documentaries but, rightly or wrongly, its fiction films have generated far greater interest than British films in the same genre. While the British are said to be pragmatic in their approach, the French adopt a more theoretical stance, using documentary film as part of new 'compilation' work and seeing almost limitless analytical possibilities in fiction film itself. Theories on film – greatly appreciated in France – excite only a weak response in Britain. Comparisons of this sort are endless, but they do not explain the important differences: the English like to understand *what* films say, what they communicate; the French are more interested in how they say it, and how they can be understood. In my lectures, I decided to redress the balance in British film studies.

In term time, I had to restrict my lectures to a few general questions; as it was my intention to capture the interest of historians, and send them rushing to the cinema, I decided to grapple with the transposition of history into film and with the problems of film analysis. Both of these questions are developed later, but the difficulties I encountered in the course of my lectures proved that I had not been precise enough in formulating the problem. I will therefore begin with a brief outline of the subject.

After having spent many hours of careful work in archives in search of historical evidence, historians often think that their conception of history is the only valid one. Very few of them accept that what they regard as historical truth has nothing in common with what other people think of as truth. Here, we are going to analyse 'historical films', and the first thing we must do is forget, as far as possible, everything we know about the periods dealt with: thereafter we will be able to understand what the people who made these films, and the people who saw them, thought of as 'history'. The focus of our work will be *The Birth of a Nation*. The people who made it, and most of the people who saw it, regarded it as exact history. Lilian Gish, one of the stars of the film, said that the makers had 'restaged many moments of history with complete fidelity to them'; a reviewer wrote: 'History repeats itself upon the screen with a realism that is maddening'.

At last, history was revealed: such an enthusiasm seems to me to be extremely interesting. How can we explain it? The producers of *The Birth of a Nation* were very proud of having reconstructed the Ford Theatre precisely as it was on the day Lincoln was killed. For them, obviously, pictures, unlike words, could not lie. Griffith, the director, asserted that in the libraries of the future, history books would be replaced by films: 'Instead of consulting all the authorities . . . and ending bewildered . . . you will actually see what happened. There will be no opinions expressed. You will merely be present at the making of history.' Speaking of historical film, he said: 'In the film play we show the actual occurrence . . . If your story traverses to a battlefield we show an actual battlefield . . . . We show you the scene as realistically as if you were looking down from a hilltop and watching an engagement of contending forces.' But the producers were not satisfied with merely restaging 'the events as they had occurred': they quoted the work of an historian, Th. W. Wilson's *History of the American People*. Far from despising 'professional' history, the filmmakers were happy to base their work on an authoritative source. Those who have looked at Wilson's *History* will know what the producers were able to find in it. The chapter on the period of reconstruction, for example, confines itself to generalities: 'The real figures of the ruin wrought no man could get at. Men saw with their own eyes what was going on at their own doors. . . . . It was there that the policy of the congressional leaders wrought its perfect wake of fear, demoralization, disgust and social revolution.' Griffith and his cast were convinced that they knew the history of the civil war as it had happened and not as it had been distorted by politicians. The film could not be anything but the truth.

Historians who tried to list the historical inaccuracies in *The Birth of a Nation* would be ignoring the fact that their job should not involve bestowing marks for accuracy, but describing how men living at a certain time understood their own history. An historical film can be puzzling for a scholar: everything that he considers history is ignored; everything he sees on the screen is, in his opinion, pure imagination. But at the same time it is important to examine the difference between history as it is written by the specialist and history as it is received by the non-specialist. In choosing historical films I hope to encourage my readers to reflect on the use of historical understanding in the life of a society.

As far as the cinema is concerned, the problem of presenting history overlaps with another question. Talking about a film is easy: looking at it is far more difficult, as it implies that we are able to notice and to remember everything that appears on the screen. But even a single photograph contains so much information that we cannot hope to see everything, even if we look at it for a long time. We generally choose what I would call 'a comprehensive viewpoint', by which I mean a more or less precise interest which focuses our attention, our understanding, on certain details. We see a picture only by selecting and building significant shapes *in* the picture, using information we have collected. When a friend shows us a photograph of his country cottage, for example, we might try – generally without even knowing it – to grasp details which illuminate what we already know, or think we know, of the friend's life-style. We could probably do the same thing with a television broadcast. Imagine a short television film with a 'non-directive interpre- tation' – a series of shots without a commentary, deprived of explicit purpose, in which each viewer could discover relations and junctures determined largely by his or her interests at that moment. There are no films of this sort, of course, but making and programming them would not be difficult. They do not exist because television programmes are kept in a frame shaped by the first years of the film industry and maintained since then.

I think it is a social fact of extreme importance that we have become accustomed to follow a 'leading thread' while watching a film, so that we would find it difficult if not disagreeable to watch 'non-directive' films. In retrospect, it seems obvious that film could not have evolved in any other way. The history of film is often presented as a slow progress towards the style of film we are familiar with today: as one historian put it, during the early years of film-making 'films were simple staged events lacking in the effective manipulations of dramatization', and now usually considered to be poor films. Films could perhaps have developed other styles, but the need for narrative guidelines dominated the film world from the start. Even documentaries were conceived and filmed in order to express a dominant idea, either with a semi-fictionalized approach or with a strong ideological bias. Grierson, who had an enormous influence on the British documentary film industry, stated that a film should persuade, be focusing on an idea or a demonstration. In the late 1920s, a young Russian director, Pudovkin, wrote a hand- book on film which is of interest because it was the work of a film-maker at the end of the silent era, involved in the 'left wing' of the Russian film industry, who was allowed at that time to experiment with anything he felt to be of interest. We can see that his main preoccupation was to lead – one might almost say condition – his audience:

> When we approach a given, real image, we must spend a definite effort and time upon it, in advancing from the general to the particular, in intensifying our attention to the point at which we begin to remark and apprehend details. By the process of editing the film removes, eliminates this effort. . . .When a spectator is dealing with actuality he can overcome them only by a given effort of attention. . . . The film spares this work . . . and endows the spectator with the energy preserved.

In clearer terms the writer of a new television handbook writes: 'The viewer's attention should be focused on the subject most important to the story at any given moment – this is an essence of cinematography. . . . The gaze of the viewer should be drawn to the intended subject or centre of interest in every scene through the design of its visual elements.'

When looking at a film, we cannot help focusing on the story; we are obliged to choose one thread and to concentrate our impressions and feelings on this thread. For the most part, books and reviews on the cinema are no more than reflections on the narrative and the characters portrayed. I am not saying that the story is unimportant, but it is no more important than any other means of expression (colours, shapes, movements, editing, sound, music, etc.) which, taken together, make up a film. Because we have been conditioned by a long tradition, I felt it was important to emphasize those other means of expression in order to persuade my Oxford audience to look at film in a different way.

I had decided to discuss two main points, citing numerous examples and giving appropriate definitions. I arrived in Oxford with a suitcase full of evidence, the greater part of which was never used. I have been told that my first lecture was a long and tedious speech. In France, my audience would have been politely appreciative and probably rather bored. This was not the case in England. In the two days that followed I received numerous telephone calls and visits, and my friends (my new friends, for I had known them for only two days) advised me not to go on in the same way. Abandoning the lectures, I entered into a lively, difficult but interesting debate with the audience. This book will try to give the evidence on which I based my analysis and the substance of the discussion which followed.

During our meetings, we first looked at the film in question. I then gave my interpretation, taking stills directly from the print to prove my point, and placing special emphasis on the process of editing. In a book, that approach is obviously impossible. Many of my readers will not have seen the films I am going to discuss. I therefore think it necessary to give a brief account of the story before making any comments on the film in question. In the course of a lecture, an audience can interrupt in order to ask questions or raise objections: it is not unusual to spend hours discussing one film. Again, this is obviously not the case in a book. I have therefore enlarged the number of case studies in the hope that at least one of the films will be familiar. In each case, my objective is the same: to understand how, why and for what purpose the past has been and is still restaged by the cinema.

I would like to thank all those who helped me, particularly the British Film Institute in London, the Centro Sperimentale di Cinematografia of Rome, the Cinémathèque universitaire in Paris, who allowed me to study the films; St Antony's College and Dr Theodore Zeldin, who invited me to Oxford; Tony Aldgate, François Garçon, Michel Lobelle, Ann Osborn, Vera Schuster, David Stafford, Kenneth Short, Charles Wenden, who attended my Monday evening lectures and obliged me to transform them into a series of discussions; and finally, Anne Beech, John Edgeler and Peter Hamilton, who corrected my English text.

Acknowledgements

Plate I   The eyewitness photograph of the Russian Revolution is reproduced by courtesy of Irène Sorlin and the same scene, as portrayed in *October*, by courtesy of *l'Avant-Scène*, Paris.

Plate II   Four scenes of racial tension in *The Birth of a Nation* are reproduced by courtesy of *l'Avant-Scène*, Paris.

Plate III   On the American Civil War, the three scenes from *The Birth of a Nation* are reproduced by courtesy of *l'Avant-Scène*, Paris, and the one from *Gone with the Wind* by courtesy of the National Film Archive/Stills Library, London.

Plate IV   Two scenes from *Long Live Italy* are reproduced by courtesy of the National Film Archive/Stills Library, London.

Plate V   Two scenes from *The Leopard* are reproduced by courtesy of *l'Avant-Scène*, Paris.

Plate VI   Three scenes from *October* are reproduced by courtesy of *l'Avant-Scène*, Paris.

Plate VII   Three scenes from *The End of Saint Petersburg* are reproduced by courtesy of the National Film Archive/Stills Library, London.

Plate VIII   Two scenes from *Rome: Open City* are reproduced by courtesy of *l'Avant-Scène*, Paris.

Plates are to be found between pages 82 and 83

I
Principles and Methods

1

How to Look at an 'Historical' Film

I must first ask my readers to be patient. Before studying the films themselves – which are, I admit, the most exciting part of our work – we must first specify the methods to be used and define the subject of our interest, which is, roughly speaking, the study of the cinema considered as a document of social history that, without neglecting the political or economic base, aims primarily at illuminating the way in which individuals and groups of people understand their own time. We will of course return to the ideas I am discussing here, but I would like to warn the reader that I am describing research which is still in progress, a stage in working out a method; I shall give very few final results, I shall ask questions to which there can be no reply and I shall point out problems for which I can find no solution.

The audiovisual age

Audiovisual material – by which I mean material that reaches the senses and establishes communication through a combination of moving pictures and sounds, particularly television and the cinema – is a part of our daily life. It is a source of much of our knowledge, information and entertainment. But as historians, we demand very little of it. The cinema is barely ninety years old, although it has drawn considerable crowds since the beginning of the century; there are few places in the world

3

today where television is unknown. And yet, until 1960, audio-visual material was almost completely neglected by historians. At the most, they dealt with it in a few paragraphs on art and culture. For reasons which are worth examining, historians have stressed the artistic aspect of cinema, failing to speculate on its documentary value, its possible influence in moulding opinion or its interest as an historical source.

In 1960, or thereabouts, the situation began to change: we now have cinema periodicals specially intended for historians, we have established organizations like the Slade,[1] and a number of universities have developed courses on audiovisual studies. I believe that television is at the root of this change. Historical documentaries are an inexpensive and convenient way of filling screen time. As editing and the addition of a commentary are usually all that is needed, a programme built up of old films involves on average one tenth of the cost of a television play. Successful series like *World at War* have exposed the public to an unfamiliar type of history – visual history, designed to strike by its evidence and through immediate contact, instead of convincing through reason and deduction.

The integration of film into the material used by historians is not the result of deliberate choice: filmed documents have been imposed on historians through the use made of them by non-specialists or by specialists with no training in history. A comparison with written sources might be useful. All over Europe, scholars have collected and corrected texts relating to antiquity and the Middle Ages. Historians were on their own territory: no one disputed their right to work on the manuscripts, and they realized that if they did not complete the task a large proportion of the documents were in danger of disappearing. The effort to construct a positive history, respectful of its sources, is inseparable from the discovery and publication of the texts on which that history is based.

If we turn to audiovisual material, I think we can distinguish three new features which completely alter the situation. First, historians have no monopoly over the material, nor are they alone in studying and disseminating it. For example, television has made most of the interesting material relating to the Second World War widely available. In this respect, the historian's task is no longer to compile otherwise unknown sources and make them available to all: he must learn instead to use material that is already widely available. If the scholars of the past had not accomplished their enormous task, there would be no positive history, no 'scientific' history. But if historians today neglect audiovisual material, it will exist in spite of them as a history through pictures. Furthermore, the public will lose all interest in specialists, and the specialists themselves will be in a curiously divided position, conducting their research shut away in libraries, but turning to television when they want information on the present. Historians must take an interest in the audiovisual world, if they are not to become schizophrenics, rejected by society as the representatives of an outmoded erudition.

This introduces the second point, that access to filmed records is very expensive. If we had to pay to consult Roman inscriptions or medieval documents, and pay again if we quoted them, historical publications would be few in number, and historiography would become the privilege of a few public foundations and wealthy individuals. We cannot discuss the cinema without bringing up the central question of money. As there is heavy demand, due mainly to the requirements of television, the film companies charge high prices. We have to make do with one film, when for the purposes of comparison we would prefer to use ten. In this book, we are going to discuss a number of films, but if the reader were to see them all it would prove to be an expensive undertaking. I hope that my accounts will suffice.

We can read a text once and then discuss it; we are all used to this kind of exercise. With a film it is more difficult: we are trained to read, rather than to watch. And here we come to the third point. Hitherto, the historian produced a new text after having read existing documents. In both, the medium of expression was the same – language. Cinema, however, although it too uses language, can manage without it. There are many films in which not a single word is spoken. In any case, when language is used in the cinema, it forms part of a whole: the raw material of cinematic expression is an indissoluble combination of picture, movement and sound. Anyone who is interested in the audiovisual – historian or otherwise – must translate a system with several components into a system with only one – language. Starting from pictures, he must produce a written text. It is an unsatisfactory method, and I accept that in writing this book, I place myself and my readers in a rather absurd position: it is difficult for us to obtain the necessary material, and we do not quite know how to use it. I am convinced that before the end of the century we will use another film medium, video, to express our feelings about cinema film. So why embark on an unsatisfactory study that will be out of date in twenty or thirty years? For the moment, we have no alternative: we must begin somewhere, and we can argue that getting used to pictures no doubt begins with getting used to reading.

We will not be considering the whole of world cinema, of course, and I would like to explain the choices I have made. I have chosen 1960 as *a cut-off point*, when television had become a common-place in nearly every country in the world and when light, inexpensive recording equipment became more generally available, at least in the West. If we were concerned only with the United States, we would naturally have to go back to 1950, whereas in other countries 1970 might have been a more appropriate date at which to end the study: 1960 is taken as an average boundary. Before then, television was of only slight importance and audiovisual material was limited to the use made of it in the motion picture industry: film equipment was cumbersome and expensive; only a few companies used it for specific purposes, which we will discuss later. Production was restricted to a few, select circles, and an inventory of the audiovisual film output of the pre-1960 period would be a brief one: most of the existing material on the Second World War, for example, has been located.

Since 1960, the television companies have been filming constantly to provide programme material. The availability of small cameras and video means that companies, political groups and private individuals have recorded on literally miles of film or tape. To take only one example: three years after the *coup d'état* in Chile there were at least three feature films and several short films on the failure of the 'Union Popular' and the events of September. We know not only the official truth – elections, parliamentary debates, speeches, processions – but we also have filmed records of dozens of incidents unknown to the press – the occupation of land, the shopkeepers' strike, confrontations between workers and lorry drivers and arrests made by the army in September and October. Of Hitler's accession to power, the cinema shows us only the official version – Hitler in the Reichstag, the screaming crowd in the streets, the enthusiasm of the victors. There exist only a few photographs of the hunting down of opponents, the prisons, and the first concentration camps, whereas we have several hours of film on the internment camps in Chile. The history of the American involvement in the Vietnam War, the *coup d'état* in Chile or the Portugese Revolution will be known through audiovisual records as much as through written ones, but an inventory of this material will first have to be drawn up, and this will need lengthy research by international teams. We have not yet reached this stage.

In short, we have a stage of limited development in the evolution of audiovisual material, followed by a stage of ultra-rapid expansion. We will restrict ourselves in this book to the first stage, which is the only one for which we can achieve a fairly clear general view. For this period, the exploratory research and archive work is well advanced. The Slade Film History Register can be consulted by subject (mines, strikes, bombing, etc.) or by period. In addition to newsreels, all British films stored in the National Film Archive are listed in a printed catalogue and the catalogue of the other films is available on demand.

How films are made

At this point, it would perhaps be useful to summarize what a motion picture is, from a material point of view. Everybody knows this as well as I do, but we must agree on the technical terms we are to use. A motion picture is first of all a strip of film on which frames are printed; during filming, as during projection, the number of frames filmed or projected is constant for a given period, generally twenty-four frames per second. The filming begins when the motor is switched on, and the sequence of frames taken continuously, without stopping the motor, is called a shot. When a cameraman comes to the end of a reel he has the raw material of a film; several consecutive shots which may have no connection with one another. The film is constructed when some passages are cut out of certain shots, and shots that the director wishes to bring together, for reasons of

7

completion or contrast, are spliced end to end. This is the editing. Several related shots, for instance showing the arrival of a person who gets off a plane, into a car, and drives away, form a sequence.

❦ It is essential to bear these points in mind if we are to understand what kind of document we are working with. It is very rare to find raw material – a shot as it was filmed by the cameraman: most if the films we see have been edited. It is impossible to reconstruct the originals, because what is not used is nearly always thrown away, for lack of room. But you must not imagine that what has disappeared was of great value: in most cases the cameraman responsible for filming an event, such as the opening of an exhibition by the king, took three times more than was necessary to be sure of having clear pictures, in which the king and the people welcoming him were easily recognizable. The problem for the historian is not that shots have been eliminated, but that what he sees is the result of a subjective choice, where the effect of editing is involved, that is, the influence that the different shots making up a sequence have on one another. On top of this, since 1930, there is the further problem of the sound track. We must remember that before magnetic recording came into general use, sound recording was an extremely delicate operation, requiring complex, cumbersome equipment. Speeches were recorded easily, because the speaker did not move, but in the previous example an enormous effort would have been needed to follow the king as he walked through the exhibition, speaking to different people. Nobody thought it was worth taking the trouble. In spite of appearances, the cinema before 1960 consists of silent films to which sound has been added. In the sequence of the royal visit, vague crowd noises, voices, applause and a commentary were added later. When we watch such a film, we are conscious of an atmosphere, and we feel a sense of involvement, but the sound effects, which play a large part in our impression, are artificial and have nothing to do with the scene that was filmed. Let us try to make a comparison: there is a great difference between a telex from a news agency reporting an event and a comment on this event in *The Times* or the *Guardian*. Exactly the same thing is being dealt with, but the article develops, shifts and modifies it. There is an even greater transformation between the filmed shot and the shaping through

8

editing and the addition of sound effects. In most cases we know only the finished version of filmed events.

So I propose to make a first distinction between the filmed document as raw material, and the film which gives an interpretation, a particular point of view. I am stressing this difference because it is generally ignored in studies of the cinema. A classification should be made among films; several studies, in particular the article by Roads on film as historical evidence,[2] have laid down rules for this and I do not think it is necessary to repeat here what you can easily find elsewhere if you are interested. Suffice to emphasize the difference between information films and feature films.

They can first be contrasted by stressing that the very great majority of feature films are fictional; the few exceptions, like Walt Disney's films on the desert, and documentaries on the sea, and on animals, are not very important. Information films are directly connected with the world of social relations, certain aspects of which they claim to reveal. To borrow a term from semiotics, we will say that they have a referent. For instance, it is decided to film a race that should interest the public. The purpose is the contest; the film of course shows only a few aspects, interpreted by the shooting and the editing, and transformed by sound effects. But the film exists only in relation to its pretext, and if we want to study it we must compare it with the referent. A fictional film is its own event; technicians and actors have been brought together, and for several weeks they have formed a social group, the manifestation of which is a long strip of film. The motion picture is both the cause and the result, it has no referent.

This involves a great difference in the way in which the audience is addressed. An information film seeks the best viewpoint of the event, the clearest picture; it concentrates entirely on the scenes and the people to be shown. A fictional film has less need of clarity and precision, but as it refers to nothing other than itself it must grip the audience, making them participate actively, guess what is not shown, and feel sympathy or repulsion with what is happening on the screen. Brecht has explained perfectly the justification and function of this phenomenon of identification; he studied it mainly in the theatre, and we shall have to make a closer examination of the mechanisms

9

by means of which the feature film involves the audience.

On the one hand we have the feature film, often unrelated to current events, and in any case conceived as a self-contained work, an enclosed universe; on the other hand, we have the information film which is only a kind of relay, a reflection that is no doubt distorted but that was originally based on direct observation of an event. It would seem that for the historian the information film is the preferred audiovisual document, the one from which he can get most. From sources of this latter type the British Inter-University History Film Consortium has made five very interesting films on the years between 1936 and 1940 (*The Munich Crisis: The End of Illusions; From Munich to Dunkirk; The Spanish Civil War; The Winter War in its European Context; Neville Chamberlain*) and the Open University has edited the *War and Society* series.[4] I am nevertheless going to criticise this kind of document. My proposition is that the information film is of undoubted but extremely narrow value, and that for the period we are dealing with, that is, for the years *before 1960*, the most original source is the fictional film.

Moving, talking newspapers: the newsreels

Newsreels were born with the cinema: in 1896 or 1897, Dickson in the United States and Lumière in France were filming scenes of daily life. Until about 1910, cinema shows had no programme; people went without knowing what they would see, just to watch moving pictures. The performances were short, and included about ten items, a·mixture of newsreels and fictional scenes. Even at that time, the principal market was already the United States. In Europe cinemas were open only a few hours a day, whereas in the United States the nickelodeons, which started in 1905, were so popular that within five years there were nearly 10,000 of them, open from morning till night; programmes changed daily, which meant that there was a considerable demand for films to renew the shows.[5] For technical reasons, mainly because they owned the patents, the market was dominated by a few companies – Edison, Biograph and Pathé. In 1908, they came to an agreement and founded the Motion Picture Patents Company which had a monopoly of production and sales in the United States. Pathé dealt particularly with newsreels; this company already had subsidiaries in most European countries, and to supply this vast circuit the company sent cameramen all over the world to make films that could be shown equally well in Russia or in England, and in the East or the West of the United States. The dominance of a company which supplied an extremely diverse clientele set a model for newsreels at the beginning of the century. This pattern did not change until 1960 and remains unchanged in countries like Italy where newsreels are still shown in cinemas.

There are various reasons for this permanence. Let us briefly mention some technical considerations, although these are not the main factor. Those of you who have used a cine-camera know how difficult panning is – swivelling the camera to follow a moving object – if a tripod is not used. The exploits of Buster Keaton in *The Cameraman*, following the stages of a gigantic fight step by step, would be almost impossible with the light-weight equipment available today; it was out of the question with the old cameras, which were far too heavy. In addition, emulsions were slow, and filming was only possible in a good light. For a film to be successful, it was advisable to choose a good position, set up the equipment beforehand, and wait for sufficient light; so the simplest thing was to film events announced in advance such as exhibitions, sporting contests and military parades. If there was a violent demonstration or a fight, the still photographers took a few snaps and the cine-cameramen arrived when it was all over.

But we must take into account other phenomena, with which historical research is directly concerned.

The first important question is the organization of the film industry and its position with regard to the public. The habit of going to the cinema spread remarkably quickly in the West, from the first decade of the century. Twentieth-century historians seem to forget that the film was a perfectly common information vector well before the First World War. In his articles, which I recommend you to read,[6] N. Pronay has shown that no English newspaper ever reached a public comparable with that of the newsreels, which were seen every week by more than half the population of Great Britain during the 1930s.[7] The newspapers have their public, whose characteristics

11

they approximately know, and for whom they adapt their style. Newsreel producers[8] do not know whom they are addressing; the same films are shown in a small agricultural town, a working-class suburb, and the West End, depending on the distribution circuit, so they have to try to please everyone.

We know the instructions given to Gaumont-British cameramen – give priority to traditional events, festivities and sport; when abroad, do not miss either official ceremonies or events in which the English are involved.

People dealing in news items and entertainment in other media often take care not to offend their public but the fear of shocking the audience never seems as acute as it is in the cinema. Film-makers have always avoided what might annoy their audience, using a self-imposed censorship to avoid any kind of 'excess'. Just before the First World War, the British Cinematograph Exhibitors' Association, fearing the loss of a part of its audience, urged the Association of Kinematograph Manufacturers to establish a system of censorship: a British Board of Film Censors was established in January 1913. The film-makers were not obliged to refer their films to this new private institution but it became more and more difficult to find cinemas ready to show a film without the certificate delivered by the Board. The cinema had created its own limits.

The big European cinema networks, of which Pathé was the best example, did not survive the First World War. After 1920 they broke up into national companies and the market was taken over by the US firms, which were now the most powerful. For their sales abroad, and for their purchases of foreign films, almost all the producers went through the United States. The circuits had changed, but the old rules endured – to reach every social group within any one country, to satisfy audiences in very different countries, to concentrate on a few well-defined fields of interest which people had become accustomed to since the earliest newsreels.

We must also take into account a conception of news which places the event in the foreground. As historians, we should wonder how, in each period, the public is informed of current events; for reasons that we do not have time to analyse, we should note a tendency in the late nineteenth and early twentieth centuries, to put the emphasis on exceptional facts, which can

12

be dated precisely and described in a few words or a few pictures. An attempt was made in the cinema to develop magazines dealing with a single subject, but they had little success and filmed news which was almost entirely limited to a series of brief, superficial glimpses of a small number of events.

Excellent studies have already been made of US[9] and British newsreels, and I will therefore deal more with German films. The Bundesarchiv collection in Coblenz is far from complete for the period of the 1920s, but the period from 1929 to 1932 is covered more satisfactorily. There, we would expect to find material on the German crisis, unemployment, rioting, the rise of the Nazi organizations, but in fact newsreels made during this time are no different from those of previous years, and remarkably similar to newsreels produced in other European countries in their general conception. Sport is prominent, appearing weekly and frequently taking up more than half of the programme. Regional festivities featuring dancing, costume and music appear to be the next most popular subject, followed by film of official ceremonies. The crisis is mentioned only indirectly and coverage of politics is confined to what might be called 'recognized' circumstances – elections, inaugurations, visits of foreign dignitaries.

Documents of this sort are of only limited value, although they are not entirely worthless. They invite an interesting comparison with the concerns of the written media in 1932. The newspapers of the period continually refer to the rise of Hitler: if we took them as our only source, we might deduce that the Germans were interested in nothing but politics. Newsreels counterbalance this impression, reminding us that the economic and political crisis overlay ordinary activities without affecting them. The same Germans who, through political meetings and the newspapers, lived in a state of permanent tension, found their country apparently unchanged when viewing newsreels at the cinema.

Filmed news was never intended to cover developments over a long period; it deals only with particular facts, occurring at a definite point.[10] It is at its best when dealing with diplomatic agitation, military preparedness or the effects of war.[11] Hardly surprisingly, the five British Inter-University History Film Consortium films all deal with the origins or the early years of the

13

Second World War, three of them focusing entirely on the fighting. The material gives us a good idea of what was at stake (such as the strategic importance of Madrid), the conditions in which fighting took place (winter in Finland), the rival forces and the principal battles.

Newsreels themselves are questionable as pieces of evidence. What can be gleaned from an analysis of them? John Grenville[12] proposes a distinction between primary and secondary evidence, giving as an example the Gaumont-British special feature on the Munich Conference and Chamberlain's return to Great Britain. The film gives us very little information on the diplomatic discussions themselves: here it provides only secondary evidence. But it gives primary, direct evidence in the sequence showing Chamberlain reading a report on the results of the Conference. Primary evidence of this sort, however, is hardly very useful. Newspapers published the report in full, and in this respect the film made no great contribution to the evidence already available elsewhere. I think we must see the film in a rather different light. The film shows Chamberlain being driven home along a road lined with crowds. The people raise their arms and the soundtrack records long shouts of applause. The evidence here is secondary rather than primary. The film-makers wanted to show that the British people supported Chamberlain's policy and that they were prepared to unite in support of their leader. The British film-makers were in fact imitating their German counterparts. Interestingly enough, the same film footage was re-edited in France for French audiences, with the French Prime Minister Daladier taking the place of Chamberlain. In the English version, Chamberlain's return is featured prominently: in the French film, Daladier's return is dealt with much more briefly. Knowing that newsreels are composed entirely of shots chosen to produce a desired effect, and with a completely fabricated soundtrack, we should not conclude that the British were more satisfied with the results of the Munich Conference than the French were. All we can say is that the film-makers themselves had two completely different sets of objectives. Films tell us all we need to know about the policies and opinions of their makers, and no more, but as we are aware of the importance of newsreels in influencing opinion, we must also understand what those policies and opinions were.

14

Newsreels show the world as film-makers would like to see it, as is obvious in their choice of topics and even more apparent in the style of the various sequences. In spite of its brevity, every part of a weekly newsreel can be edited in various ways.[13] Official ceremonies, for example, are described in suitably solemn manner. The Prince of Wales visits allotments given to poor country people: we see the Prince arriving, speaking, smiling, digging, cutting corn. His exploits are not of intrinsic interest and might even be described as faintly ludicrous, but the film-makers were interested in making the point that the Prince was prepared to try. Today, we can learn little of value about the Prince of Wales from the film, but we can at least gain some information about rural life in the 1930s by examing the faces of the ordinary people ranged behind him in the film.[14] Another reel[15] covers the street fights between Communists and fascists in London: a few brief shots and a shouted commentary make both demonstrations appear shocking and offensive.

We are obliged to treat newsreels as 'distorted' or rather as 'directed' images of society. Events that were of little importance at the time are endowed with a greater significance through repetition. Penelope Houston underlines this point: 'Look at enough news film and one begins to feel that the most constant image of the 1930s is of a mounted police charge into an unarmed street crowd. But I realise, as I write this, how little real idea I have of the facts. How often was this scene actually enacted, in London, or Paris, or Madrid, or Berlin? How far is it an impression gained from well deployed screen use of a few unfailingly dramatic shots?'[16] Newsreels give us a highly selective view: if we want to use newsreels as evidence we must expose the concealed rules governing that selectivity.

Newsreels illustrate diplomatic and military history, but they might also be useful in another way if we were prepared to consider them as ethnographical documents.[17] If we look, for example, at film of German crowds leaving a stadium, and if we ignore the clothes, the uniforms and the surroundings and consider only the mannerisms, the way of walking, the priority given to women and children, the composition of the groups, we are presented with a number of interesting details. We can guess that half a century ago, social life modelled behaviour in very different ways, but we lack the means to prove it. In this

15

respect, films are a potentially useful source of evidence, but perhaps we are still too close to the period and should leave research of this sort to the historians of the twenty-first century.

Imagine that a catastrophe destroyed all newspapers everywhere with the sole exception of *Life* magazine; who would dare to use this sole source as a basis for writing history? What happens with newsreels is rather like that. This is not an imperfection peculiar to the cinema, but a situation connected with the production and distribution of newsreels in the first half of the twentieth century. This fact must be acknowledged, and we must limit the use of news films to the restricted field for which they are suitable, and look elsewhere – in fact to feature films – for an instrument for research.

History and historiography

Up to now we have discussed the relationship between the cinema and historical research as though the purpose of this research was obvious to everyone. I am not sure that we are in complete agreement on this point, and before considering the use of feature films I think it is essential to make it clear, at least as far as I am concerned, how I see the historian's work.

In the first stage, history is an attempt to clarify – to sort out what is probable from what is false, to establish the chronology of events, to show the relationships between them, to detect periods of strong social or political tension and define their characteristics. We can call this positive history, the methods of which were devised two centuries ago and have lost none of their value. Today we must go beyond this stage. We know that history is a society's memory of its past, and that the functioning of this memory depends on the situation in which the society finds itself. Out of the almost infinite mass of incidents and encounters which perpetually occur, a certain number are identified and described, and in this way become fixed as events, particular moments, the memory of which will be passed down and adopted by later generations. Sometimes it is a matter of chance whether a name or date stands out or disappears, but we should not attach too much importance to this. The essential part of what remains was made to be kept; even if we restrict

16

ourselves to material traces, we find what was built to last – the towns, the houses of the powerful, the palaces. Our task is not only to reconstitute the past; we must also understand how, and according to what interest, the bases of our future documentation accumulated. We must realise that our work is largely conditioned by the organization of the period in which we are interested.

Most societies, at any rate Western societies, create their history as they evolve. And in these societies certain groups, social classes, political parties and socio-professional communities define their own version of the past. To clarify matters, we will use the word 'historiography' to refer to the work of historians (or any other people) based, in principle at least, on all the available documents, and we will call the descriptions proposed by the groups belonging to the same society 'historical traditions'. I will make this clearer by an example that I would like you to bear in mind. In the second part of this book, we shall be working on Russian films about the October revolution. In Russia it has always been the rule to refer to history and particularly to the experience of the revolution; before the opposition was crushed by Stalin, it defined its position, against the party leaders in terms of its own version of the events of 1917. The conflicting trends in the Bolshevik Party were marked by revisions of the previously accepted historical traditions. Today, now that the opposition is re-appearing, it presents the reassessment of October and the period of Lenin as an essential stage. The Russian example is particularly obvious, but the same phenomenon can be found in many other countries.

The historical tradition defended by each group and class is of course only an instrument for talking about the present; the conflicts that divide a society, and the goals pursued by the opposing forces, are transposed in the semblance of past events. So I think that historiography – the history of history – is the ideal instrument for approaching the study of the problems that are current concerns in a society and for understanding the picture it has of its future.

I now come to what seems to me the second aspect of historical research – an aspect complementary to and inseparable from positive research. With the methods available to us – defining the socio-economic base, analysing production methods

17

and yields, studying quantitative data – we describe a period or a social sphere from the outside. But our research remains firmly rooted outside its object unless we can go beyond our scientific problematics and try to discover how the society we are dealing with defined itself, how it interpreted its own situation.

Let us return to the example of Soviet Russia. For a decade, the Bolshevik Party was simply not strong enough to administer a country of that size without some additional support, and so the Bolsheviks recreated a precariously privileged class in the form of a vast bureaucracy. Half a century later, we can now see this process as a whole, and we can begin to understand its significance and the various stages in its evolution; we must now discover how those who were involved in the process understood it, and the extent to which their actions were guided by their perceptions. In research of this kind, the greatest obstacle is the dearth of documentary evidence. The leaders of a political struggle have of course left their own accounts of the period, but how can we discover the point of view of those who did not write in newspapers or speak at congresses, but who nevertheless had an important part to play in a period of open struggle? At this point, we must turn to other material, including feature films.

Not all films are of equal interest, however, and we will first of all discount mass-produced imitations of an earlier success, on the grounds that these simply cashed in on a fashionable and popular theme. Mass production would be of interest if we were studying public reaction, but that is not our concern here.

On the other hand, the success of a new film must be taken into account, although I admit that this criterion is a very ambiguous one: bad films can be transformed by good publicity and vice versa, but we have no other method of assessment. We can measure the size of audiences and the length of runs, and this will give us a rough index of the correspondence between the message of a particular film and certain public expectations of that film.

We will also consider the character of a film. Nearly all films refer, if indirectly, to current events, but references of this sort are frequently obscure. For reasons of economy, we will concentrate on overtly political films. In view of what we have

18

said about the importance of historical traditions, I think it would repay our interest to analyse historical films in which we have a chance of finding a view of the present embedded within a picture of the past. Finally, I have chosen films produced during periods of tension, rather than those that were released in a period of relative calm.

To sum up, I would therefore propose four rules for selection: the originality of a film, its relationship to current events, its favourable reception by the public and the fact of its being produced and distributed during a time of crisis. On this basis, we could analyse several films from the same period (those films made on the tenth anniversary of the Russian Revolution in 1927, for example), but as we are attempting a comprehensive view, rather than an exhaustive one, I think it would be best to select a number of different examples, rather than restrict our choice to films made at a certain time. In 1914–15, for example, when war broke out in Europe, very few historical films were made, and yet *La Marseillaise*, *La Grande Illusion* and *Gone with the Wind* were all made at the time of the Spanish Civil War, when the signs of German and Japanese agression were first apparent and war seemed imminent. Not all historical films were exceptional: many of them were mass-produced. In studying the film I have selected, I will say why I consider it to be original, why it can be classified as an historical film, what kind of reception it had, and – because we are concerned with 'history in film' rather than 'film in contemporary history' – with the period covered in the film itself, rather than the period at which it was made.

What is an 'historical' film?

Before beginning the individual analyses, I think it is essential to raise a few general questions about the nature of the historical film and the methods of research already in use.

When we want to characterize a film briefly, we try to isolate the features it has in common with other films, so that it can be classified as a type. Most of the types that we are familiar with – westerns, thrillers, comedies, science fiction, horror – developed within the world of the cinema, despite their literary origins,

19

and they no longer exist except as cinematic types. The peculiarity of historical films is that they are defined according to a discipline that is completely outside the cinema; in fact there is no special term to describe them, and when we speak of them we refer both to the cinema and to history. This is a point that should be of interest to historians: it would seem that audiences recognize the existence of a system of knowledge that is already clearly defined – historical knowledge, from which film-makers take their material.

A spectator watching an unfamiliar film can type-cast it within minutes. In the case of the historical film, what are the signs by which it can be recognized as such? There must be details, not necessarily many of them, to set the action in a period which the audience unhesitatingly places in the past – not a vague past but a past considered as historical. The cultural heritage of every country and every community includes dates, events and characters known to all members of that community. This common basis is what we might call the group's 'historical capital', and it is enough to select a few details from this for the audience to know that it is watching an historical film and to place it, at least approximately. When the period is less well known, or does not belong to the common heritage, then the film must clearly stress the historical nature of the events.

A well known American film, *Intolerance*, illustrates both these processes. The film consists of four stories, three of them taking place in the past and one in the present, which are shown alternately rather than in chronological sequence. Two episodes, the life of Christ and the religious wars of the sixteenth century, are easily recognizable: they can be identified by the costumes, the attitudes, famous scenes and occasionally portraits. But one of the episodes is set in ancient Babylon, a period virtually unknown to audiences, so the film provides abundant detail to establish the period, informing the audience that a certain object was found during excavations, that a particular custom is described in Greek or Babylonian texts. By compensating for the gaps in the audience's knowledge, it emphasizes the historical nature of what is shown.

What I think is important in both cases is the understanding that is formed, with no difficulty, between the film-makers and the audience: for both, something real and unquestionable exists, something which definitely happened and which is history. The contingent aspect of the historical tradition, with which historians are deeply concerned, is completely ignored by the producers of historical films. It must be said that this type of film is not an historical work: even if it appears to show the truth, it in no way claims to reproduce the past accurately. So I think that when professional historians wonder about the mistakes made in an historical film, they are worrying about a meaningless question. They would do better to concentrate on other problems.

We have noted some of the methods by which a film identifies itself as historical and allows the audience to find its bearings. In this way every historical film is an indicator of a country's basic historical culture, its historical capital. Which characters do not even have to be introduced, which have at least to be named, and which need to have some details given about them? What scenes, meetings and events are recognized unhesitatingly? When, and on what points, do explanations have to be given? Behind the common knowledge, we can detect what is much more important: the underlying logic of history. What facts does the film select? How does it develop them? What connections does it show between them? The historical film is a dissertation about history which does not question its subject – here it differs from the work of the historian – but which establishes relationships between facts and offers a more or less superficial view of them. The understanding of historical mechanisms as developed in the cinema is another field for our research.

~ Historical films are all fictional. By this I mean that even if they are based on records, they have to reconstruct in a purely imaginary way the greater part of what they show. Scenery and costumes similar to those of the period represented can be based on texts and pictures, but the actors alone are responsible for the gestures, expressions and intonations. Most historical films (though not all – this does not apply to *October*) combine actual events and completely fictitious individual episodes. It is very seldom that a film does not pass from the general to the particular, and arouse interest by concentrating on personal cases; this is one of the most direct forms of the appeal to identification, an appeal which is in fact not specific to the cinema. Fiction and history react constantly on one another, and it is impossible to

21

study the second if the first is ignored. The same type of analysis can be applied to an historical film as to any feature film.

Every film has its own 'history'

When we begin the study of a film, the first question that arises is which document to use. Some of my readers may undertake research in this field, and I would draw their attention to this point. A film is analysed from a copy, but a copy is not like a book; it always has a career and sometimes a history. Its career is the use that has been made of it previously; a copy wears out and gets torn, and to repair it the damaged parts are removed. Before a film is shown, its condition should be checked, and any cuts noted, so that the missing passages can be replaced from another copy. But this is a comparatively minor thing. We must also realize that many production companies print copies for the domestic market (domestic prints) and copies suited to foreign audiences (foreign prints). We must always bear in mind the origin of the print used and the audience it was intended for. The essential thing is the history, in other words the way in which the film has been marked by the political variations of its time. Many films that we are going to study have undergone important alterations. For some of them there are no more than the scissors of the censor to account for and things are quite simple: for a long time *La Grande Illusion* was shown without the passage in which a German woman and a French soldier live together; the original version was not restored until 1958. With *October* and *The Birth of a Nation* things are far more complicated. I think it useful to give some information on the subject. Erudition is only the first and by no means the most interesting stage in the study of films, but it is absolutely necessary because all too often people discuss a film without knowing they have seen completely different films with the same title.

October was filmed and edited in a few months, at the end of 1927. In many of the authoritative studies of the Soviet cinema the film is said to have suffered cuts in a number of scenes because they dealt with Trotsky. That is not true; Trotsky played a very small role in the original print: the shots showing him were cut out but their omission only shortened the film by a few minutes. The cut shots were not burnt, as had been done for those cut in *The Birth of a Nation*; instead, the cut scenes were deposited in the Moscow film archive. The film, in its first version, was shown for several months in Russia after its release. However, audiences found it somewhat disappointing; the general impressions were that it was too difficult to follow and too intellectual. As a result the film was stored away and forgotten. A German company, which had acquired a print, finding it too long and subversive, made a concise version and sold it under a title borrowed from John Reed's book, *Ten Days that Shook the World*. In 1966, the Russians took the first version out of storage and sold it to Western companies. As the Western newspapers, even the communist ones, had given the film good reviews, the government decided that the film was a useful propaganda vehicle in Soviet Russia and abroad; but *October* was still said to be too difficult for 'average people' and another, shorter, re-edited version was assembled: all the subtitles were modified;[18] and the sequences in which oppositions were used (one photograph followed by the same photograph horizontally reversed; when Kerenski is endlessly climbing the steps of the Winter Palace inversions are extremely important in emphasizing his helplessness) were simplified. As we shall see later, the time scale is broken up: in the second part of the film, night and day constantly overlap one another; the 1967 version tries to 'restore' the chronology by editing first the day shots and then the night shots.[19]

Here again things are simple: it is not difficult to ask which of the three different versions is going to be shown. Nobody can tell us where a print of *The Birth of a Nation* comes from. It is well known that the original 13,500 feet version, which showed the negroes in a hostile, racist manner, was strongly criticized; the producers cut out 500 feet which have never been recovered.[20] In the following years the film was projected all over the United States; depending on the audience, the distributors[21] sometimes shortened the copy, sometimes altered the editing, sometimes added, cut out and modified subtitles. The producers themselves made changes[22] and in 1930, Griffith himself issued a new short sound version.[23] It is impossible today to say which is the original print or how many prints are in distribution.

My conclusion on that point will be extremely clear: you must never study a film without referring to the origin of the print you have seen.

Problems of interpretation: from Kracauer to the present

Only what is relatively important politically is censored, and here we find another indication for measuring the popularity of films. When we follow the career of the prints, and reconstitute the original, we are again only doing a job of pure erudition, to which the methods of positive historical research are well suited. The uncertainty begins when we try to read and to interpret the film. Historians seem to experience a particular difficulty in this field. Thirty years ago, two books by Kracauer, *From Caligari to Hitler: A Psychological History of the German Film* (1947) and *Nature of Film. The Redemption of Physical Reality* (1961), opened the way to a sociology of the cinema, but they were not followed up. In spite of their inadequacies we are still compelled to quote from them. Kracauer developed two different points of view, which are not contradictory, but for which he proposed no synthesis. In *Nature of Film* he tried to show that feature films are realistic, in spite of their fictional character: 'Film is uniquely equipped to record and reveal physical reality and, hence, gravitates towards it. . . . The only reality we are concerned with is actually existing physical reality – the transitory world we live in.'[24] If we ignore the plot and the characters, we discover aspects of life which the camera has recorded all the more accurately because the cameraman did not even notice them. Take a film like *The Servant.* Today we are interested in the story and we think the setting unimportant, but in a hundred years time historians will find in it valuable information about dress, homes, public places and relationships in London in the middle of the twentieth century. This is what I have called the ethnographical aspect of the cinema; Kracauer was right to draw attention to it, to show that it changes according to the period and the director and points out that certain social spheres are often shown while others, such as the country and factories, are forgotten. Looked at in this way, films are only a series of documentary illustrations;

24

the frames remain, but the film disappears as a system of expression with a specific character. As it is difficult to work with film, for material reasons, and as there are very good collections of stills in the archives, it is possible to avoid the cinema altogether, if this is all we expect from it.

Kracauer also drew a parallel between the unhealthy atmosphere in the German cinema in the 1920s and the political situation under the Weimar Republic. There is certainly a connection between the two, but the author does not show where it lies; he underlines a few major trends in the cinema – mysticism, a feeling for nature and an exaltation of the irrational – that he also finds in Nazi propaganda, but this parallel, which is sometimes forced, proves nothing. Starting from an interesting intuition, Kracauer was content to give brief impressions, never really analysing the material of the cinema and never wondering what links there were between films and the society which produces them. I will return to these questions later.

Since 1960 there have been studies of individual films, but I know of only one attempt at a methodological synthesis – a work written by six Danish historians, *Film Analyses. History in Film*. As the book raises important questions, I will discuss it at some length.[25]

The authors look at films in relation to the historical and social circumstances in which they were produced. They think that while all films reflect a background reality, this reality is not directly reflected but rather transformed by a series of processes. The book begins with an outline of the socio-historical position, and then analyses twenty-three films produced in the United States and Western Europe in the fifty years since the end of the First World War, beginning with Lang's *Doctor Mabuse* (1922) and ending with *The Godfather* (1971).

The authors argue that during this period, the rise and crises of US capitalism have forced the entire world into a ceaseless motion called development, which has destroyed the old social order. As capital tended towards an even greater concentration, independent producers were reduced to the status of wage-earners: 'The centralizing tendency of capitalism and *proletarianization* of independent producers led to a new world where

25

self-sufficiency has been abolished, a world strange and threatening for those who based their way of life on self-sufficiency.'

Most people who work in the film industry are wage-earners, but their situation is such that they are in many ways placed in the same position as independent producers – whether they sell their products, if they are writers, freelance journalists, musicians – or whether they are allowed enough freedom in their work that they become less conscious of the economic background determining it. 'The intellectuals are to a high degree in the same position as the *proletarianized* independent producers but the mainly immaterial characteristics of intellectual work can lead to a concealment of the economic circumstances in which it takes place, so that there is in this work process the basis for a mixture of real insight and mystification.' Films are not a direct reflection of reality, but give a distorted image of society, restricting social conflicts to a limited environment, transferring from the social to the individual plane and arbitrarily shaped by the conventions of the genre.

Let us look at John Ford's *Stagecoach* as an example of the most widespread types of distortion. First, some social conflicts are transposed and take place in the framework of a mini-society, a small, closed universe. Secondly, the subject matter of social conflict is transposed to the personal, individual level; the hero's problems with agriculture and the break-up of the family (remember that the film was produced in 1939: its social background is the economic depression of the 1930s) are seen as being caused by personal conflicts between the hero and certain wicked individuals. When these conflicts are resolved, the hero can return to his farm and restore the family idyll. Thirdly, *Stagecoach* is a western; the course of events proceeds within the limits of the conventions of a particular genre which requires a fixed organization of the story material.

The general approach in *Film Analyses* is at least an advance on Kracauer. The latter never separates a film from its 'author'; he imagines that a film, like a book or a painting, has a single creator whose biography throws light on his creations. The Danes realize that such a notion cannot really be applied to the cinema: a film is always made by a team. To a large extent a writer or a painter is an independent producer: he does not need to find a publisher or a dealer until he has completed his work. But film-makers have to find financiers before they can begin, and during shooting they are constantly making compromises with the actors and technicians. The director is a leader and an arbiter, but he has nothing of the author; for reasons of convenience his name may be attached to the title of the film, but the details of his life cannot be used as elements for an explanation. If we want to put films back into their context, which is very important, we must consider the circuit as a whole – the financing, the shooting and the distribution. Kracauer also has a tendency to tell the story of the film, to concentrate on the scenario, and to comment on the psychology of the characters. The Danes, on the other hand, try to get away from fiction, and, beneath the anecdote, to discover the hidden expression of social conflict.

In spite of this progress, I see two serious objections. The first concerns the connection made between the background and the film. The socio-historical analysis in *Film Analyses* seems to me a little too simple; even if it were taken further, the technique of defining a model and then trying to find proof of it in films is still not a very satisfactory method. With this procedure, we are sure to find at the end only what was postulated at the outset. The twenty-three studies lead to constantly recurring conclusions: the middle class is more and more threatened with losing its freedom, and independent work is giving way before monopolies. This book, as I have said, covers half a century of the cinema in the United States and Europe: if, over fifty years, thousands of films have only repeated the same thing, dealing with the cinema is a waste of time.

In logic, when we are trying to classify terms, it serves no purpose if we have a category into which all the items can be placed, because it allows no distinction to be made. The same applies to an explanatory model which does not show the differences between films. Instead of describing society and then seeing how it is transposed to the cinema, we should move in the opposite direction – start with the films, study their specific characters, group together those which have features in common and separate those which are different, even on secondary points. But such an analysis cannot be made simply by seeing the films; it demands a preparation that many commentators prefer to dispense with.

27

Film-making and film-analysis

How are films made and produced? News items or events or even a novel, or the biography of an important person might suggest suitable themes: the film-maker's first job is to write a short account of the subject and to present it for a producer. This simple, untechnical plan is called a *treatment*: Renoir and his scriptwriter wrote several unused treatments for *La Grande Illusion* and one of them is easy to get hold of:[26] it is quite different from the final film. If a producer and a group of actors are interested in the scheme, the director or the scriptwriter rewrites the text in order to give a full list of shots, described in their order, with stage directions and technical terms clearly marked; this is the scenario. There is a good scenario of *October* written by Eisenstein himself[27] but, once again, it is far removed from the three finished versions of the films we can see today. It is difficult to put into practice what was decided beforehand and important alterations occur in the course of production. Two examples illustrate the point. One of the most spectacular effects of *October* is the opening of the main bridge of Petrograd; the carcass of a dead white horse, which is slowly raised with the bridge, eventually falls into the water; the scene was not even in the original scenario and was introduced later on: one morning, whilst filming another scene, the director, seeing the opened bridge on the sky-line, decided to include its slow and irresistible motion in the film and to dramatize it by adding a carcass.[28] *La Grande Illusion* ends with two French prisoners of war escaping from the camp through snow, mud and cold. The snow, which produces a very impressive effect, was not in the scenario; it had snowed just before the sequence was shot and the quite accidental effect of snow enhanced the mood of the scene.

Another difficulty may arise from the novel that the film was inspired by. It is tempting to make a study of the transposition of the written text to the screen, to list differences and likenesses, to dwell on the novel and on its relationship with the film, in a word, to take into account the sources. It is well known that the subject of *The Birth of a Nation* was suggested by two novels by the Reverend Thomas Dixon;[29] many apparently unnecessary or secondary details can be easily explained by referring to these books; for instance, the scene where Ben Cameron, injured, is visited by Elsie in hospital, follows the book closely, which explains why it is so long; we are then told that the same character is to be executed 'on a false charge' but we do not know what this charge is: the book is more precise; the military surgeon tells Ben's friend that the young man was 'sentenced by court-martial as a guerilla. It's a lie, but there's some powerful hand back of it'.[30] The novel is less ambiguous than the film, but, as we shall see later, this lack of precision about the causes of events was one of the salient features of the film;[31] the film itself was greatly admired in spite of its vagueness.

If we were interested in the process of film-making it would be important to compare the novels and the scenarios with the film. If we only want to study the films in their final form, however, as they were shown to the public, if we are asking what the films show us about their period, such comparisons are less relevant. Publishers print 'the text' of some films; one must bear in mind that there is an enormous gap between a shot-analysis and dialogue: dialogue only gives the cues, the spoken part of the film; the book published with the title *Grande Illusion* is not very useful because it does not include information on centring, motions, stage management or editing. On the contrary Theodore Huff did very well when he described the making of *The Birth of a Nation* giving, shot by shot, any necessary information on shooting, staging and editing:[32] although it is rather a good work, I think the writer did not pay enough attention to the changes which were made from one print to another – especially from the silent to the sound version – and I prefer to use a more comprehensive analysis.[33]

A film is not simply a story played out by actors, even if the plot and characters are very important. It is also a series of shots which exert an influence through their content and through their relationship with one another. Again, it is a succession of information through language and, in sound films, a musical accompaniment and sound effects. When we first look at a film, we react to certain particular aspects of the picture. If we try to explain our feelings, we can find that our remarks are misunderstood or that they are not intelligible to others. One reason for this lack of precision is that in discussing our feelings about a film, we fail to provide enough detail to

29

expand and substantiate our comments. Feelings are rarely a particularly useful basis for discussion or argument. If we want to argue about films – and as historians we have to argue about documents – we must begin with a description of what we are arguing about, namely films. Of course, the particular, specifically emotional quality of a film is only in part reducible to words and sentences. A description is no more than a brief discussion document. Semiologists would describe it, barbarically, as a meta-text, by which they mean another text, a by-product of the first, rewritten in terms which enable historians to understand one another. A meta-text enables us to gauge the importance of data like style, shooting and editing. Many people maintain that a verbal description of this sort merely stifles intuitive creation and comprehension. They may be right but they miss the point completely. Intellectual, theoretical research is an abstraction: if we want to understand a film, we must ignore its presence; if we want to discuss it, we must isolate it and examine it from a distance. Objective consideration of this sort is probably less satisfying than pure, unalloyed 'feeling', but at least it can form the basis of further discussion.

A filmed story and its constituent images cause us to react with approval or disapproval. We accept what we have seen or we reject it, and after the performance we all enjoy discussing what we felt. I have often observed that audiences are disturbed by the portrait of negroes in *The Birth of a Nation*, and that they react with very violent criticism. Too many discussions on the cinema consist only of obvious remarks and hasty judgements. It is easy to say that *The Birth of a Nation* is a racist film which condones lynching and violence. This may be true, but it is far too obvious a comment to serve any purpose. If we want to understand the reason for this racism, and its place in American life, we cannot be content with such general remarks. We must get a grip on the film, and to do so we must analyse it more deeply.

Many essays on the cinema try to assess the meaning of a film in terms of the director's purpose. In my opinion, a film *has* no meaning, and we should not be concerned with the purpose of the film-maker. As both of these statements are highly contentious, I will try to make them more precise.

On the question of meaning, I would say that a film does not *necessarily* demonstrate anything. If it does make a point, it does so in such an obvious way that it is simply not very interesting. *The Birth of a Nation*, for example, suggested that blacks were a threat to the South and that the Ku Klux Klan were right to attack them. This point is made perfectly clear in the film, and we would waste valuable time in discussing it further. A film shows various things, and poses many questions. We cannot hope to find and clarify them all. We must choose a middle way between discussing the obvious and losing ourselves in a maze of largely unanswerable questions.

What about following the director's intentions? Griffith certainly had a purpose in filming the American Civil War, and we can study what he wanted to 'explain' and why he used particular details in his film. But Griffith is not the film. If we wanted to write his biography, we would have to decide to what extent his life and his experience are involved in his films. But he did not make the film single-handed: many older and younger people from all over the United States worked with him and had an effect on the film. And the thousands of Americans who saw the film and enthused over it did not care about Griffith's 'purpose'. *The Birth of a Nation* was a milestone in Griffith's life, but to the extent that we regard the film as a document of social history, we are concerned only with analysing the finished work and studying its effects.

History in 'historical' films

One film mixes together a lot of information. Some of it is shaped by the cultural habits of a period or society: some of it is new and unfamiliar. Put together, old and new make the film; as far as we are concerned, it is important to know how details, notations and pictures react upon one another. A film is made in more than one way; there are many connections, each of them structuring the whole of a film or a part of it, sometimes only one sequence. A good method for examining a film in detail is to take one or two themes and see how they are treated throughout the film. For us, history provides a convenient starting point. What is shown of it? Are the 'historical' scenes long and detailed or short and imprecise? How are they edited?

31

Most books and reviews on the subject of history in film compare the events shown in film with a written description of those same events, but such an approach is ineffective. What should we compare? The history of the American Civil War as we now know it and a film of the war made in 1914? It would be an absurd comparison. We are in a position to see many things and relations which were unsuspected at the time: after the black revolt of the 1960s and 1970s we do not look at American blacks as people did before the First World War. We must, instead, compare the film with the version of history given at the time, but in 1914 there were many versions of the war, many accounts, none of them with a monopoly on the truth. *The Birth of a Nation* is one such account, no more or less so than any other book or film. If we were studying an historical text written at the same time, we would not compare it with the film version to see if it was true. We would instead try to understand the political logic of the account given in the book, asking why it emphasized this question, that event, rather than others. We should keep the same preoccupation in mind when analysing films.

As my argument is rather theoretical, I will give an example. Take Austin Stoneman, a character in *The Birth of a Nation*. We can try to identify him by looking beyond the film to the House of Representatives, where a parliamentary leader called Thaddeus Stevens had considerable influence during the Civil War and in the period of Reconstruction. During the war, Stevens was an aggressive extremist: in 1864 he spoke of the need to 'exterminate' the rebels, and at the end of the war he urged the President to reduce the South to a 'territorial condition'. In this respect, the character of Stoneman closely resembles Stevens – but I would add that such a conclusion is not particularly interesting. Stoneman or Stevens – what is the difference? Let us go further: if we want to deal with the 'context', our comparison should not stop there. In many ways, Stoneman and Stevens are very different. Stevens was elected in 1848, whereas Stoneman was 'rising to power' in 1860; Stevens never married, whereas Stoneman had two children; Stevens never visited the South, whereas Stoneman travelled there 'to see his policies carried out at first hand'. More important, Stevens's close friend, Charles Sumner, supported the same

32

programme and was one of the senators whose hostility towards the South wrecked Johnson's and Lincoln's policies. In *The Birth of a Nation*, Sumner urges a less dangerous policy in advocating extension of power to the newly free negroes.

Stevens or not Stevens? We cannot decide. Why is this so? We will have to accept that it is impossible to list all the characteristics of class, group and character given in the film. We can enumerate some qualities, but we can never be sure that we have exhausted the possibilities or that we have grasped the relevance of a particular quality. Is it important that Stoneman was married, or that he very often remained seated when speaking to other people? We cannot answer that without putting Stoneman – or any other character – into a system of mutual relations. Most phenomena are only inadequately described if they are analysed piece by piece. The appearance of any element depends on its place and its function in the pattern as a whole. The shots do not simply stand 'additively' next to each other, but assume quite different shades of meaning through this juxtaposition. Our vision does not involve mechanically recording the elements, but grasping significant structural patterns.

I know that the word 'structure' is anathema for many historians. Structural analysis is not a pure formalism, nor a self-sufficient system: the structures do not exist by themselves, at least when we are working on a limited object like a film; they are conceptual models which help us in describing the organization and mutual relations of a particular complex whole. The structural analysis begins by discovering opposing principles (Stoneman as anti-Lincoln, for example) and goes on to emphasize the process of development of the opposed characters, groups or alliances.[34]

In 'reading' a film, we must make a detailed examination, on the screen and more slowly on the viewing table, of all the elements in a film, to assess material and to see how it stands in relation to other material. At this stage we must ask: what is happening? How does it work? What is the film stressing? What fictional mechanisms is the film using, and behind them what social mechanisms are concealed? It is not a matter of 'explaining' the film, nor of finding out what the film 'means'. Under the unifying veneer of the story, multiple threads run through a film, some of them vanishing immediately, while others are developed at length. Analysis must draw out this multiplicity, showing that several approaches are possible to any one film.

Next, we must ask whose ideas are being expressed through the film, and for whom it is intended. Comparisons will be made between producers (financiers, studio executives, intellectuals) and consumers (the audience, and in a sense the whole of society), stressing the points of agreement and the conflicts.

In the course of this book I will give few results; at present, our main task is to define a method and try it out. We will not get much further than that in an introductory work.

Notes

1. 'In January 1969 the Slade Film History Register started to comb the film collections systematically for material of use in the study of the twentieth century . . . The main selection criterion was to include every newsreel item ("story") which related to personalities (politicians, statesmen, inventors, artists and "ordinary people") who made news, events (wars, strikes and elections) and subject themes (aircraft development, welfare services, economics, women and society, fascism, etc.) . . . Selections were based on the issue sheets of the newsreel companies and their accessions registers, together with additional information from any catalogues which existed, shot sheets, and the viewing of some of the material.' ('The Slade Film History Register' in Frances Torp (ed.), *A Directory of British Film and Television Libraries*, London, 1975). The lack of finance resulted in the closure of the Register at the end of 1975; its files can be consulted at the British Universities Film Council, 72 Dean Street, London.

2. C. H. Roads, 'Film as historical evidence', *Journal of the Society of Archivists*, 1966, p. 183. See also R. M. Barsam, *Nonfiction Films*, London, 1974, chapter 1 and William Hughes, 'The evaluation of film as evidence', *The Historian and Film*, London, 1976, chapter III.

3. Created in 1967, the British Inter-University History Film Consortium comprises the history departments of the Universities of Birmingham, Edinburgh, Leeds, Nottingham, Reading, the London School of Economics and Political Science, Queen Mary College, London. See John Grenville, 'The historian as film-maker,' in *The Historian and Film*, chapter 7 and Tony Aldgate, 'The production of "Spanish Civil War" ' in *University Vision*, 1974, 11,

34

p. 16 and 12, p. 42, and Tony Aldgate, *Cinema and History, British Newsreels and the Spanish Civil War*, London, 1979.
4. The third-year history course 'War and Society', prepared by the Open University, includes 32 lectures. Students receive, alternately, one radio programme every fortnight and one TV programme every fortnight. The 16 TV programmes comprise, for instance, 'The social consequences of World War II,' 'The Afro-American and World War II,' 'Guerilla Warfare in Algeria'. See Arthur Marwick, 'Film in university teaching' in *The Historian and Film*, chapter 8 and *Archive Film. Compilation Booklet*, The Open University, 1973.
5. 'Today it would be hard to find a nickelodeon in the country that is not furnishing a change of program every day. In some instances...two changes a day are offered.' *Views and Film Index*, 28 December 1907, in Lewis Jacobs, *The Rise of American Film*, New York, 1939, p. 53.
6. Nicholas Pronay, 'British newsreels in the 1930s,' *History*, 1971, p. 411 and 1972, p. 63.
7. 'By 1934 the circulation figure for the cinema was already 43% of the [British] population [excluding the young people] . . . In 1938–39 over half the population, excluding the very young, saw each week what was communicated by means of the screen.' Pronay, ibid., 1971, pp. 412–13. See also Aldgate, *Cinema and History*, p. 54 ff.
8. Gaumont-British, Movietone, Pathé, Paramount, Universal.
9. R. Fielding, *The American Newsreel*, Norman, University of Oklahoma Press, 1972.
10. According to N. Pronay, the newsreels were very popular among the working class for their 'personification of political issues and their directly personal style; by way of contrast the cult of impersonality adopted by the BBC and by the documentaries appealed to the middle class'. Pronay, 'British newsreels in the 1930s', 1972, p. 69.
11. 'The newsreels of the 1930s belonged much more to the world of journalism than to the film world.' Ibid., p. 63. See Aldgate p. 34 ff.
12. J. A. S. Grenville, *Film as History. The Nature of Film Evidence*, University of Birmingham, 1971.
13. We cannot agree with N. Pronay (1972) when he says, 'The "stories" were constructed to move as fast as possible . . . The professed reason for this technique was to cut before anyone in the audience became bored. It was, however, also another way of saying 'cut' before anyone could have had a chance of going over the story again in his mind . . . Much the same applied to the sound tracks: the points were made to sink in through speed, loudness and repetition.' Ibid., p. 63.
14. British Movietone News, 24 April 1933, included in the Open University programme quoted in note 17, below. See 'Great Britain 1750–

1950: Sources and Historiography', The Open University, 1974, p. 16.
15. British Paramount News, issue no. 664, 8 July 1937: 4. 'Blackshirts and Reds clash'.
16. Penelope Houston, 'The nature of the evidence', *Sight and Sound*, 1967, vol. 36, no. 2, p. 91.
17. By selecting some short sequences devoted to precise aspects of social life and editing them the Open University had opened this field; its programmes on 'Images of the working class in films of the Thirties' and 'Slum clearance' used feature films, newsreels and documentaries. The OU's television programmes have been drastically reduced by lack of money.
18. Alterations often give information on what is supposed to be understandable for an 'average citizen' in 1967. For instance the first subtitle, which was originally 'February' has been completed by a caption telling the audience that February was the first step in the Revolution!
19. Unfortunately the most common version, distributed by the BFI, is the last.
20. We can imagine what the cut shots were by reading some reviews written after the first screenings. For instance *The Moving Picture World* says: 'We are told both in pictures and in titles that African Slaves were brought to this country by Northern traders who sold them to the South. Puritan divines blessed the traffic, but when slave trading was no longer profitable to the North, the "traders of the seventeenth century became the abolitionists of the nineteenth century" ' (13 March 1915). This sequence was suppressed.
21. At that time a distributor acquired all the rights (including changes) for the whole of a State.
22. The second caption tells us: 'All pictures made under the personal direction of D. W. Griffith have the name "Griffith" in the border line . . . There is *no exception* to this rule'. It is easy to distinguish the captions written by the producers from those which were made by the distributors. Very often two or more different captions, having the name 'Griffith' in the border line are edited at the same place in different prints.
23. Billy Bitzer, Griffith's cameraman, writes: 'Ten years after the first showing, Mr Aitken [the producer] who still owned *The Birth of a Nation* consulted me and I deemed it best we insert film twins – two identical picture frames coupled where one had been. Thereby we doubled the original twelve reels to feed into the new, more rapid projector.' *B. Bitzer, His Story*, 1973, p. 112.
24. *Nature of Film* (reprinted in 1965 as *Theory of Film*), p. 28.
25. *Filmanalyser. Historien i Filmen* by Michael Bruun Andersen,

36

Torben Grodal, Søren Kjørup, Peter Larsen, Peter Madsen, Jørgen Poulsen, Copenhagen, 1974. Quotations taken from the introduction, translated by the authors.

26. See A. Bazin, *Jean Renoir*, New York, 1973, p. 172.

27. Sergei Eisenstein, *Three Films*, London, 1974.

28. Having given Eisenstein's account we may add that another film devoted to the Russian Revolution, *The End of St Petersburg*, which was shot during exactly the same period, includes some shots of the same opened bridge, which means either that one of the two directors (which one?) was influenced by the other or, more likely, that this bridge was seen as a symbol of the Romanovs' capital. With regard to the white horse, we must remember all the dead horses in Dostoevsky's novels. Bridge and horse are not mentioned in the original scenario of *October* (see n. 27). It is interesting to see they were 'spontaneously' added to the film during the shooting.

29. In 1915 many people thought that the 'author' was Dixon, the writer of the novels which Griffith drew his inspiration from. See *Fighting a Vicious Film*, Boston, 1915, a pamphlet against the picture in which the film is attributed to Dixon.

30. *The Clansman. An Historical Romance of the South* and *The Leopard's Spots. A Romance of the White Man's Burden, 1865–1900* whose epigram is very symptomatic: 'Can the Ethiopian change his skin or the leopard his spots?'

31. Below, p. 93–94.

32. Theodore Huff, *A Shot Analysis of D. W. Griffith's 'The Birth of a Nation'*. New York, 1961, p. 62.

33. 'Special Griffith', *L'Avant-scène du Cinéma*, 193/194, October 1977. All the captions are given in English.

34. In the lecture he delivered to the seventh Conference on History and the Audiovisual Media (München, September 1977), 'A structural analysis of the film "Sisimiut" with reference to an assessment of the applicability of semiotics in historical film research, Karsten Fledelius gave an excellent restatement of the question. The main objection is that the structural analysis is too time-consuming but it enables us 'to observe some patterns or "modes" of expression which seem to possess, several of them, some ideological values. Perhaps these were not realized by the film-maker, at least on the conscious level, but nevertheless they are there and they exert their influence on the message of the film as the potential of meaning is either narrowed or broadened by certain ways of building up the syntax of the film. In this way structural analysis becomes of fundamental value for the "close reading of the film – the sign analysis"' (p. 40). See also Karsten Fledelius, 'Film Analysis; the Structural Approach' in *Politics and the Media*, edited by M. J. Clark, Oxford-New York, 1979, p. 105–126.

II

The Events
as They Occurred

*The nineteenth century
pictured by the twentieth*

2
The Reference Periods

Historiography can be conceived of as a method rather than as a specific field of research. Men, countries, societies: we cannot know what the precise aims of historians are with regard to them because historiography has no object in itself. Writing the history of lands, events and institutions means putting them into a system which is, more than anything, a chronological system. Historiography is built upon a scale of time with a starting point, a graduation and an end. Provided that a convenient scale is being used, everything – the earth, a car driving along a street, William Shakespeare, the minutes we have lived through since this chapter began – is or could be an object for historical study. When reading books by historians of the nineteenth century, we immediately understand that history for them was not what it is for us and, consequently, their historiography was different from ours: in looking at political or diplomatic life, they used scales and starting points which do not work for the social or economic life with which we are concerned. Princess Anne's life – as far as it is related to its chronological development – is as 'historical' as the general evolution of Europe since the First World War. By common, tacit consent, the writer and his readers, the historian and his public, decide that the first and not the second subject (or vice versa) is worth telling. Film-makers are not labelled historians and cannot share experts' opinions; for our study – I must remind my readers that we are trying to define the conception of historical mechanisms as expressed in films – it is very important to determine what film-makers regarded as 'objects of historiography'. And that means that we should first examine the time scales used by them.

The beginning of national histories

The starting point is necessarily an artificially selected date; everybody knows that there are no 'breaks' in time and that 'periods' or 'ages' are never separated from previous 'epochs'. Once this commonplace assumption has been made, we must add that it is not absolutely true. *The Birth of a Nation* came out exactly half a century after the end of the Civil War and *La Marseillaise* a century and a half after the outbreak of the French Revolution. Was it just the right time in each case for an anniversary assessment? In the United States of 1915 or in the France of 1937, the Civil War and the Revolution were both moments in their respective histories, familiar to every native, and an already distant memory. At that time the most serious crises that the two countries had gone through were still, for most people, what we might call the original shock, the date used whenever a reference point to measure the past was needed. For us, the Second World War serves a similar purpose. In our way of speaking, 'since the war', is a ready-made expression, used even by those born long after the war. But there is a big difference between a specific starting point – revolution, civil war – and a more general one, such as the Second World War. Our common scale of time is more or less divided into three parts – distant periods, the twentieth century (wars, crises, dictatorships), the generation since the war. For a Frenchman or an American of the early twentieth century, the reference point was much more than a mere break in 'the march of the time', it was the symbol of a major split, the end of a wonderful, brotherly life for some people, the dawn of an egalitarian, democratic society for others. We are not concerned with deciding if such a transformation occurred either in 1789 or in 1866, but we must keep in mind that belief in a general, momentous upheaval.

During the nineteenth century and until the middle of the twentieth century, the Revolution was the 'highest common factor' for Frenchmen. Revolution was like a 'meta-language', a suitable yardstick against which one could measure everyone's position was in French political life. The right reproved and the left supported the Revolution, 'all in one piece', whereas Liberals preferred the 'good years' of the Revolution, before the Terror, and Bonapartists regarded the best of the period to be the rebuilding of the country by Napoleon. It was of course possible to select only a part of the Revolution; for instance, during the main part of the nineteenth century, both the left and the Bonapartists, although their views were poles apart on the form of government, thought that the men of the Revolution had carried out a good foreign policy in Europe.

In the United States, if opinions were less evenly divided, opposition between Republicans and Democrats coincided, to a large extent, with the border line between North and South with the result that many white people in the South, who were more conservative than Republicans, used to vote for Democratic candidates. The US cinema provides us with an example well suited to our general subject – the study of films as a source of social history. We will see that *The Birth of a Nation* marks an important change in the cinema industry in the United States, the point when a new generation took over from the pioneers. When studying the history of US films, I was struck by the lack of films dealing with the Civil War from the early beginnings of the cinema up to 1908.[1] I thought at the time that the pioneers, who were all born before the Civil War, did not want to look for the subject of a scenario in the crisis because the memories of that period were too vivid, whereas the younger film-makers, born after 1865 (I mean Griffith, Ince, Zukor, and so on) had no reason to avoid the subject. In her book, Lilian Gish tells us she did not know too much about the Civil War and had to read a lot before she understood what happened in the 1860s.[2] For me, that was a problem of generation. But let us look at the theatre. We find numerous plays devoted to the Civil War. An essay written on stage portrayal of the Civil War[3] shows us that, during the first two decades following the conflict the heroes were invariably Northerners, while the Southerners were made the villains. At the end of the century, soldiers on both sides are considered equally brave; very often the hero is a Northerner, the heroine a Southerner (or vice versa) and a conflict results between love and duty. At the beginning of the twentieth

43

century, the theatre concentrates on the suffering entailed in war-time. My hypothesis was wrong. The first, second and third generations after the Civil War were equally sensitive to the national tragedy and the pioneers of the cinema had no particular reason to avoid the subject. Why does a change occur around 1908–10? I suppose we must look at the audience. At first the films were regarded as a mindless spectacle, reserved for poor people and immigrants. Most of the films were meant to be understood by a non-American audience; they had no subtitles and were very simple stories. Immigrants would not be interested in the Civil War, which movies therefore avoided showing. But by 1910, more and more people, even native Americans, were interested in films. As it was necessary to find new dramatic subjects, the film-makers turned to national history. As refined, cultured people did not go to the cinema, scriptwriters could easily gain inspiration from the theatre; the films of the years 1908–14 have simply repeated the same themes used in plays fifteen or twenty years before: love and duty, love between North and South. In this sense, *The Birth of a Nation* is a very 'standard' product but, as we shall see later, there is in this film, eventually, no conflict – North and South are 'one and unique'. Can we speak of a conflict of generations? Possibly, but first of all we must consider the difference of social rank, the conflict between 'native' Americans, who knew 'their' history and, being rich, cultured people, went to the theatre – and the 'new' Americans, who, being ignorant of the national past, and with only modest incomes, were content to go to the cinema. We have here a collision between those who saw, on the stage, the up-to-date products of literature and those who were content with the products based on already obsolete plays. *The Birth of a Nation* was extremely important because, for the first time, old and new Americans attended an historical film dealing with national history. Around 1910 a great many Americans were in the mood for films treating of the Civil War and in referring to such a frame of mind we shall use the concept of 'readiness'. I propound an hypothesis that we shall examine later: an historical period cannot be pictured if audiences do not feel disposed (for reasons that are to be discussed) to take an interest in it.

France and the United States offer two examples of political self-definition with reference to the past. Instead of expressing views on the present time and the future evolution of society, people adopted attitudes and values appropriate to an out-of-date period. The thousands of immigrants who landed during the late nineteenth century were not concerned with the Civil War and that – together with capitalist growth, and the gap between local and federal problems – makes it difficult to compare the United States with France. However, it is worth considering what functions could be served for Americans by referring or not referring to the 'original shock'. Looking at films can give us some information on that point.

A comparison of the major countries of the Western world before the First World War tells us that some had a 'reference point' and some did not (for example, England and Spain). The processes by which historiography is broadcast, related, taught to children; the manner in which it is used to express or to conceal the questions of the day; the justifications taken from the past for keeping or overthrowing the institutions, constitute a central part of our study. And, in this context, we cannot ignore the basic divide between countries where people referred to a 'starting point' and countries in which the past was not focused on a specific date. We must add that such a distinction is too simple. Contemporary Italy offers a third possibility that could be described as the 'false reference point'. Italian political speeches constantly refer to the period of the 'Risorgimento'. The founding of the Kingdom was actually the beginning of a new nation, which did not exist before, whereas France and the United States already existed in 1788 and in 1860 respectively. But for the majority of Italians, 'unity' was an empty word. Italian towns and villages had been living for centuries under the distant domination of powers which, whether or not they originated in the Peninsula, were always foreign. The House of Savoy was as foreign as the Austrians or the Spanish and, being a new, modern, bureaucratic monarchy, it was able to make people pay and obey. In *The Mill on the River*, a miller, living in the recently annexed Lombardy region, opposes the taxes imposed by 'the damned Savoys' and eventually burns his mill, so as not to be accused of tax evasion. We cannot say that this film, which came out in 1949, showed that the Italian monarchy destroyed small, rural mills

45

in Lombardy but it does show that hostility towards the House of Savoy and its unifying policy remained strong even after the Republic had succeeded the monarchy. Only the intellectuals, the governing élite, used to refer constantly to the founding period. But in a country which did not have a universal franchise until 1913 and where two-thirds of the population were uneducated and had no opportunity to express their opinion, only speeches from the ruling class were heard. The Risorgimento was more important in European historiography than in the political self-definition of the Italian people.

Three traditions

We have identified three categories of relationship between a society and its reference period; the basic role of the referring period in defining and typifying political and ideological positions (for example, the French Revolution); the noticeable but limited function of the most important historical epoch (for example, the American Civil War); and the superficial and purely artificial significance of those periods which are habitually quoted (for example, the Italian Risorgimento). The scheme is by no means exhaustive; the referring period does not play the same role in every social group or every area – but we only want to emphasize a difference and point out how the past can be either still active or completely obsolete in a society.

Considering our classification, we might suppose there is a link between the social importance of the referring period and its 'invocation' in film. In fact, there is no direct connection. The film industry which is most interested in the national past is neither the French (strong relationship) nor the Italian (weak relationship), but the American one.

I take it, incidentally, that giving exact statistics is impossible; many of the films have been lost and we only know them from old catalogues; some were not even listed and, consequently, our estimate is necessarily approximate. That being the case, in what sense can we assume that a film deals with an historical period? A subtitle, a picture clearly representing a specific period, some words uttered by one of the characters (we shall return to the indications marking the historical nature of a film)

46

could indicate that the events, or some of the events, take place in the period concerned. This reference is often very superficial; many Italian films, particularly those made during the fascist era, are romantic, sentimental stories, with a vague historical background – but that imprecision is interesting in itself: why do people not want to show the Risorgimento and its problems in Mussolini's Italy? And, if they avoid giving precise information, what is the minimum required to make viewers understand that the film is devoted to events that happened during the Risorgimento?

From the earliest history of the cinema there have been about 800 American films on the Civil War as against 80 Italian films on the Risorgimento and 40 French films on the Revolution. It is difficult to compare the histories of these three film industries. Although the American film industry became increasingly powerful in the period after the First World War, outpacing the French and Italian industries within a short time, before 1914 both France and Italy were able to compete with the United States. Hence it is not irrelevant to our argument to compare the output of these three national film industries during the first two decades of the history of the cinema, a comparison which shows that some 400 American films were produced as against 30 Italian and 20 French films during the same period.

Most of these films are short stories with a main character who is first introduced, then placed in a perilous situation and eventually rescued or sacrificed. That short, succinct description is sufficient to discriminate between the three types of films. American films often run towards a happy ending whereas, in the European films, more often than not, their heroes are killed. Italians die as martyrs in the cause of Italy,[4] Frenchmen are victims of the Terror and we discover, at that point, a fresh distinction: Italian films do not introduce a political dimension: every Italian is supposed to like Italy and to be ready to lay down his life for unity. French films are, generally, politically oriented: the heroes side with the right or with the Liberals, against the revolutionary government. The years of the Revolution are seen as a period of crime and excess; although a few films take the monarchists' part, more often they show innocent people despatched to the guillotine. It is of some importance to note that French films rarely dealt with France's foreign wars. Even during the First World War, when extreme measures were taken in the name of patriotism and the cinema was used as a means of 'magnifying' the importance of France, no film was dedicated to the defence of the country in 1792–5 or to the liberation of oppressed nations by French armies, whereas Germany and Austria were constantly accused of oppressing Poland, Alsace and the slave minorities. The only two films[5] which deal with the army do not focus on war or enemies but recall the history of 'La Marseillaise', that song written by the young officer Rouget de Lisle, sung by soldiers travelling from the South of France to the front line, and adopted as the national anthem under the Third Republic. Here again, we must not miss the political significance of those two films: to a large extent, shooting La Marseillaise was making a 'republican' film against the monarchist ones.

By giving a general survey of both the French and Italian cinemas, in a very narrow, specific sector, we begin a major debate; I am drawing my readers' attention to this question, which is a little outside our subject, because I see here an original theme for research. It is generally admitted that French opinion, around 1910, accepted the coming war as unavoidable, whereas the majority of Italians did not want to go to war. Recent research shows that Frenchmen were not enthusiastic about war in 1914 but, for a few years, had been resigned to the prospect of mobilization. In Italy, the Socialist Party frankly opposed the war (in other countries, Socialists supported 'national unity') from start to finish and many Liberals and Catholics clamoured for immediate peace. Is it possible to say that there is no connection between cinema and opinions, attitudes, behaviour, that films do not 'influence' people? We should be cautious in making such an inference. In the Europe of 1914 there were many other more important media of information: speeches, newspapers, clubs, school, church and so on, each of them being relied upon as the most credible source on some topics within a more or less wide range of issues. There was (and there is still) no reason for every source to be connected with all the questions of the day and historians ought to pay particular attention to the omissions or contradictions which appear when they collate all the vehicles of information. Before the First World War, the cinema was not considered as a 'medium' affecting all social institutions and little control was exerted over it; the people involved in film-making produced only what they thought audiences would appreciate. We must emphasize that, as far as national history was concerned, French producers did not consider war as a suitable subject for the cinema, although Italian film-makers were of the opposite opinion. Our concept of 'readiness' helps us to understand what happened in the Italian studios; many Italians and especially the Italian working classes – which at that time were the most important part of the cinema audience – were not in the mood to become enthusiastic about the victories of the Risorgimento. Dramatic events and adventures were able to raise interest but, due to the prevalent anti-militarism, a critical view was taken of any film which glorified war or showed victorious soldiers as if that was the only important aspect of war; film-makers avoided the Risorgimento as a subject, as far as possible; when they had to deal with it, they tended to focus on the painful and distressing aspects of the conflicts and battles involved. There was certain 'readiness' to view important historical events in a particular light in France; both the French Revolution and the more general subject of war were viewed in a way that suggests another hypothesis: these two subjects were too important and too sharply defined not to provoke a violent reaction when they were screened. As we shall see later in studying *The Birth of a Nation*, filming a subject which has created political and social scandal is virtually impossible. Sociological theories on 'cognitive dissonance' may help us to understand the situation.[6] Going to a film show means, at the same time, to become a part of an unknown collectivity, to abandon oneself to pleasure and relaxation. People who go to a cinema do not want to undergo an initiation process in order to join the audience or to realize they are at variance with it: in other words, everything that puts an obstacle between the spectator and the screen is regarded as a source of annoyance; being isolated in darkness and ready for enjoyment, the audience will not tolerate being implicated in a controversy. The lack of consensus over the Revolution was so fundamental that it could not be eliminated or even minimized: the only way to avoid dissonance, in this very peculiar place that is a cinema, was to prevent such a topic from being screened.

But all that is purely negative – what films do not show – and we shall get a more positive view when we turn towards the US cinema. The large-scale reconstruction of famous battles was a speciality of the American studios at the beginning of the twentieth century; the naval encounter during which the Spanish fleet from Cuba was destroyed by the US fleet was reconstituted, entirely in the studio, so impressively that the Spanish Government bought a copy as a document; films about the Civil War all have battle scenes and the climax of one of them, *The Battle of Gettysburg*, is an immense cavalry charge. In the years just before the war, when it seemed imminent, a great many books were published trying to describe and assess what the coming war would be like. We must study this literature if we are to understand the state of mind in which governments and public opinion approached the crisis of 1914. In Europe, the cinema does not play an important part from this point of view; in the United States, on the other hand, a number of battles were shown on the screen before 1917. If we are to know what Americans knew of war, according to the films, we have to compare the filmed battles and to summarize the information the films gave us.

The characters and their point of view

The characters are the human beings who act in films. It is not necessary to emphasize the fact that, in 'classical' films, there exists a small cast of characters whose adventures are followed throughout the film; the cinema could use many other devices but it rarely does and we can take it for granted that in most ordinary films made in the Western world, the spectator will be presented with one or several heroes. The only factor in question is their identity.

For Italy, the answer is a simple one: the hero is Garibaldi.[7] Of course, there are many notable exceptions; the main characters are sometimes unknown people and, often, other less well-known leaders of the Risorgimento. However, Garibaldi and his followers, the 'Garibaldini', outnumber the others; five of the first ten films dealing with the Risorgimento are dedicated to Garibaldi or to his 'thousands'; of the four pictures on the same topic made between the end of the First World War and the introduction of sound, three show 'the hero of the two worlds'.[8] We shall study seven Italian films, four of which include Garibaldi as: (i) the central character (*The Red Shirts*, *Long Live Italy*); (ii) a profile, a distant silhouette we never see in close-up but whose name and influence are felt throughout the film (*1860*); and (iii) a threat from which Sicily is eventually saved (*The Leopard*). But we are anticipating; we shall see later why, and in what circumstances, Garibaldi became an 'ambiguous' hero; during the silent era he was exclusively pictured as a great man. We are not trying to distinguish truth (the 'historical truth') from falsehood and we do not have to decide if Garibaldi was consistent or was in fact a fickle politician. Rather, we are looking for 'images' and beliefs, pictures and assertions about events. We are not obliged to verify evaluations and we want only to estimate how beliefs and images were instrumental in achieving desired goals. While facing new dangers every day, Garibaldi as seen in films never won a battle and yet never lost heart; with him, unity was not achieved, war led to hopeful defeats; he stood for the pessimistic, and at the same time praiseworthy, respectable version of the Risorgimento: consensus over the man concealed dissensus over the events. (See plate IV.)

We do not find heroes on that scale in either American or French films. We sometimes see Lincoln, Grant or Lee, Robespierre, Danton, Bonaparte, but not many films are centred on them and they often come into view only fleetingly, at the beginning or at the end. The heroes are unknown, fictional characters. But whilst French films do not merit a lengthy description, the greater number of American films demand classification into several thematic categories. Hence, there are four main thematic possibilities:

1. *Cowardice and redemption*, in other words a shortened version of Stephen Crane's well-known novel *The Red Badge of Courage*. Soldiers – Union or Confederate – cannot stand up to the enemy's attack and abandon their post. Thereafter: (i) having conquered their fear, they return to the battlefield, acquit themselves gallantly, assure a good result to their side; (ii) relatives, friends, serve as substitutes for them and

51

are killed in their place; (iii) the cowards are killed. In any case, honour is saved.

2. *Fault and pardon*. The frightened or exhausted soldier, longing for his parents or his girl friend, fails in his duty; he ought to be punished with death but is saved by an intelligent superior who is often Lincoln himself. Indulgence symbolizes reconciliation every time it is granted to an enemy or coincides with the end of the war.

3. *Spying*, which might be only one of the various missions undertaken by soldiers, is so frequently pictured that it forms a series by itself. Draw the curtains, push open the doors: you will find a concealed observer. Spying is an individual feat that requires self-control, swiftness, fitness for making friends: non-combatants, women or children, excel in allaying suspicion and hearing without fearing detection. Cowards find here an opportunity to grasp crucial information (the plans of enemy) and to bring it to the general who gives his pardon.

4. *Duty against feelings*. Divided families, father against sons, brother against brother and, more often, tortured lovers.

There are, of course, ways of combining two or more possibilities but the combinations are not limitless and it is important to realize that, in the early days of the cinema, people regularly saw the same narratives; moreover, the four basic combinations have remained unaltered. We now understand why great men are so scarce in American and French films: films follow minor episodes in major events and that is fortunate for us because we are able to determine which type of man or woman is singled out as a main or a secondary character, a hero or a coward.

During the projection, we see human beings and objects from the characters' point of view. Semiologists make a sharp distinction between point of view and narrative voice[9] and their researches help us to go further in our analysis of pictured history. Narratives are stories, events or parts of events set in order to be told to listeners or spectators. How do spectators come into contact with the events? Are they suddenly put in the middle of the action, as if they walked along a street and looked through a key-hole? Or are they advised they are going to be told a story? The prologue of *The Leopard* is a stroll in a large park; led by the camera, we see a huge iron gate, wander through wide paths, look at statues, ending up in front of a palace; prayers can be heard through one of the palace windows, so we jump through the window and enter the chapel. Of course, all that is purely artificial: we would never have been allowed to visit the park and it would be impossible literally to jump from the terrace to the second floor – but that is not the point; in this 'narrator-less' film, things seem to happen before us. Such a solution is not common in historical films; most of the time, there exists a narrative voice, which is supposed to be a go-between and to tell us the story. The main character is occasionally the narrator: in *The Wanton Countess*, Livia Serpieri, speaking in voice-over, provides us with information on her own feelings and on the situation. More frequently, we read a caption, with a date and details concerning the period; here, the narrator is a hypothetical person, someone who could be 'the historian' or 'the voice of historiography' and that person, who often only appears with one of the subtitles, takes a major part in the film. It is as if there was a pre-existing reality outside of the story, known to every spectator, from which data necessary to our understanding of the film could be taken. Speaking with the authority that history (common knowledge) gives, the narrative voice tells the audience: remember, in that year, something happened.

'Point of view' is the place or situation from which characters perceive events.[10] In the simplest situation, the point of view coincides with the main character's vision; most of the time, in *The Wanton Countess*, we follow Livia, we see the town, her friends, her lover and all is seen in terms of her interests. We may also receive several points of view, from various characters; so, in *The Horse Soldiers*, we in turn view events through the eyes of John Wayne, William Holden and Constance Towers. Sometimes, leaving the heroes, we look at the scenery as if we were alone and had the point of view of the narrator. Interestingly, in many historical films, the 'narrator viewed' sequences are the only glimpses of history we are shown. For instance, in *The Wanton Countess*, the battle of Custozza comes under this heading. A relative 'objectivity' (by which I mean a viewpoint which cannot be identified with any of the characters

53

involved in the story) is restored when history is implicated and, in this case, the point of view is the narrator's one.

To what extent are we concerned with such a purely semiotic distinction? At first we might say that, in an objective framework (data on historical situations) a purely subjective, fictional story takes place and that history is only used in order to make this story look credible. But we must remember that framework and characters react one upon the other; there is a constant interaction between them which is particularly tangible when we compare narrative voice with points of view, and various points of view with each other. Let us briefly list the possibilities:

1. No asserted narrative voice. History is not supposed to be external to the film, although this does not mean it is excluded: we shall see that there are many ways of introducing history in films; it is seen from the point of view of one of the characters or a few points of view are intercut; in this case, we shall consider the relationship between the 'objective' point of view (our entering the palace at the start of *The Leopard*) and the characters' point of view.

2. Delayed narrative voice. In its first part, *The Wanton Countess* has no narrative voice: after the introduction of Livia's voice-over, we are enclosed in both the countess's point of view and her narration. This is especially noteworthy as history is reshaped in accordance with the interests and frame of mind of the same character.

3. Narrative voice opening the film and then disappearing. In this case, which is the most common, how is the voice supplied and what serves as a substitute for it?

4. Narrative voice distributed throughout the film. When does that voice occur? Does it cross-cut the whole of the film? Does it break in at specific points? A special case is, of course – see *The Birth of a Nation* – the same voice opening, interrupting and closing the film.

5. Double narrative voice. Here, the film points out and distinguishes history and story. In *Gone with the Wind*, captions giving information punctuate the picture, whilst Scarlet's voice-over explains the heroine's feelings.

My purpose is not to catalogue combinations but to make it clear that, by studying the 'voices', we may disclose whose interests are presented in the film. Look at this very simple contrast: we wander in Prince Salina's foot-steps almost throughout the whole of *The Leopard*; we are told that unity is progressing favourably, in conformity with the hopes of the king, the ruling class and the Prince himself – but we end with the same Salina anticipating his own death: the external view (Italy in the making) is undermined by the character's subjective view. On the contrary, *1860*, which recalls the same episodes, constantly mixes the points of view, before ending with an 'objective' picture of the Italian soldiers: the film tries to eliminate any subjectivity and to make the general conclusion – the same as in *The Leopard* – correspond to the final vision.

Timing

Establishing the historical period in a film is usually quickly done. The first shot of *La Marseillaise* is a subtitle, '14 July 1789', and that is enough for us to know that the film deals with the French Revolution. Introducing characters and plot is more difficult. Spectators need time to identify and locate the men and women they see on the screen. More generally, individual actions unfold slowly, and we find in historical films that very often a complex editing process is used to make the audience familiar with the heroes. We said that historiography implies a starting point and a scale of time: how are those components units employed in the film? As that question is a rather complex one, we will consider it with an example.

Long Live Italy relates – once again – the liberation of Sicily and Naples from Bourbon rule. Just after the credits, while a green, white and red flag, is flying on the screen, a voice-over starts: 'in 1860 . . .'; so, the narrative voice delivers the conventional account of the position. 1860 – or any other date – is the starting point; it is so vital that we find it even in films for which a precise date is unnecessary. *The Brigand of the Wolf Cave* shows the 'pacification' of Southern Italy. After Sicily and Naples had been liberated, the South of the Peninsula was annexed by the new kingdom. Since many local people refused to submit to the 'King of Savoy', the Italian army had to fight the rebels for several years. The episode called forth in

55

The Brigand could have happened at any time in the decade following 1860 but the picture opens with a caption indicating 1863 – information which does not matter a bit for the film. As we already know, there is no narrative voice in *The Leopard;* it thus appears natural that, following the opening sequences of the film, Prince Salina should open out a newspaper and start reading aloud, in the course of which he announces a date; further information on the period is then given by women who comment on the situation.

Starting points demarcate two periods: *before* and *after.* Before, there was history (what spectators know of historiography and which changes according to their culture); after, the story matches with history. Those points are not by any means simply calendar dates: they are rather days or years which are felt as significant by the audience. Many Americans do not situate 4 July precisely in the past – but there is no American to whom it is an ordinary, unimportant day. Some dates have a symbolical value and, simply by being quoted, catch the spectator's attention. A subtitle in *The Birth of a Nation* reads: 'And then came the fatal night of April 14th 1865'. Fateful, glorious, terrible: days like 4 July or 14 April are larger than life, momentous; taken together, those dates constitute the symbolical time, the series of dates which seem to exist by themselves – opposed to the series of ordinary days and years which make chronological time, the regularly divided time that we use in our business and which has no signification unless it is related to our activities and projects. In both cases we may speak of time, for both are designated by the same indices that are used to label 'dates' – but they do not have the same function in social life.

Historical films sometimes bring chronological time into play (*Long Live Italy* begins on 4 April, the second sequence opens on 15 April; we are then told that Garibaldi landed in Sicily on 11 May and so on). There are examples where this is not the case, but historical films are always a form of narration, unfolding a story told from beginning to end and implicitly assuming a time dimension, because, of course, it is impossible to develop the story without this essential element of time. *Long Live Italy* provides us with a first approach to the categories of narrative time:

1. Sequence II: in Genoa, Garibaldi welcomes friends; visitors enter into or go out of the field, but the camera focuses on Garibaldi, panning when he moves, stopping when he stops. With this 'full-length time', time of action and time of projection coincide.
2. Sequence I: in Palermo, men get hold of guns, attack soldiers, are taken prisoner and finally shot: all is finished in less than four minutes; it is 'shortened time'; time is suggested by the alteration occurring from the beginning (men awaiting the hour of insurrection) to the end (shooting) not by the full details of actions.[11]
3. Sequence VII: the Garibaldini are advancing up a hillside; we catch glimpses of the Bourbons at the top of the hill; the Garibaldini come to a stop; shooting; a succession of shots alternatively from the Garibaldian and Bourbon points of view, long shots of running people, medium shots of hand-to-hand struggles, all edited very quickly. Later on, we are informed that the Garibaldini beat the Bourbons. There is neither a beginning nor an end and the editing process suggests an 'undetermined duration'.

Time is not limited to those three categories which, all together, make 'narrative time': we find other variants.[12]

4. End of Sequence II; Garibaldi and one of his supporters go to bed; fade;[13] the sleeping comrade in daylight; he is awakened by Garibaldi's voice: we have skipped over the night and the fade coincides with a 'break' in the time sequence; many more important breaks will occur in the rest of the film;
5. Sequence VIII; long shot of a bivouac; panning from right to left; two men enter the field and walk towards the left while the camera is panning; they stop and begin to drink but the camera leaves them before they finish; focus out, soldiers in long distance; focus in and panning to the right, Garibaldi in medium shot; panning to the left and so on. The camera shots, completely disconnected from any action, do not take account of people moving in the field and only describe something which could be 'rest' or 'waiting'. Time

57

does not exist except as time of editing: that is another break in continuity – but completely different from the first, for 'editing time' is like an extra time, added to the narrative time.

We are eventually led to enumerate five categories:

full-length time
shortened time $\left.\right\}$ narrative time
undetermined duration
break
editing time

Is that point really worth making? Let us consider it further. Editing time brings us back to the 'objective' view. We constantly find that external vision which cuts into the film as if it told 'the truth'. We know that everything is artificial in films but, if we are not very careful, we shall never detect the tricks by which some sequences are made more credible, more 'historical' than others. Pictures are mixtures of the three sorts of narrative time intercut with breaks and it is interesting to consider what is eliminated, by which I mean not what is suppressed in comparison with other narratives of the same event, but what is assumed in the film and not shown. In *Long Live Italy* we see Garibaldi discussing with the Bourbon officers who prepare their retreat from Sicily but we do not see them leaving. The Garibaldini, at least as they are shown in *Long Live Italy*, spend their time in bargaining with agents of the King of Naples and, even after having liberated Sicily, never begin governing the island. It is as if history were reduced to diplomacy, never concerned with management or administration. Obviously, the fact that events are fully described, or shortened, or of vague duration is a mark of what is considered as important. Our three categories of narrative time correspond with three scales of time: which of them is the most frequently used in a film? And is the time scale organized according to the 'timetable' of a great man or a countess or a group of soldiers?

58   We should not be content simply with the realization that

time is described and evoked in several different ways and according to the interests of one or another group of individuals in the films that we are examing. Hence, in the first sequence of *Long Live Italy* the question is posed: 'What time is it?' People are waiting for the right moment; they go out: too late, time has betrayed them. In sequence II, Garibaldi and his supporters consider whether the time has come. We could describe the entire film only by taking account of the individual moments and we could do the same thing with any historical film. Remember *Gone with the Wind*, for instance: the doctor has no time to save wounded soldiers; Scarlet barely has time to leave the burning city of Atlanta, and so on.

Of course, all this is often no more than a means of creating a sense of suspense and catching the attention of the spectator. But we must not forget that the question of time is basic to our conception of history; we are used to considering that every event depends on propitious circumstances and that nothing happens unless it is in the nick of time. Garibaldi did not manage to liberate Italy in 1848: that was too early. But in 1860, the time had come: is not such a sentence typical of historians? We are tempted to make sharp distinctions: Scarlet deciding to escape from Atlanta saves her life whereas Garibaldi leaving Messina to invade Calabria creates Italy. However, their behaviour is described in the same way: emergency, decision, results. Up to now, we have not spoken of 'historical time' for that category does not exist in itself; it is created by the choice of a starting point, the matching of different categories of time, the constant reference to the 'right moments'. Historical time is one of the tools a society uses to illuminate its origins and, being so, it is an object for historical study. But what about films? Is it not enough that we look at our list and answer: films are based upon categories such as full-length time, editing time, and so on, which are absolutely specific, untranslatable in spoken or written historiography and, for that reason, deserve special research; by comparing films we rediscover the fact that time is not a flow of homogeneous, constant transformations but rather a juxtaposition of dissimilar moments. Some periods of time are eventful and auspicious; other times seem empty and difficult. In other words, periods are not seen as equivalent, but are represented as full or empty, good or bad times.

59

The nature of evidence

We emphasize the starting point but, in this respect, historical films do not seem to differ from other films. Many feature films – not to say the majority of them – have a starting point; a man meets a woman, bullocks move off towards the railway station and the story begins. We immediately call attention to the particular nature of an 'historical outset': what happened before the meeting or the herd's departure is of no importance or will be revealed during the course of the film, whereas history is known (or supposed to be) to everyone. We may assume that historical films are distinguished by something we could call (for we are dealing with cinema) the double exposure of time, with the superimposition of symbolical time on other forms of time. Many Italian films take place in a vague period which, from the costume detail, is understood as being the second half of the nineteenth century. *The Wanton Countess*, which should be seen as a classical drama (a young lady, who married an old gentleman, falls in love with an attractive, shameless young officer), has always been regarded as an historical picture because the fiction is dated and because date, and surroundings – 1866 in Venice – refer to a stage of the Risorgimento. What I would like to suggest is that the 'historical nature' of a film is never obvious in itself; if we were absolutely unaware of the context (I mean: the circumstances, as they are known and accepted in the cultural sphere in which the film was produced) we would look at *The Wanton Countess* as a melodrama, in which characters were dressed in splendid uniforms and battles were vividly reconstructed. 'Historicity' is so weak and unstable that it has to be underlined so as to force the audience to admit that it is seeing a filmic reconstruction of the past. In addition to that, recognizing men or landscapes can be a part of the pleasure we take in looking at films as pictures. Let us consider the beginning of *The Horse Soldiers:* star spangled banner and rank of horsemen coming towards us, then turning as the camera pans with them: how many times have we seen such an opening shot? We are immediately informed the film is going to deal with the US cavalry: officers meet in Sherman's office; shortly after we see General Grant and, of course, characters acquaint us with the problem: the US army is marking time, it will eventually be necessary to create a diversion at the rear of the Confederate army. Opening shots and subsequent information having marked the starting point, officers gather and a photographer takes a picture of the group. 'Thank you Mr Brady', they say; if we are an 'average' viewer, we are diverted by remembering how photographs used to be taken but, if we have a more specialized interest in the period, we recognize the allusion to the man who was called 'Lincoln's photographer' and who took thousands of photographs during the Civil War. In both cases, the scene makes no real contribution to the progress of the narrative (we never see the photographs), but it rings a bell, reminding us that we are 'not in the present'.

Historical films are rich in details of this sort. The 'innocent' spectator is happy to spot them, unaware that he does exactly as he is meant to. The number of historical details, and the way in which they are spread throughout the film, give us a great deal of information about what was considered as 'historic' by the men who produced it: in this respect there is much to be gained from a closer examination. Film-makers are restricted in their choice of 'pieces of evidence'. There are no more than five possibilities:

1. Written documentation. Short texts are inserted in the film as captions. Newspapers are commonly used in this way, sometimes to report an important event. Newspapers are twice quoted in *The Birth of a Nation*, for example, once before Lincoln's election and once after the assassination. On both occasions they underline events which alter the history of the United States and affect the lives of the principal characters. In *La Marseillaise*, before the revolutionaries storm the Tuileries, we read a series of newspapers and leaflets informing the audience that the patience of the 'patriots' is exhausted. The use of newspapers is not a purely passive one, nor do they appear only as a means of providing information. People handle the papers, read and comment on them. We see a number of American magazines in the Cameron home, as Dr Cameron comments on them to his family, and we can recall a very similar episode at the beginning of *The Leopard*. In *La Marseillaise*, after we have seen the anti-royalists leaflets, we meet the Marseillais

themselves – the 'patriots' who have come from Marseilles to support the Revolution – as they examine one of the leaflets. *Long Live Italy* provides another interesting example of the use of newspapers: we leave Garibaldi as he is deciding to sail from Genoa to Sicily, and we will not see him again until the first fight with the Bourbons; information on the journey and Garibaldi's landing is given in a series of newspaper headlines, and as the pace accelerates we gather that news of the expedition is spreading rapidly throughout Europe. We could describe this as a common, almost obsolete device, for in the same film we also see the telegraph office besieged by journalists, all anxious to be first with the news. From our point of view, the use of such devices to underline the importance of events is interesting. There is no 'grammar' in the cinema, in the sense that there is no generally accepted convention or system governing the transmission of information: film-makers often resort to rather conventional means, which are effective because they are immediately understood by the audience. In general, people are so familiar with the use of newspapers as a means of conveying urgent and important information, that we find the same device used to cover events in the Civil War, the Risorgimento and the French Revolution. Did the Marseillais read and discuss leading articles in the Parisian press in 1792? Did an aristocrat living near Palermo rely on newspapers for his information? The films themselves cannot answer the questions, but looking at films produced at different times (1915, 1936, 1960) and set in completely different countries and circumstances shows that newspapers are a basic component of filmic expression. We have to understand the function of newspapers in historical films: they provide evidence (proof that Frenchmen were hostile to the king, for example, or that Southerners were apprehensive about Lincoln's election), and at the same time they provide a point of reference for the audience, who are familiar with newspapers and understand how they are used.

2. Newspapers are not the only documents used. Film characters write a great deal, and in each of the films we study, we will be looking more closely at the function of the letters, reports and texts that appear. Here, we only want to stress the

documentary value of what is written in this way. The young Bonaparte, for example, writes to his mother, and the letter serves to tie the present (his modest income) to the future (his greater expectations). Writing is an action like any other: in issuing permits to foreign visitors, Garibaldi proves that he is master of events; the Civil War officially ends when Lee signs his surrender; Ben Cameron is saved from execution by the discharge order drafted by Lincoln. Documents used in this way confirm that an event happened; conversely, the use of written sources provides an assurance of the 'historicity' of the film. But that does not exhaust their use. In comparing films on the same topic, we discover that some documents are more significant than others. In both of the two films on the French Revolution discussed below, Brunswick's manifesto, warning of horrifying reprisals if the king is dethroned, is presented as a turning point. Many of the Civil War films, and particularly *The Birth of a Nation* and *Gone with the Wind*, refer to Lincoln's appeal for volunteers (in calling up soldiers, the President created a Federal Army, which was understood by Southerners as a declaration of war). It is pointless asking if Brunswick's manifesto was crucial in rousing the patriots against the king. The manifesto itself seems to be more than just a document: it is part of the 'common knowledge' of French history[14] and films inform us of that knowledge.

3. Films can also use drawings or stills, which are like snapshots of actual scenes. Engravings or photographs – reproduced or closely imitated – are 'brought to life' in the same frame by actors.[15] Instead of an exact reproduction of a drawing, we sometimes find an allusion: many of the sequences in *The Leopard* or *The Wanton Countess* are shot in the style of Italian painters of the 1860s; walking with Livia in Venice or observing with her the sky-line in Aldeno (her country estate), we glimpse a street corner or a view of the landscape which reminds us of a familiar painting. Town and country have a period look to them, and the audience sees them clearly labelled as images of a past time (plate I).

4. Films also use familiar episodes as evidence. In any culture, certain anecdotes or phrases are known to everyone, and only have to be mentioned to bring a particular period to mind. Nelson's behaviour at the battle of Trafalgar is an

obvious example of this sort of anecdotal 'short-hand'. Re-enacting such scenes is a device that historical films often mis-use.[16] (See plate III.)

5. Portraits can also be used to pinpoint the period. Danton, Lincoln, General Grant may not appear as major characters in particular historical films, but a glimpse of their portrait helps the audience to identify the period in which the events are taking place.

Many films give the impression that they are weighed down by excessive attention to detail, all of which provides exactly the same information and merely repeats information already given in the opening scenes. But the more a film uses particular indications of this sort, the more confusing it becomes to a foreign audience. Audiences – and there are many of them outside the Western world – who do not know that Italian unity was a burning issue in nineteenth-century Europe, see films on the Risorgimento as rather tiresome stories of decadent families. Historiography, far from being universal, is subordinated to national traditions. In studying historical films, we must allow for the cultural backdrop against which history is defined.

Starting with some obvious differences, we have tried to define points that enable us to analyse any particular historical film. Using this theoretical framework, we can now proceed to examine films in their social context. I hope to draw some conclusions about the relationships between three particular societies and some of the historical films produced in those societies.

Notes

1. See *The Civil War in Motion Pictures*, Library of Congress, Washington, 1961.
2. Lilian Gish and Ann Pinchot, *Lilian Gish, the Movies, Mr Griffith and Me*, London, 1969, p. 136.
3. Willard Welsh, 'The war in drama', *Civil War History*, 1 September 1955, pp. 251–80. See also Nicholas Vardac, *Stage to Screen*, London–New York, 1968.
4. Ordered by the government, the first Italian film on Risorgimento, *The Fall of Rome* (1905) was devoted to the conquest of Rome by

Italian troops in 1870; shortly after several films showed how Rome had been lost by Italians and reconquered by pontifical soldiers in 1849. During the silent era, only two films related Italian victories.

5. The first was produced in 1897, the second in 1913 and there is no connection between them. To be exact, I must add a third film on the war during the French Revolution; it is devoted to a young drummer who, being captured by the enemy, shouts to give the alarm to French soldiers and is killed; I draw attention to that film because we found young heroic drummers both in American films on the Civil War and Italian films on the Risorgimento.

6. See L. Festinger, *A Theory of Cognitive Dissonance*, New York, 1957.

7. For a general view of Garibaldi in Italian films, see Guido Cincotti, in *The Italian Risorgimento in the Theatre and Cinema*, Rome, 1962, pp. 226–7. 'The only authentic myth that our history has managed to create and nurture with constancy, Garibaldi, passes unharmed through the most fantastic adventures'. *The Fall of Rome* (in which Garibaldi was not involved) ends with Garibaldi (and some other 'architects of unity') emerging from clouds. 'The Italian cinema enters into a disastrous crisis at the end of the first world conflict. As always Garibaldi saves the situation and succeeds in finding a place in the squalid patchwork of the Italian cinema of the twenties . . . When the Italian cinema is reborn from its own ashes, at the introduction of the sound . . . it automatically turns to the emblematic personality of the Hero of the Two Worlds.' In describing the facts Cincotti does not try to explain why Garibaldi was the 'only authentic myth' of the Italian cinema.

8. According to the title of the second of those films. Garibaldi fought in Latin America during civil wars and in Europe.

9. See B. Uspensky, *Study of Point of View: Spatial and Temporal Form*, Centro Internazionale di Semiotica, Working Papers and Pre-Publications, D, 24, Urbino, 1973, and Seymour Chatman, *Cinematic Discourse: The Semiotics of Narrative Voice and Point of View in 'Citizen Kane'* (ibid., Centro Internazionale F., 69), 1977.

10. 'Point of view is the *stance* or position that someone takes in respect to the events of the story, and that someone may be a character or he may be the narrator (if there is one). The term "point of view" has at least three separate senses: firstly, a literal sense, that is, the spot from which someone *perceives* something – by means of eyes, ears or whatever; secondly, a figurative sense, that is someone's world view, ideology, *Weltanschauung*, his general conceptual orientation; and finally a transferred sense, that is, someone's interest-vantage, his situation in respect to profit, welfare,

65

well-being, quite independently of his awareness of them', Chatman, p. 7. We shall consider, in our analysis, the point of view of all these three senses.

11. A variant is cross-cutting. In sequence VI, we are with the Bourbon governor of Palermo; suddenly, we see country men meeting in the street of a village and deciding to get flour for Garibaldi; back to the governor; back to country men, back to the governor; the two series are supposed to be simultaneous and connected (the governor mistrusts the country men who are afraid of being surprised by the soldiers of the governor).

12. Flash-back and flash-forward, which are in current use in feature films, are scarcely distributed in historical films: there is no example in the films we are going to study.

13. Fade: darkening of the picture until it has disappeared and then lighting of the screen disclosing the picture.

14. Another way is the 'reported' quotation. Well-known texts or sentences are given not by their authors, but by supporters, or enemies, who comment on them. Before unity, many Italians wrote books about the future of the Peninsula; instead of giving the texts, *1860* stages some ordinary people who, chattering on the train, in a pub, in streets, tell us the various conceptions of unity.

15. Let us mention, in *La Marseillaise*, the encounter between Marseillais and aristocrats, the assault in the courtyard of Tuileries, which are very close contemporary drawings and three episodes in *The Birth of a Nation* – when the appeal for volunteers is signed, when Lee surrenders, and when Lincoln is assassinated – which reproduce pictures. The latter adds to stills captions specifying the books from which the documents are taken. The method, still in use with *Intolerance*, is considered out of date after the 1920s: cultured people do not need references and 'ordinary' people do not understand them.

16. We could fill a book with such filmed episodes which are particularly developed in films whose makers intend to get a popular audience, such as *La Marseillaise* or *Long Live Italy*: in these films the king of France and Garibaldi do exactly, say absolutely what they have to do or to say.

3

The French Revolution

I will begin with the smallest group – French films on the French Revolution. Although films on this topic are few in number, they do not occur at random points in the history of the French film industry. With the advent of the talkies, French films on the Revolution fall into two distinct categories, the first coinciding with the success of the Popular Front, the second occurring at a period when the Cold War was at its height. This second group will not concern us here, as it consists mostly of fairly crude exercises in pro-French propaganda, with love affairs taking the place of quality or stagecraft.[1] Using examples taken from the first category, I will begin by setting up the problem of the relationship between films and their socio-historical context.

Singing La Marseillaise

We will discuss only two films:[2] *Napoleon Bonaparte* (1935) and *La Marseillaise* (1937). Despite the title, *Napoleon Bonaparte* in fact does not cover the whole of Bonaparte's life, and can be divided into three sections: the end of the monarchy; Captain Bonaparte's return to Corsica, and his adventures on the island (a French 'western' dealing with events from an obscure episode in Napoleon's life); General Bonaparte's first successes. We shall concentrate here on the first period, in which Bonaparte is an idle witness of events in Paris.[3] *La Marseillaise* is the story of a small group of young men from Marseille, particularly the mason, Bomier, and the clerk, Arnaud, who join in local political conflicts, enlist in the battalion raised in their city, and travel on foot from Marseille to Paris to help overthrow the monarchy.

Both films recall the same facts and events: the club meetings, the popular rising on 10 August, the assault on the Tuileries, the royal family seeking refuge in the Assembly, and the overthrow of the monarchy by the republic. But there is a much more important coincidence: the song of La Marseillaise itself. In *Napoleon Bonaparte*, the song is presented by Rouget de Lisle himself who, as a young army officer, teaches the song to the crowd in the Club of Cordeliers.[4] In *La Marseillaise*, the Marseillais adopt the song as their war anthem, and because they sing it as they enter Paris, it is rebaptised with their name. We must remember that the French national anthem has a very particular political significance.[5] In the France of the 1930s, 'La Marseillaise' was still the symbol of Republicanism, as it had been at the end of the nineteenth century, but it was also a patriotic symbol for all Frenchmen, unlike the 'Internationale', which was sung only by revolutionary parties. 'La Marseillaise' was sung by everyone – to the right or the left of the political spectrum – who was prepared to defend France against external threats, particularly from Germany. By the 1930s, the national anthem served a rather ambiguous purpose. The French Communist Party, for example, sang only the 'Internationale' until 1934. From then onwards, they used 'La Marseillaise' in preference to the 'Internationale'. In the two films we are discussing, then, the national anthem is not used in important sequences undeliberately.

Before deciding 'how' it is used, we must consider the context in which it is used in both cases. Both films place particular emphasis on external affairs: the war against Austria and Prussia, the succession of defeats suffered by the royalist forces, the invasion in the North-East of France. In clubs and during meetings, speakers constantly refer to the perils which menace national security. Citizens are encouraged to join the army, and both films contain long sequences devoted to the enlistment of volunteers. There is no doubt that they are referring to the patriotic implications of 'La Marseillaise' as a symbol of nationalist revival.

In 1935–7 the dangers were indeed very real. Germany, in the process of re-arming, had called for a reconsideration of the Versailles 'diktat'. Many Frenchmen, seeing France as diplomatically isolated in Europe, thought that the real issue was the modernization of the army, together with national union. The country was bitterly divided, and the external difficulties were exacerbated by the internal crisis. Hardly surprisingly, neither film is concerned with the beginning of the Revolution, the hopes of 1789, the political and economic rebuilding of 1790–1; the action moves immediately to a more dramatic point, to the period when internal and external difficulties had to be resolved. Both films, in dealing with events in the past, deliberately invite comparison with events in the present of the 1930s.[6] Starting with the same events, the films offer two very different solutions. In *Napoleon Bonaparte*, the camera pans over the crowd as it sings under the direction of Rouget de Lisle, catching various faces, costumes, attitudes; everyone in the crowd, from the middle class to the proletariat seems to share in the same enthusiasm. The king is then dethroned but the film does not insist on Louis XVI's responsibility and, when the 'patriots' go to the Assembly, they only affront the Queen, 'the Austrian'. The Tuileries are quickly conquered, but late at night, the rabble – the worst section of the lower class – hangs aristocrats and makes noise in the streets – whilst a new bourgeois government is already transforming the society and organizing an army. When the 'patriots' of *La Marseillaise* are strong enough, in their town, they expel the aristocrats: some of the latter might be good fellows but, due to the situation, it is not possible to trust them. In this film, a long sequence covers the fighting in the Tuileries, during which we see aristocrats ambushing the patriots and killing one of the central characters, the mason Bomier; thus, the victorious patriots shoot the defenders of the palace.

We can now measure the political conclusions of our pictures. *Napoleon Bonaparte* suggests that internal difficulties could be promptly solved because there are few internal enemies; the whole of the nation should face the external perils – without forgetting another danger, the scum of the populace, which might overthrow the society if it had an open field.[7] In *La Marseillaise*, however, there are two considerable dangers, inside and outside, which are inextricably mixed; before advancing towards the border line, it is necessary to disarm the agitators and, if necessary, to put down their rebellion.

The peasantry in the French Revolution

The second sequence of *La Marseillaise* opens with a countryman killing a pigeon; arrested by forest wardens, he ought to be judged by the landlord but friends set him free; taking refuge in hills, near Marseille, he meets Arnaud and Bomier:

'Are you escaping king's justice?'
'Not the king's – but the aristocrats' one'
'So am I.'

A medium shot, with the hills of Provence, rocks, distant bushes, encloses the clerk, the craftsman, the peasant, all the workers who long for better justice in France. But, when news comes from the town announcing that Revolution is in progress, the three men part company; the town-dwellers go back to Marseille; as their companion says, they are the men of the future, whereas he has nothing to do but to vanish; his disappearance is consistent with the political line of the film: peasants have no part in *Napoleon Bonaparte* or in *La Marseillaise* and revolution is accomplished by and for the middle class.

Recent research on the peasantry in contemporary France shows that although they formed the bulk of the working population, supplying privates for the army, and especially the infantry, they did not benefit from the sudden burst of economic growth, and remained on the fringes of society.[8] French politicians, intellectuals and scholars (among them historians) paid little attention to the peasantry until the major upheavals of the third quarter of the twentieth century, when, in less than twenty years, the peasantry were reduced to roughly 15 per cent of the population. Those who survived became the subject of renewed interest in the form of enquiries, historical studies, books and films. French television – a public utility service – broadcast a number of programmes on rural problems, scheduling no fewer than three films on the role of peasants in the French Revolution in a one-year period.[9] As television is beyond the scope of this present study, I will not analyse these films in any detail, but all three emphasized the class war in the countryside: instead of placing all aristocrats in opposition to the majority of the French population, they drew a clear distinction between the propertied and the unpropertied classes, pointing out that landed aristocrats were not the sole exploiters of the landless peasantry. Enclosures and the allotment of common land were the central focus of the struggle. The films throw the unity of the oppressed peasants into relief, suggesting further struggles over partition and the distraint of wealthy farmers on the land.

Historians may be right when they say that there is nothing very new in this, but they should remember that a television audience is unlikely to know very much about class wars in the eighteenth century, although they are perfectly capable of understanding the similarities between the Revolution and the struggles of the last decades of the twentieth century. In the Fifth Republic, country people express their opposition to the further redistribution of land and the officially sanctioned migration from country to city in riots, street closures and violent demonstrations. The French economy is at a critical point. Industry is adversely affected by concentration and by factory closures. The 'end of the peasantry' is often seen as the end of a way of life. France can no longer survive in glorious isolation – it must now depend on others. In another way, and at another time, the country people of France resisted the end of the old rural community during the Revolution.

Historical films are concerned with the problems of the present even if that concern is expressed only indirectly. On the surface, they deal with historical events, like the assault on the Tuileries or the enclosure of common land; but from the vast range of possible choices, film-makers have singled out those characters, circumstances and dates that have a direct bearing on contemporary circumstances. We could say that the past is narrated in the present tense, or that it is rebuilt on contemporary references. This is a general rule, and its application varies according to period and country: political potentialities depend on the reference period and its importance to the society concerned. In our studies of specific films, we shall be calling attention to the contemporary facts, attitudes, characters concealed in historical settings, but we cannot stop there. We would

71

not be able to draw any inferences from historical films if we did not already know what was happening when they were made. Take the case of France in 1936: French film-makers seemed to be working in a vacuum, producing dramas and comedies of manners that made no direct reference to the problems of the day.[10] The film-makers' obsession with the Revolution is interesting, but we can find similar references to the past in less sophisticated documents such as books and magazines. Interesting though it is, the immediate relationship between an historical film and the period in which it was made is not fundamental and gives anything but complementary data.

If this is the case, what *can* we learn from films? We will be discussing this point in some detail, but I think that a brief summary of the issue would be helpful. Current knowledge of history is relatively predefined at any given time: film-makers know more or less exactly what cultured people know, and they stage productions which are apt to echo the preoccupations of their audiences. *Napoleon Bonaparte* and *La Marseillaise* deal with the same period in 1792, and with the same events: the difference lies in the editing of shots in sequence, in the composition of the film, in short, in the process by which audiovisual material is transformed into meaningful expression.

To arms!

As the call for volunteers is dealt with in both films, we shall start there. The sequence is isolated, parenthesized, illustrating a situation already familiar to the audience. In *Napoleon Bonaparte*, Danton addresses the crowd, warning them that France is in danger and exhorting the patriots to defend themselves.[11] The patriots from Marseille meet in their club and realize, as they listen to news of the army, that the aristocratic commanders of the royal regiments have failed in their duty and have thus left the country open to attack by the Austrians: they decide to enlist. We, the audience, are now fully aware of the danger.

A drummer appears in medium shot. While he is beating his drum, the camera pans to the side and then downwards to a recruiting sergeant. As soon as the camera is stationary, the sergeant begins to speak excitedly: we do not see the people he is addressing; in fact, he is telling *us* of the defeats of the French Army, urging *us* to enlist. His voice rises higher and higher, ending in a rattle. Filmed from below, he looks like a huge strange bird, as he raises his arms. Volunteers come forward, but again we do not see them: a register and a pen appear on screen; hands take the pen, sign, replace the pen and disappear. In counter-point to this rather dull sequence, we have two sound effects: in the background, a chorus sings a military song; in the foreground, the volunteers give their names and particulars in voice-over.

In *La Marseillaise*, Arnaud and his friends go to the registration office. Bomier, a young craftsman, would like to accompany them, but as an undischarged debtor he must remain behind, alone. We see him at home: the camera scans the apartment of a poor widow, glimpsing the furniture, the costumes, cross-cutting with shots of Bomier and his mother. She would prefer Bomier to stay safely in Marseille, but knowing that he is anxious to join his comrades, she agrees to pay off his debt so that he can then enlist. Bomier sings a revolutionary song, and leaves. We follow him, still singing, through the street, and join him in the queue as he jokes with his friends.

In *La Marseillaise*, the sequence is enclosed in a continuous, linear narrative. Take virtually any character and imagine the following succession: something happens to the character; he reacts; there is a change in the situation. We could easily take the whole of the film and break it down into similar narrative structures, starting with the smallest ones (Bomier cannot leave; he speaks to his mother who resolves the difficulty; Bomier is allowed to leave), and moving up (the enrolment sequence and so on) to the largest, which is the film itself. Many films are composed entirely of such three-step structures[12] and rely on the staging of details, the setting or the editing process to stimulate the viewer's interest. The editing in *La Marseillaise* is in what we might call a flowing style: we do not see how things hang together; the action seems to move easily, 'naturally', from one event to another. As we see Bomier running from home to the recruiting office we hear him singing – we know, from the song, that he is happy, and we know why he is so satisfied. As we follow the characters, we gather information. We learn that the young patriots are proud of enlisting, that the soldiers of the 'patriot' army are honest men; we see a modest family, the streets of Marseille, a recruitment office. Although the basic, three-time model is a very simple one, it offers numerous possibilities:

1. The model can be extended indefinitely, like a nest of tables, or it can be added to (the enrolment sequence, for example, is an addition – not strictly necessary – rather than an integral part of the model), or the model can be broken, or disrupted, by deliberately omitting one of the three stages.
2. The model can be staged in different ways, depending on the choice of character and circumstance and the style of shooting and editing.

Even allowing for the difference in the way this model is used, we cannot make a strict comparison between *Napoleon Bonaparte* and *La Marseillaise*. In the sequence from *Napoleon Bonaparte* that we analysed earlier, we saw the use of the narrative model – and we assume that in the majority of films that model is always at work. But the two films we are considering here are very different. The sequence from *Napoleon Bonaparte* tells us nothing new. If we could see the young volunteers, we might be able to learn something about them – their age, their costume, their social status – but we are deliberately prevented from seeing them. They give their names and their occupations to the recruiting sergeant, but these details are partially obscured by the common act of signing the same register, and by the revolutionary song which, far from being an accompaniment, nearly saturates the soundtrack.

We see here one of the differences between the two films. *La Marseillaise* is concerned with the individual destinies of certain characters – Arnaud, Bomier and the others. There are no separate stories in *Napoleon Bonaparte*. The men and women we see on screen are not faceless, anonymous nonentities: in the enrolment sequence, they give their names loudly; in other sequences, we see many faces only once and for only a few seconds, but the images are so sharp and precise that we feel we could recognize them again, even though none of these carefully individualized people appear in other sequences. The film tends to develop a collective excitement, giving little importance to the fate of individuals.

Although *Napoleon Bonaparte* is less didactic than *La Marseillaise*, it is no less concerned with historical specification. Thisleads us to a second important point. History is 'external' in *La Marseillaise:* as we said in the previous chapter, the period is established right at the start of the film, in a caption; the historical quality of the film is enhanced by the various devices we discussed earlier.[13] But in the sequence we are discussing here, nothing is gained in stressing its 'historical' nature. The same sequence could be used in any other film where a young fellow wants to leave with his friends and is prevented from doing so by lack of money. The film is in fact narrated on two levels, each of them corresponding to a specific time: symbolical time for the historical dimension; narrative time for the young men's adventures. Of course, the two levels interact: Bomier leaves home singing an apparently martial song, for example, but we can easily distinguish anecdote from the presupposed historical framework in which it appears. Separating the historical from the anecdotal in *Napoleon Bonaparte* is rather more difficult, for the film constantly pushes history to the forefront, insisting on the way of telling (filming) it. The importance of the register book in the enrolment sequence is interesting in itself: the book itself probably still exists in an archive, where we could examine it and find the proof (the only remaining proof) that these men enlisted in 1792; the minute-book we mentioned earlier[14] is a written source, but it is not produced as evidence – it plays an active part in the film. This brings us to an important point: narrative voices increasingly envelop the picture. *Napoleon Bonaparte* is constructed as an evocation. In 1815, the young novelist Stendhal, who wants to write Napoleon's biography, meets some devoted followers of the Emperor, who reminisce. Immediately after the enrolment sequence, we see the old recruiting sergeant, now a veteran.[15] As Stendhal's interlocutors bear witness, the past and present seem to merge[16] and we are forcibly reminded that historiography cannot ignore the importance of the narrator. *Napoleon Bonaparte* is historiography in the making, whereas *La Marseillaise*, taking the 'reality' of history for granted, lets us see some of its features.

Having urged us to enlist, the recruiting sergeant ends his speech with a piercing sob. With arms raised, he is a ludicrous sight. The audience, embarrassed by the shrill voice and the clumsy movements, remembers for a moment that it is attending a performance. The picture is full of broad hints, of which we will look at one example: while Danton and the crowd are singing the Marseillaise, in the former church of Cordeliers, Robespierre, listening to them anxiously, comes and goes in the sacristy; he stops suddenly under an eagle-topped lectern, and we see Robespierre in close-up, with the eagle behind him and the Marseillaise echoing through the room. It would be impossible to misunderstand the significance of this shot: the future exists in the present; war-like enthusiasms (the Marseillaise) will lead from the Republic (Robespierre) to Napoleon (the eagle). This chronological confusion is not confined to the past – the present is also drawn into the film. As we explore with the camera the church where people sing, we come across two men, seen from behind. One of them turns to face the camera, and shouts ' *You*, do sing with us!'

The spectator placement

The problem that arises from any feature film is to explain the functioning of the narrator and the nature and effects of spectator placement: specifically describing and accounting for in detail a film rhetoric in which the agency of the narrator in his relation to the spectator is enacted jointly by the characters and the particular sequence of shots that show them.[17]

An audience watching *La Marseillaise* feels comfortable. Arnaud and Bomier are introduced very early in the film, and throughout, the audience sees characters, situations, even phrases that are familiar; spectators know what they are looking at (a survey of the year 1792) and in whom they are supposed to take an interest. At the same time, they are not involved in the film. The cast is simply too large to invite identification with any one character, which is a constant temptation in fictional films. The audience is firmly 'outside' the film, watching it as if they

were seeing events from abroad. Imagery used in this way reinforces a conception of historiography: the men of the
Revolution are presented as individuals and also as members of
a determined collective – we see Bomier as a good son, fond of
his mother, the patriot as a human being, and we glimpse
Bomier the honest craftsman, building a chimney, behaving
like a good fellow, and so on. Characters are not interesting on
their own; they are meant to make us realize that the Revolution
was carried out by ordinary people.[18] What we see as history
was the daily life of those who lived at the end of the eighteenth
century. By implication, what we do now might be important to
historians of the future.

La Marseillaise does not represent the French Revolution
as a romantic epic, whereas *Napoleon Bonaparte* stages it as a
huge storm. The difficulty – at least for people who try to
describe films – is that the sensation of whirlwind is created by
the filming; analyzing *La Marseillaise* is easy, for the narration
is shaped in the structure we have mentioned above; rendering
an account of *Napoleon Bonaparte* is artificial and necessarily
inadequate. However, I must give an example of what is shown –
what is isolated – in the picture. We are in the church of
Cordeliers; Rouget de Lisle starts singing his song; the camera
pans, quickly and nimbly, over the crowd; we grasp faces,
expressions, motions, without being able to define anything
precisely. Suddenly, the company is on its feet; in an extremely
swift editing process, we glimpse faces of howling men and
women; the camera pans again, but in jerks, as if it moved in
fits and starts; papers falling from the ceiling (transcripts of
the song) deluge the audience. There is a short breathing space;
silently, people take the papers and begin to read them. And
once more, the crowd becomes enthusiastic, the camera pans
frantically, arms, faces, mouths, hands are edited together;
apparently meaningless shots[19] such as the head of a medieval
sculpture are intercut with shots of the crowd, while singing
voices are underlined, and nearly drowned by the thunder of an
organ. This long sequence – like the major part of the other
sequences – is self-sufficient. With *Napoleon Bonaparte*, historiography is an intense thrill;[20] historic moments differ from
ordinary life; something happens, in the proper meaning of
the word, and the film, instead of unfolding a tale, aims at

77

expanding what is, by nature, transitory. Symbolical time, which mingles with full-length time in *La Marseillaise*, is strongly marked by editing time in *Napoleon Bonaparte*.

The latter film puzzles historians: they cannot decide whether it is true or false, as they would be able to do with *La Marseillaise* for the film does not deal with events or, when it does, it emphasizes the importance more than the development of these events. Anyway, *Napoleon Bonaparte* is a form of historiography, which breaks up the rule of continuity and seeks to convey the significance of a particular day. In the framework of classical written historiography, there is little room for intensity. Must we consider it less relevant than the linear concatenation of causes and consequences on the pretext that we cannot produce evidence? For the audience, *Napoleon Bonaparte* was 'history', and we must seize this opportunity to investigate an unfamiliar historiography pattern.

Actors and circumstances

So far, we have been considering two apparently very different films, but in some respects there are close similarities. In both films, events are fleshed out and given meaning through speech, although dialogue is not used in the same way in the two films. In *Napoleon Bonaparte*, the dialogue consists of short speeches, mixed with shouts, calls, applause and isolated words, whereas speeches in *La Marseillaise* are used to give a full account of the position. Nothing happens without being voiced, always in a similar way – the classical 'two-step flow' between the leaders, the go-between and the mob. The Marseillaise sequence in *Napoleon Bonaparte* is built on this principle: at the outset, the leader, Danton, is completely isolated from the mob; the crowd clamours for Danton, who is apparently unable to leave his associates, Robespierre and Marat; Desmoulins, Danton's supporter, has to intervene before the leader and the crowd can meet. The editing we have just described relies on Danton's merging with the mob (shots of Danton intercut in the sequence), which is impossible until the meeting of the two has been arranged. The proclamation of the Republic and the notification of the first reforms are then edited in the same manner, using

78

the leaders, the go-between and the mob. For their part, the characters in *La Marseillaise* never stop talking, almost as if the audience would miss the point unless kept fully informed at every possible opportunity. Again, the leaders (club officials, officers) decide, and the crowd and soldiers act on their instructions, while a few characters – notably Arnaud – act as go-betweens.

Is it surprising that although the films differ in so many respects, there is so little discrepancy between them with regard to actors and circumstances? Not really, if we bear in mind that both films deal basically with politics. Political change is conceived of in terms of the functioning of a system that people were already familiar with in the 1930s. Thus, in the film, the significant images were those of the hierarchy of concentric groups and the absolute authority of the spoken word. All forms of political activity are shaped by the prevalence of words and the delegation of authority which, taken together, constitute French parliamentarianism. In order to tackle the problems of the day, the film-makers resorted to the patterns of meaning and the values which were usually associated with politics at the time.

Our starting point was a narrowly defined one, but I hope that it is now clear why it was convenient to our purpose. In comparing only two films, we have been able to draw new inferences. We have noted that, in staging the past, film-makers often treat of the present, but what do we mean by the 'past'? Once we have isolated the individuals, the traditions and the anecdotes which provide the clues to the historical period, we can draw two important conclusions:

1. The cinematographic conception of historiography – in other words, the way in which men and their relations in the past are described – is a very specific one, and does not necessarily coincide with the historian's conception of historiography.
2. Films do not supply a total 'reality' when dealing with the past. They translate aspects of the past by choosing a few people, placing them in a particular setting, making them act. The image thus produced cannot be interpreted unless we examine certain characters closely and look at the functioning

79

of the system in order to understand the interpretation of social hierarchy it implies.

In other words, an historical film is a reconstruction of the social relationship which, using the pretext of the past, reorganizes the present.

Notes

1. *The Lame Devil* (1948), *Caroline Love* (1951), *If Versailles was Told to Me* (1954). The first film is dedicated to Talleyrand; this man, credited with restoring the diplomatic status of France after Waterloo, was a fine subject for films, novels, historic studies when France, after its obliteration during the War, was again in a weak international position.
2. To be precise, we must add to our list *Under Terror* (1935) which carries on, in the 1930s, the above-mentioned tradition of anti-revolutionary films (see p. 47).
3. *Napoleon Bonaparte* is one of the films which had a turbulent history. In its first version, shot in 1925–6, issued in 1927, it lasted 10 hours and was simultaneously projected, for some sequences, on three screens; despite its awesome length, it did not go farther than General Bonaparte's departure for Italy (remember that Bonaparte left for Italy in spring 1796 and assumed power only in autumn 1799): in that form, the film was, of course, useless. It was re-edited, in a two-hour print, with a soundtrack, in 1935 and it is this second version projected in cinemas ever since then that we are going to analyse. In 1971, a four-and-a-half hour version, with soundtrack, was edited for television.
4. Cordeliers were Franciscan friars, so called because of the girdle ('corde') they wore. During the Revolution, many convents were used by political clubs.
5. See above, p. 48.
6. Just an amusing example which proves how deeply rooted in the problems of the 1930s our films are. When The Marseillais hear Rouget de Lisle's song for the first time, one of them says it has been taught to the patriots 'by a choral society of workers': there were no choral societies of workers in 1792 – but there were lots of them in the 1930s and they played an important role in persuading the Communists to sing 'La Marseillaise'.
7. Now, we understand why Bonaparte only witnesses the events in the

first part of the film: all the Frenchmen being involved in mobilization. Bonaparte is no more than one among thousands. As we mentioned in the previous chapter, the editing underlines the relationship between the crowd hanging aristocrats and Bonaparte looking at the executions while he is writing to his mother: the young officer is laid by, reserved for another occasion which, the film seems to say, will be the time of re-establishment of law and order.

8. Theodore Zeldin, *France, 1848–1945*, vol. I, Oxford, 1973, pp. 131–97; Eugen Weber, *Peasants into Frenchmen. The Modernization of Rural France, 1870–1914*, Stanford University Press, 1976.

9. The films are: *1788* (the year before the outset of the Revolution; in the countryside, people meet to elect their deputies to States General; conflicts arise between poor peasants and landlords); *The Big Fear* (countrymen setting fire to the castles in summer 1789) and *An Enemy of the People* (partition of common land in two villages of the Somme in 1793); these films were shown in 1977–8.

10. For the French cinema of the 1930s, see Goffredo Fofi, 'The cinema of the popular front in France "1934–1938" ', *Screen*, winter edition, 1972–3 and Elizabeth Grottle Strebel, 'French social cinema and the popular front', *Journal of Contemporary History*, XII, 1977. Both give information on the shooting of *La Marseillaise*.

11. A sentence of his speech has to be reported: 'Frenchmen, maintain your race'. It is a quotation from an authentic Danton speech but, in 1792, the word 'race' had not the same meaning as in 1935. Is that not a revealing mistake?

12. The narrative model is so important, for film analysis, that we shall develop and illustrate it in another chapter; see below, pp. 85–86.

13. Above, pp. 61–64.

14. Above, p. 73.

15. 'Stendhal's scenes' were especially shot for the 1935 version; the scenes of the Revolution were taken from the silent version, with a post-synchronization.

16. For instance, a poor old woman starts telling Stendhal what was happening on the night before 10 August 1792: walking in the room, she eventually turns her back on the audience; she suddenly turns round and looks young, beautiful, as she was on that night of 10 August.

17. Nick Browne, 'The spectator in the text: the rhetoric of *Stagecoach*', *Film Quarterly*, winter 1975–6, p. 27. On the same question, see also Edward Branigan, 'Formal permutations of the point of view shot', *Screen*, 16, no. 3.

18. We only speak of Bomier, because he is the main character in the sequence we are analysing. Other personages, such as Louis XVI quarrelling with the queen or the aristocrats in exile, are described as ordinary people.

19. Apparently, for one might find an explanation, for instance the unceasing tradition of French bravery, or the continuity between medieval and modern France or the new system (the crowd) overwhelming the ancient one (the medieval religion). In any case, the intercrossing creates a strange impression in the middle of the sequence.

20. While speakers are announcing some of the decisions taken by the revolutionary government, a man says: 'Isn't it wonderful to witness the birth of a Republic?' Many people begin weeping for joy.

I. In filming **October**, *great care was taken to reproduce accurately the historical events as seen by eyewitnesses. Above is a photograph taken in St Petersburg in July, 1917; below the same event as portrayed in the film.*

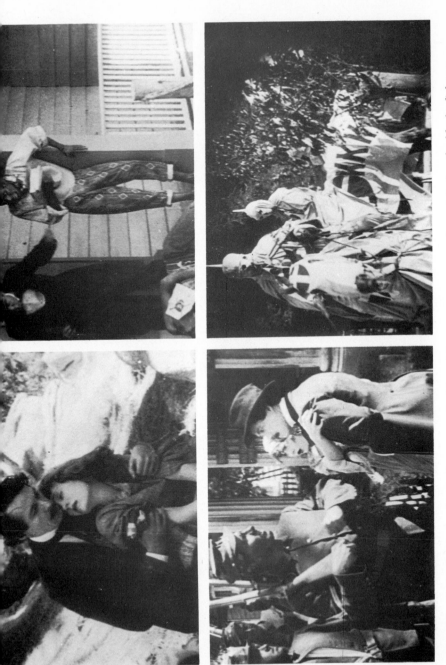

II. **The Birth of a Nation** is much concerned with racial hatred in the American South. The first victim is a white girl (above left); the whites wreak vengeance on the black murderer (above right); but the two races are unevenly matched — the blacks fight on foot (below left), the whites have the advantage of horses (below right).

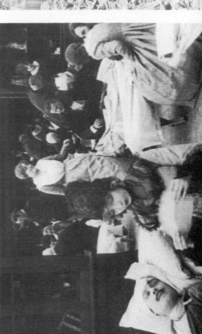

III. *Restaging the American Civil War: the surrender of the Confederate Army, with General Lee on the left, General Grant on the right (top left); the assassination of Abraham Lincoln (top right);* 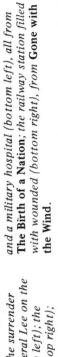 *and a military hospital (bottom left), all from* **The Birth of a Nation**; *the railway station filled with wounded (bottom right), from* **Gone with the Wind**.

IV. *Restaging the Italian Risorgimento: Garibaldi after the landing in Sicily (top) and the Red Shirts on the march (bottom) from* **Long Live Italy**.

V. **The Leopard** *contrasts the different classes of nineteenth century Sicily. In the scene above the aristocracy (Prince Salina, left) confronts the new bourgeoisie (Chevalet, the government official, centre) while the peasantry look on; symbolically, in the bottom scene, the future (the new bourgeoisie) depends on, is supported by, the past (the aristocracy).*

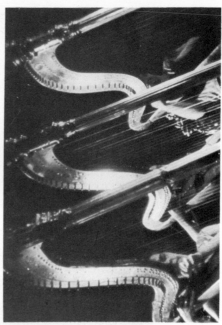

VI. Class war and the battle of the past with the future emerge in harsher form in **October**: (left) the proletariat wait for the appointed time; and (right) machinery is used to symbolize marching (revolutionary) time and harps motionless (bourgeois) time.

VII. *In* **The End of St Petersburg,** *the conservative peasant at first sides with the bourgeois establishment by informing on the workers (left); nevertheless he is thrown in jail (top right); and in response joins the revolution (bottom right).*

VIII. **Rome: Open City** *provides us with a cross-section of Italian society at war: a worker, a foreman and a priest are united in the Resistance against the Germans (top); but the resisters are killed and their children trail back to Rome (bottom).*

4

The American Civil War

Are we now saying that we can only understand characters and events in historical films by referring to the years in which those films were produced? It is certainly true that film-makers have an unerring instinct for selecting the facts and the circumstances that suit them – films on the French Revolution concentrate on the end of the monarchy, rather than the Reign of Terror, for example – but without neglecting contemporary references, we must go further and wonder whether the problems raised in films were necessarily the ones that excited passionate public opinion. From that point of view, *The Birth of a Nation* teaches us that films, by manufacturing a fanciful history, occasionally disclose carefully concealed problems.

The Birth of a Nation

The film opens with three sequences which could be described as a prologue. The Stoneman family lives in the North; the father is a politician in Washington, and his daughter, Elsie, stays with him while his two sons visit the Cameron family, and their three sons, in the South. We are shown the quiet, happy life of the Cameron family. The Stoneman boys arrive in Piedmont, where their friends live; the Cameron children accompany them on their country walks, visit a cotton field and generally enjoy themselves.

The film is then divided into two parts: the Civil War and the Reconstruction. The war begins with Lincoln's call for

83

volunteers. The Stoneman boys return home, and shortly after enlist in the US Army. The Cameron sons, meanwhile, join the
Confederate Army. The film does not attempt to show the
entire war – we see only particular episodes in the conflict.
First, Piedmont is invaded by the Union troops, but is liberated
by the Confederates. We see Atlanta under siege, and we attend
the death of the younger Cameron and Stoneman boys.
Eventually, we see Ben, the surviving Cameron son, lead a
desperate assault at the battle of Petersburg, during which he is
wounded. At the military hospital, Ben meets Elsie Stoneman,
who is a nurse (plate III). Ben is wrongly accused and condemned to death, although we are told nothing of the charge.[1]
His mother appeals to Lincoln for clemency, and Ben is freed.
He goes home and begins to rebuild his house. Peace returns,
but Lincoln is assassinated (plate III).

Stoneman becomes the man of the moment, although we are
not told why, and he does not appear to be the head of the
party. He goes South in order to accelerate the politics of
integration. His daughter meets Ben Cameron again, his son
courts Margaret, the eldest Cameron daughter, and the young-
sters spend some happy days together. Meanwhile, the carpet-
baggers persuade the blacks to vote for them; a mulatto,
Silas Lynch, is elected as lieutenant-governor; the blacks,
convinced that they are now masters of the South, persecute
the whites (plate II); the 'faithful souls' (those blacks who do
not support the carpet-baggers) are whipped and occasionally
killed. Thinking of the blacks as primitives, Ben decides to
frighten them; masked and dressed in white, he travels with
some friends through the countryside. The Ku Klux Klan, the
'invisible Empire of the South' is founded.[2] A renegade called
Gus, one of Lynch's friends, decides he would like to marry
Flora, the second Cameron daughter; meeting her in the
forest he pursues her; panic-stricken, Flora jumps over
a precipice and dies (plate II). Led by Ben, the Klansmen
murder Gus (plate II) and throw his body in front of Lynch's
house. Black soldiers search the Cameron house, but as Ben is
not at home, they arrest his father; Phil Stoneman kills one of
the soldiers; the Camerons escape and hide in a cabin which,
shortly after, is besieged by the soldiers. Elsie Stoneman goes to
Lynch's office to plead with him; he silences her and decides to

marry her immediately. Ben and the Klansmen arrive on horse back (plate II), the blacks run away, Elsie and the Camerons are rescued. Ben and Phil marry Elsie and Margaret.

When you are dealing with more than 1,000 shots in a film – and there are 1,599 shots in the longest version of *The Birth of a Nation* – you cannot hope to deal with all of them, without reclassifying them into groups. In a 'classical' film like this, it is possible to define a number of formal characteristics. To begin with, the film contains dividing lines, a kind of punctuation (if by punctuation we mean a break in the visual continuity) separating the groups of shots. The break is usually marked by a fade, but it is also sometimes indicated by a subtitle. We will distinguish here between strong breaks, marked by a fade plus caption, and weak breaks, marked by one or the other.

We must also take the editing into account. We have already spoken of the montage – the combination of shots in a certain order, and the effect this has on the meaning – but we have yet to list the main groupings of shots. As a 'typical' narrative film, *The Birth of a Nation* is an excellent starting point. In it, we find two sorts of editing, which I will call continuous and discontinuous; both types can be further broken down into two subdivisions.

A continuous montage may be descriptive or narrative. Descriptive editing lines up shots that complement one another, either because they deal with closely-connected characters or objects (as in the description of the Cameron family at the beginning of the film), or because they move from a general scene to a particular detail of that scene (the visit to the cotton field, for example). In narrative montage, the successive stages of an event are shown, the best example of this being Lincoln's assassination. Narrative editing usually coincides with the use of narrative time.

Discontinuous montage juxtaposes shots that relate to different series. Cross-cutting, in which scenes taking place simultaneously in different places are intercut, is an early and well-known example of discontinuous montage: we find this technique used at the end of the film, when shots of the people besieged in the cabin are cross-cut with shots of Ben's troop coming to rescue them. Parallel montage, in which shots of

85

different people linked by a common action appear in turn, is another familiar example: when the Stoneman sons leave for the war, we see them on the road, then their sister in front of the house, and so on. Another form of discontinuous editing, less commonly used, exploits contrasts, particularly of form and movement: we see this in the battle for Petersburg.

The superficial classifications proposed here do not aim merely at classification. Editing is a means of expression peculiar to the cinema; allowing for the obvious differences, it could be compared to the literary style of a book, and we shall see that it is of great importance in determining the meaning of a sequence.

The effect of a montage sequence is directed or modified by the use of subtitles. *The Birth of a Nation* is a wordy film, in which language is used a great deal. For a total of 1599 shots we have 211 captions – one subtitle for every $7\frac{1}{2}$ shots – but the total is not particularly significant. The place and function of the various groups of captions is more revealing. There are practically none in long passages like the Petersburg battle sequence or the last-minute rescue. We will discuss this in greater detail below, but for the moment, we will simply note that the captions fall into three main categories. The smallest group (30 subtitles) transcribes the words spoken by a character.[3] As a general rule – and I would like to stress this point – the characters speak very seldom; they express themselves through gestures (like the prolonged handshakes when the Stonemans arrive at the Camerons) or by facial expression (Phil Stoneman's pleading expression when he courts Margaret Cameron, or the sad silence of her reaction). We shall see that the use of either speech or silence is important. The film itself speaks, rather than the characters, in two different ways: at certain moments, subtitles are used to introduce events or characters, and these we will describe as pointers;[4] at other times, subtitles are used to express an opinion, which we will describe as comment.[5]

Be historical, at any price

86   The film's pretext, the Civil War, is established at once: North

and South are compared three times;[6] two 'comments' contrast federal power and the power of the states:

101: 'The power of the sovereign states established . . . in 1781 is threatened by the new administration.'
140: 'Abraham Lincoln uses the presidential office for the first time in history to call for volunteers to enforce the rule of the coming nation over the individual states.'

We see in turn the blue and grey uniforms, the Confederate flag and then both flags.

We have seen[7] that the historical nature of a film can be marked in two ways – either by showing well-known scenes or faces, or by indicating, particularly through dialogue or subtitles, that it is set in a specific period in the past. *The Birth of a Nation* makes abundant use of both methods, often together. As the film also underscores characters, scenes and documents in captions referring to historical texts,[8] it deserves to be called a 'doubly historical' film. This constant concern to establish the credentials of the film betrays a wish to be historical 'at any price'.

We will briefly examine the historical clues. First, the dates. There is no shortage of chronological detail. Shot 3 opens a period: 'The Abolitionists of the nineteenth century demanding the freeing of the slaves.' Shot 10 gives the starting point: 'In 1860, a great parliamentary leader, whom we shall call Austin Stoneman, was rising to power in the House of Representatives.' Shot 532 dates the death of Lincoln: 'And then . . . came the fated night of April 14th 1865.' Shot 532 closes the period: 'The negro party in control of the House of Representatives . . . . An historical fascimile of the state House of Representatives as it was in 1870.'

The period is clearly defined – the 1860s – but no precise dates are given for the war itself; the assassination occurs in the middle of the period, and is established with maximum precision. After shot 832, no further chronological information is given.

The film uses texts and drawings as documentary evidence.[9] Three famous scenes are also included: the famine in Petersburg, where the besieged residents have only a few grains of maize left; the surrender of the Confederate Army, with Lee on one side, stiff and perfectly controlled, and Grant on the other, rudely smoking his pipe (see plate III); and finally the assassination of Lincoln in a public theatre (see plate III).

Apart from Grant and Lee, who appear briefly in order to sign the surrender documents, and a short sequence in which Senator Sumner appears in conversation with Stoneman,[10] there is only one portrait in the film – that of Lincoln. I will discuss this special treatment later, but here I want to emphasize the care with which the character is identified. The first newspaper quotation refers to him indirectly, informing us that in the 1860 election Lincoln stood as the Northern candidate against a Southern opponent. A subtitle, introducing Lincoln, appears prior to the scene in which we see him examining the appeal for volunteers. Although he is perfectly recognizable, another caption breaks into the shot to name him again. Every effort is made to ensure that he is immediately recognized on each of his three appearances.

The documents and the set-pieces always lead back to the same sequences: there are one or two points in the film where reference, memory and historical tradition meet. We may describe these points as 'events', if we use the word 'event' to describe a brief action which dramatically alters the subsequent narrative – which certainly applies to Lincoln's assassination. What I think is particularly important in this film is the emphasis with which the events are thrown into relief. They are enclosed in specific cinematic units, fairly brief, in which subtitles and documents invariably play a part. Moreover, they are depicted with only one type of montage – continuous narrative editing. Take the signing of the appeal for volunteers as an example. In the preceding scenes, the montage consists of a varied succession of brief shots. The signing of the appeal is heralded by a subtitle, which also announces the reference document. An extended shot shows Lincoln examining the paper he has been given; another caption stresses the significance of the scene. We then see Lincoln signing the paper, meditating alone and beginning to weep. I will not describe the assassination itself in any detail, as the scene is a particularly precise reconstruction of the incident and would make tiresome reading.[11] We should note that the film uses a particular technique to underline the event, however: the sequence squares exactly with what we have called 'full-length time';[12] in *The Birth of a Nation* this cinematic temporality is the mark of the event.

The three major events – the signing of the appeal for volunteers, the surrender of the Southern Army, and the assassination of Lincoln – create breaks in the film, through their structural organization. The first two events mark the beginning and end of war and the third forms a division between the two parts of the film. If we consider only the events, we have a sort of diagram of the war: the North wins the election, and the South sees this as a threat; the President makes the threat concrete by mobilizing volunteers; war breaks out; the South loses; calm is beginning to return when Lincoln is assassinated. This a brief outline, using only a few facts, and strongly emphasizing the President's initiative. But the events which the film brings out – using the techniques that we have listed – occupy a very limited place in the film and, what is more important, are set in a continuity, in a whole that includes them. The problem is thus to find out what happens between them, what train of ideas leads from one event to another or, again, how history develops behind the event.

Between the first and last dates, the notion of time is confused. *The Birth of a Nation* offers no chronological identification marks, and even seems to ignore the duration of time. To take only one example, we see that two facts which were separated by nearly six months – the capture of Atlanta and Lee's surrender – are placed together as though one immediately followed the other. Through indirect signs the audience realizes that years have passed: a subtitle, a letter, changes in the appearance of Ben and his youngest sister. Whereas full-length time points out events, duration is not used as an historical fact, but simply as a component of individual existence. The film separates the event (a definite fact which is recorded in documents and has consequences in the form of other events) and evolution (a succession of years during which individuals live and change).

Today, we see the Civil War as the first great modern war, because of its exceptional length and the scale of the material resources used. The film ignores both these aspects. So, what does it show of the war?

North and South

To determine this, we will analyse the sequences coming between the two events which enclose the fighting. For this, we will start from strong breaks marked both by a fade and by a subtitle. We find three breaks, separating four episodes, which we will number:

Episode 1, the shortest: the departure of the Stoneman brothers;

Episode 2, the departure of the Southerners, with the Camerons among them;

Episode 3 is heterogeneous. It is devoted entirely to the Camerons, but first we are at the front with Ben, then with the family, and then with Ben again. If we were considering only the story, we would distinguish at least three episodes here, whereas the film strongly links the shots in this section: this is a case where we realize that a detailed study of the editing is essential in order to read a film;

Episode 4 deals with the battles, Atlanta and Petersburg, with, as we have already seen, an absence of breaks which, for an uninformed audience, makes the battle seem consecutive.

Episodes 1 and 2, the departures of the Northerners and of the Southerners, should be compared, or rather contrasted. This is a vital passage in the film, one of those which best show the differences between the Stonemans and the Camerons, and we will mention them again from this point of view. Here, we will examine only the distinction between the North and the South. The Northerners are allowed a very brief scene: eleven shots with only one subtitle. Elsie comes out of the house with her two brothers; she kisses them; they pass a hedge and come to the road; there is a kind of barrier separating the brothers and their sister; a parallel montage shows, in turn, the boys leaving, and the girl waving, imitating a soldier levelling his gun and aiming, and then going back into the house. The Southerners have 58 shots and 8 subtitles. The episode begins with a subtitle referring to the first Confederate success: the South already has a military past when, in the North, girls are playing soldiers. The montage of the episode is completely different from that of the first; several shots show the crowd cheering the flag; then we are in the Cameron home where the sons are saying goodbye to the family. The Camerons, isolated at first, come out and mingle with the crowd, while the sons join the troops and march between two close rows of civilians.

This is the only clearly marked contrast between North and South in the whole of the film. This distinction is not particularly original in itself and it had already been used in the cinema. In 1913 a film called *The Battle Hymn of the Republic* dealt with the mobilization in the North; the story begins with a picture of the resistance encountered by Lincoln's first call for volunteers. The President, who has realized that the recruiting offices are empty, is worried, and his associates try to rouse public opinion from its indifference. The important point is not that this had already been brought out in the cinema, but that *The Birth of a Nation* stresses this contrast alone, and ignores everything else that separates the two parts of the United States. The differences, perfectly obvious at the time, between an industrialized urbanized society, protectionist and abolitionist, and a primarily agricultural society, faithful to the great estates, to free trade and slavery, are completely ignored. We must note this surprising omission and try to explain it.

Episode 3 is easier to place, and the subtitles which begin and end it offer an interpretation: the individual suffering caused by the war. Here is another point to be emphasized: the effects of the war are essentially personal. Subtitle 214 provides a first link between the misfortunes of war and private life: 'Two and a half years later. Ben Cameron in the field has a letter from home'. Shot 215 opens with a partial view of the Southern quarters, but the field is immediately occupied by Ben, on whom the following shots concentrate. Ben reads a letter from his family, and this is followed by the family reading a letter from him; from the letter we move straight to the Cameron girls, who are in town and have to go home because of a raid by the Northern troops. Implicitly, for Ben, who is at the other end of the chain, what happens in Piedmont is not distinguished from what happens to the Camerons. The Northern attack, first launched in the streets of the town, is very soon brought down to the invasion of the Cameron home. The arrival of a Southern company, which drives the Northerners away, is taken first in the square in Piedmont, and then limited to the same house. There is nothing to show whether the Camerons are par-

91

ticularly affected, or if the whole town has suffered; out of 60 shots dealing with the attack, only 16 are taken out of doors; we know the adventures of only one family. The same construction, repeated three times – for Ben in his camp, for the Northern attack, and for the Southern operation – moves from a general viewpoint to a particular case. The scene of the Northern attack finishes with pictures of the broken furniture, a fire that the women are trying to put out, and the injured father: the effects of the war are reduced to the misfortunes of a single family. The other allusions to the consequences of the fighting that appear here and there in the film are of the same type. When Ben returns home, the dead sons are mourned, and then the people begin to mend what has been destroyed. Margaret refuses to marry Phil simply because she thinks of her dead brothers. The war has killed, it has destroyed – these are things that affect only one generation. But the film makes no mention of any profound damage or lasting effects on the economy or the society of the South.

Series 4 deals with two great battles. The episode that we are concerned with begins with general bird's-eye views: a valley, galloping horsemen, firing, smoke – a vast picture which aims at reproducing the general impetus of an attack. We very soon move on to an entirely different system, where the frames consist of closer shots showing only details (a small group of soldiers, or one man) and a discontinuous montage, constantly passing from one side to the other. The close-up photography gives a savage quality to the battle; instead of the mass movements of the beginning we have hand-to-hand fighting. Certain pictures are given a particular emphasis, like the one where we see a soldier driving his bayonet into his enemy's belly. This cruel war also has moments of heroism with, for instance, the man putting a flag in the muzzle of an enemy gun or the officer saving an injured man. All this is perfectly clear. It is more useful to stress the effects produced by the contrasting montage. For the first time the two sides are treated identically; the shots follow one another without always making it clear which side is being shown. The alternation, which creates a tension, also establishes a certain fusion: the characteristics of war are identical on both sides – the same relentlessness, the same wounds, the same heroism. The North is now placed on the same level as the South. If some readers are not convinced of this, I may remind them of two details. Caption 290: 'On the battlefield. War claims its *bitter, useless* Sacrifice'; the sacrifice is claimed both from North and South; the subtitle goes on: 'True to their promise, the Chums meet again'; the 'Chums' are the surviving Stoneman and Cameron boys; they meet on the battlefield and die together, arm in arm. Caption 311: 'While women and children weep a great conqueror marches to the sea'; the 'great conqueror' is General Sherman. The comparison between the first and second episode brought out the inferiority of the North; the last episode makes both sides equal.

A war with no cause

The stages of the transformation are missing, and I repeat that the film ignores duration considered as an historical factor. Why has the North caught up with the South? Why, if the two armies are comparable, does the South surrender? *The Birth of a Nation* neglects these questions; it shows only snapshots, precise facts at precise moments, but never an evolution, and it sees only effects without a cause. Each event, whether political or not, is imposed with no explanation. Why is Stoneman elected? Why does the South fear the election of Lincoln? Why does the President appeal for volunteers? Why does Booth assassinate the President? Rather than continue this list of unanswerable questions, I will simply remind you of one particularly obvious case: Ben, as a prisoner, is sentenced to death, but we do not know why he is sentenced.

The war – the subject of the first half of the film – has no explanation. The first nine shots seem to be leading to the black problem, but they are not followed up; in fact the question of slavery is hardly mentioned in the episodes which deal with the war. Immediately after this prologue with no sequel, we move on to the introduction of the families, and then the war.

In the absence of any explanation, we may compare all the events to see if there are any common characteristics in the way they are set in motion. I notice two in particular. First of all,

93

chance. Think of the assassination of Lincoln and the origin of the Ku Klux Klan; the detailed descriptions provided by the film clearly bring out the part played by chance. It is by chance that the bodyguard is away just when Booth is hanging round the box, and it is by chance that Ben sees some children playing at ghosts. But chance must be put to work, which brings in the second characteristic: individual initiative. An event occurs when a man acts and through his action alters the course of things; this is why the last-minute rescue occurs several times in *The Birth of a Nation*, whereas it generally happens only once, at the end of a film. And when Ben is sentenced to death what matters is not the reason but the outcome, Lincoln's intervention to prevent the execution.

In the film that we are concerned with, history is reduced to a series of events corrected or modified by chance or by human action. There are no causes, no gradual evolution or transformation, simply a succession of facts that the observer has to reconstitute with the help of documents and restore as faithfully as possible. Are we to conclude that the makers of the film are victims of the dominant historical conception of their time, and that they are content to reproduce in pictures what professional historians have said in their books? This would be a possible hypothesis if the film stopped at the death of Lincoln. But *The Birth of a Nation* continues after the assassination and we have to ask ourselves how it is that history, formally absent from the second part, nevertheless plays a part in it.

The historical demonstration is first of all a guarantee; the first part, based on records, appears so authentic that it is difficult to believe that the second is completely imaginary; we find the same characters on both sides of the break formed by 14 April; Lincoln's intervention in Ben's favour, and the presence of the Stonemans in the theatre on the evening when the President is assassinated, are justified in this way: the direct link with a famous man, who undeniably existed, gives a certain historical consistency to the fictional heroes and the trials they experience. The historical part also uses mechanisms – chance and human intervention – that serve again in the second part. In addition to these points, which are far from negligible, I see another, more important question. In giving a version of the war which ignores slavery, the film completely separates the war and

94

the black problem. The differences between North and South are systematically ignored; the effects of the fighting are reduced to a series of personal dramas; the war becomes a heroic tragedy which ends in the surrender of one of the contending forces. The function of the first part is to detach the slavery question from the crisis between the American states, and to bring it up again elsewhere, in another context. Lincoln's signing of the appeal for volunteers is accompanied by a subtitle we quoted earlier (Shot 140) and which might be thought to offer an explanation of the war: the latter, if we are to believe this text, satisfied an internal need, and was an essential stage in the development of the United States. But nothing in the rest of the film confirms this suggestion, and there are no references anywhere to the powers of the states or Federal power. This subtitle, which is quite unnecessary, is an additional camouflage, another way of drawing attention away from abolitionism.

We are now in a position to assess the part played by history in the film. It is used, strictly, for a political demonstration; the historical thesis put forward in *The Birth of a Nation* is neither 'clumsy' nor incomplete; it forms a system by which a problem – the Civil War – can be set aside and its 'place of application' transferred elsewhere, here, to the realm of individual decision and effort. The use of chance or individual initiative to explain events is not a weakness in conception. It is a means of ignoring the differences between the Northern and Southern production systems, the economic function of the slaves, and in doing so it makes the conflict between black and white the result of chance – the death of Lincoln – and then of the action of one man – Stoneman. The interesting point for us is not the history, but the way of organizing the presentation of this history.

The war of races

The first part of *The Birth of a Nation* evokes a war, the second part shows another war. The sequence that leads to the conflict is clear in the second episode: Ben sends a challenge to Lynch who takes it up (plate II). On both sides, they organize, they gather their troops; it starts with some skirmishes, then the fight begins in earnest. A comparison between the

95

two wars will bring out what differentiates them. The Civil War is a war without hatred. In front of Petersburg, Ben fights against Phil: the day before that, they were friends: nothing but a mere geographical coincidence separates them and they will be friends once more the following day. Between Ben and Lynch, only death can settle their differences. The two armies of the Civil War are identical, they use the same weapons, act with the same heroism and defend the same principles. In the war of races the antagonism is total: the blacks are the foot soldiers (plate II), the whites are the horsemen (plate II) and this difference is essential; besides the enormous superiority that it gives to the whites the horse evokes a legend that has its source in the conquest of the American territory. In many ways, *The Birth of a Nation* resembles a western: it is visible in the race between Ben and his companions to rescue the besieged cabin. The masters of horses are also, by implication, the masters of the country: the blacks only succeed in concentrating their forces on two specific points, Piedmont and the cabin; the whites, thanks to their mobility, are everywhere at once, invincible and innumerable (plate II). The blacks have no discipline whatsoever and fight in chaos; remember on the one hand when the whites come to Lynch's house and, on the other hand, the siege of the cabin by the blacks: the two scenes were made in parallel and it is the film that emphasizes their contrast; the blacks are restless, they gesticulate, trample: in the twinkling of an eye the whites are the masters of the place. There are two parallel violent deaths which are introduced in almost similar frames: the death of the second Cameron son and the death of the second Cameron daughter; the first one is squeezed between the two battles; it appears as a straightforward episode and does not call for vengeance; the dramatic death of the young woman requires vengeance and becomes the point from which white resistance spreads out.

It would be easy to continue with the parallel but we know enough to see what separates the different parts of the film. After Lincoln's death, things are exactly the reverse of what they were before, the situation in the second period is like the negative of the first one. The link between the two is possible thanks to the existence of Stoneman. He appears briefly at the beginning of the film and then disappears during the war. It is interesting to note that he is introduced immediately after what should be called the prologue, in other words, after the nine isolated shots that make a brief allusion to the blacks at the beginning of the film. These scenes open with a violent affirmation: division comes about with the blacks; then there is a quick and ironic presentation of the meetings held by the abolitionists: coming just after those shots, Stoneman is indirectly characterized as a ridiculous man and as a divider of people, as a trouble-maker. As we have already pointed out, it would be useless to try to identify him: he is not a portrait nor does his presence intend a precise allusion to a well-known politician; he is essentially the anti-Lincoln. We have already noted that there are few subtitles reporting someone's words and the characters speak only infrequently: Lincoln is not used to speaking much and acts through writing; Stoneman, like his friend Lynch, does not stop talking. Lincoln characterizes simplicity itself: remember the way in which he greets Ben's mother; Stoneman likes being surrounded with people and accepts scandalously undemocratic homages. Lincoln expresses his feelings and does not hide his emotions; Stoneman play-acts and never tries to help anybody. Here again, the editing provides an excellent clue: the episodes concerned with Lincoln are mounted in a narrative continuity which gives them a strong unity; the episodes dedicated to Stoneman are either static or built around rather strong oppositions. We are eventually left in no doubt as to Stoneman's programme or his ambition.

The historical logic of the film demonstrates its efficiency: after Lincoln the position is neatly reversed; a mere inversion is enough to change from good to evil, from unity to division.

It will be easy to understand the reversal that took place if we pay some attention to the initial situation of the blacks. They only appear three times in the first section and that is sufficient to define their role in the beginning of the film. After the young Stonemans arrive in Piedmont, the friends go over to the cotton field and then to the black neighbourhood. Two identical scenes demarcate the visit to the plantations; in fact, they could be the same scene cut in editing. It is an extensive view, shot from above, of a field in the middle of which two blacks are working; the coming of the whites obliterates the blacks; the youths examine the plants, continue with their love affairs and,

97

when they have finished, they leave, vacating the landscape where the blacks remain alone, wrapped up in their work. In their neighbourhood the blacks greet the visitors and start dancing; the friends watch a while and then leave; the subtitle accompanying this scene, perhaps deliberately, is very precise: the blacks are slaves.[13] The Stonemans, however, do not seem embarrassed: they follow their friends, admire the flowers, pay scant attention to the dancing of the slaves. Their attitude confirms what we had already noted, that the black question does not create an immediate opposition between the Northerners and the Southerners. The blacks are almost invisible, they are part of the landscape in which they have their well-defined tasks; at best, they are to be glanced at, like strange objects, and the film devotes only a few brief shots to their dancing.

The blacks re-appear during the Northern attack on Piedmont. The operation centres on the sacking of the Camerons' house, and the film identifies where the responsibility for this lies: the initiative comes from a white abolitionist. We know with what prudent reserve the abolitionists are presented in the prologue; the attack episode confirms that judgement: abolitionism leads only to revolt and destruction; the white man has decided that the blacks are capable only of following and destroying.

The intervention of Stoneman brings with it total confusion. Stoneman claims he wants equality between the blacks and the whites: in reality, he puts the blacks above the whites. While he remains seated when receiving visitors, he stands up for only one man, Lynch. The assigning of rights to the blacks brings about the suppression of these same rights for the whites, as we see when the vote takes place.[14] Under Lincoln, the black militiamen obey the white officer; under Lynch, the white officer obeys the orders of the blacks. In the past, the blacks were objects of entertainment; with Lynch, a white man, the old Cameron, is chained (enslaving him) and offered as entertainment to the blacks. Many other details confirm that point, but more important is the fact that, in the second part of the film, the blacks become visible. I use this term deliberately: people we could not see, who were never present suddenly become visible. In the first part, we almost ignore whether the Camerons have servants or not; remember the introduction to the family: we see the dogs, cats and other pets, but only one glimpse suggests that there are also black servants in the house. After the Northerners' attack, the Camerons extinguish the fire by themselves, repair the destruction and attend to the wounded father without any help from the slaves. Suddenly, when Lynch arrives, slaves appear who seem to be familiar with the place; at the end of the film, the 'faithful souls' 'take a hand', acquire a role and help to rescue the family.

The whitewash

There is another even more remarkable aspect: the screen is progressively submerged by the blacks. Under Lincoln the blacks do not walk in the streets of Piedmont. After the arrival of Lynch a shot shows the Cameron house with Ben and his sister coming out of it; a detachment of black soldiers overthrows the youths and parades, covering the whole screen: the whites are now obliterated just as the blacks were previously (Plate II). In all the scenes which appear after this episode the whites are drowned in the middle of the black. Let us take only one example, the shot where we see the election: on the right hand side a soldier and a black onlooker; on the left hand side, the black voters. A voter coming out allows us to glimpse a white secretary, who immediately disappears; when a white voter enters, he is thrown out. The editing helps to produce the same effect. Eight shots are dedicated to the scene in the Courts in which the blacks judge, plead and demonstrate; only one shot, the fifth, shows white people, and it is framed by scenes showing blacks. This scene is itself shut between two shots in which Ben, confined in his house, is telling his friends about the ill-deeds of the blacks. With a Court/private house opposition, the film creates a contrast between private and public places. The first step of the black conquest is the invasion of public places, streets, meeting rooms, assemblies, from which the whites are completely eliminated; the second step occurs when the blacks become the masters of private places as well, invading the Cameron houses and imposing their law even in Stoneman's house. The intervention of the Ku Klux Klan is presented as a real cleansing. Here, it is important to observe the editing

99

process. Let us go to the point when Stoneman comes back and Lynch tells him he wants to marry his daughter. Several alternating shots show a crowd of shouting, gesticulating blacks and horsemen galloping on the plain; we then meet a setting we already know, the Piedmont public square. The montage shows, in alternation, partial views of the fight and general views of the public square; each time the scene returns to the public square the horsemen have progressed. Finally, they cover the public square: then, we have partial views of blacks running away who are, each time, replaced by whites. What seems to be worth pointing out is the use of colour, the carefully built opposition between black and white, darkness and light (plate II).

The actions of the whites can be compared to a crusade. In the film, little room is given over to the religious idea: there is no praying for the dead boys, no Pastor, no cult. The first two actions of the Ku Klux Klan, led by only a few men, are mere reprisals (plate II), but, as the Klan expands, it takes the Cross as its symbol. Klansmen are shown meeting by night and giving orders to a messenger: they show him a cross and he runs away to summon the clans. Later, two horsemen, one of whom is carrying a cross and the other a torch, are galloping through the country as other horsemen appear on all sides. The demoniacal nature of the blacks is strongly suggested: they meet in a disreputable place, a 'dive', they drink more than is reasonable, they are the people of the bottom, of the land, the people that creep and crawl. The two sides use spies and, as the film carefully differentiates them, it is interesting to compare them: the white spies ride horses and show themselves in the open, on Piedmont's public square; the blacks spying on the Cameron house do not look through the window, they appear at the bottom of the wall, in such an absurd position that it only makes sense because it creates – for the spectator – an association with the image of a malevolent devil. The blacks stick to the ground, the whites come from the skies, their horses give them wings, they fly through space in an instant and they wear white tunics that recall a heavenly militia. The film works with elementary contrasts but it does not intend to create frightening effects; it is not a horror film, the invaders are not monsters that have come from another universe, they are primitives rather than vile beings.[15] This medieval European imagery, representing Hell and the struggle of the angels against the devils, does not seem to have anything to do with the United States in 1914, and it seems to me that we have here a potentially interesting topic for further research – the study of the survival of demoniacal aspects of medieval religion in twentieth-century America.

With Stoneman in power, the institutions which previously guaranteed order now serve disorder; the classes that were at the bottom of society rise to the top; institutions perform in a way contrary to all previous expectations. The direct cause of this is clear: it is the change of leadership. The immediate effects are well described but this statement does not allow us to pass beyond a very superficial level of analysis; we speak of precisely defined reasons whereas the film bathes in an atmosphere of hatred, fear and contempt towards the blacks. Apart from the immediate cause, what is the underlying peril that threatens the whites?

First of all it is interesting to note that racial hatred appears to have no economic base; it is remarkable how these problems have been eliminated from the film. We ignore what the Stonemans and the Camerons are, what they do for a living. The plantation we see at the beginning might belong to the Camerons although it is impossible to prove it. Immediately after the Civil War, the Camerons seem to be poor, wear shabby clothes and work with their hands, but they are soon wearing their former clothes and seem to have no occupation; the elegant Ben seems to spend most of his time courting Elsie. It is important to note that the only time we hear about work is when Ben is looking for help to capture Gus: the young man goes to the blacksmith, two strong men leave their hammers to walk after him, one of them enters a bar and gives five drunken blacks a thorough beating. The young blacksmith is treacherously shot down as he comes out of the bar. On the one hand, the only white worker is eliminated and we do not know who the rest of the family are. On the other hand, the blacks do not seem to have any economic function – only the whites have useful jobs.

The Stem family

The blacks make no material demands; they destroy the

furniture of the whites but they do not loot, they do not take anything. The only thing they want is to be able to marry white women. I insist upon this marriage question, although it could be misunderstood. It is obvious that the blacks are presented as brutish rapists of white women and that their sexual appetite is part of their demoniac aspect: the youngest of the Cameron girls kills herself rather than be touched by a black; in the besieged cabin both Doctor Cameron and the ex-soldier are ready to kill their own daughters rather than let them fall into the hands of the blacks. But the blacks only think about marrying. The most important law voted by the Congress – which has a black majority – is the right for blacks to marry whites: when Gus approaches the young Cameron, he proposes to her.[16] Lynch demands Elsie's hand; when he has mastered the young lady, he does not think of raping her but of marrying her.[17] The suspicion of rape reinforces the foul, unbearable nature of black domination but what is really scandalous is the overthrow, the fact that blacks think they could be allowed to marry the whites. What we should try to understand is the fear of miscegenation, of intermarriage, which is quite separate from the disgust aroused by sexual relations between blacks and whites.

The film ends with the unity between the Northerners and the Southerners, unity which is friendly at first, consolidated by the fighting against the blacks and ratified by a double marriage. Let us see how the marriages are presented. On the Southern part, we have a perfect family. There is a strong break, in our sense of the word – marked by a fade plus a subtitle – between the presentation of the Stonemans and the presentation of the Camerons. After the beginning of the film, five subtitles describe the Cameron house and the people who live in it. The scene is organized in a continued descriptive montage: we go from one overall view to a particular view, moving from the outside, as a stranger would perceive it, to the inside. First, we have the street and the house: we come nearer so as to distinguish the flight of steps, the colonnade; we stop on the flight of steps, we are inside; we discover, in the same shots, the place, the family and these shots establish the ties between the members of the family, as we see Ben with his parents, with his father, with his youngest sister, with his two sisters. The presentation of the characters, the fondness they have for each other, the affection they share, all this occurs in the frame of the house, the colonnade which remains visible in the background. Except for the final scene when the black menace has deprived the Camerons of their roof, the family meets only in the house. The strength of the family ties is constantly reasserted: we have already noted that the whole family participates in the departure of the boys to the war; how, during the war, the fate of Ben and the fate of his parents are linked; the continuous correspondence and complicity between them. I will add only two new details: the battle of Petersburg is interrupted by a shot in which we see the Cameron family praying for the boys; at the end of the battle, we only see the dead and it is through the Cameron house, indirectly, that we know Ben has survived; the news is given in a letter; in peace, as in war, letters unite the Cameron family. At the end of the Civil War, the mother rescues Ben; at the end of the war between the races, Ben rescues the family. The birth of the Ku Klux Klan is narrowly linked to the family: it is in the house that Ben gathers some friends to tell them about the blacks' wrongdoings; the women sew the white tunics; when Lynch orders the search, Ben hides the tunic at his house, which is illogical as the police would certainly search it but understandable if we remember the symbolic value of the place. Besides, the blacks are conscious of it; their only action, in the first part of the film, is the sacking of the house; with Lynch, the climax of their rampage is the invasion of the house.[18]

We have been talking of the importance given to the house in the narrative, but we should also consider the importance of the visual effects produced by the film. I pointed out the first appearance of the house: the building, clearly visible on the right-hand side, diagonally; other buildings, hardly distinguishable, at the bottom: the street on the left. The same frame is systematically retaken, later on, every time we approach either Piedmont or the Cameron family; it is from this shot that we view, very quickly, the central public square and other houses in the town; all of the important developments – the departure of the soldiers, the incursion of the Northerners, the conflict between Ben and Lynch, the coming of Stoneman, the arrest of the Cameron family, the final battle – take place at this geographic point. The family – or the house, as we know it is the same thing – is the stable element in the film; all of the important events take place around it.

Let us now look at the Stonemans: they do not constitute a family. I should say now that we will not find here the classical opposition between the rural family of the South, attached to the land, and the urban family of the North, divided by industry. No town other than Piedmont appears in the film. Moreover, it is specified that the Stonemans also have an estate in the country. As we already know, the film refuses to see the Civil War as a conflict between two different types of society: the Stonemans and the Camerons have the same life-style, the only difference being that the Stonemans are not a family. The Stonemans are presented in two different blocks, separated by a subtitle; we first meet the father and the daughter and then the brothers with their sister; the presentation is made without real montage, with only one backdrop (the living room) for the father and his daughter, another (the garden) for the children. The differences between the Stonemans and the Camerons are obvious: there is no mother; the two parts of the family (father – sons) are completely separated and we never see Stoneman together with his three children in the entire film; the Stonemans have no house and, except for three shots, we always meet Austin Stoneman in an impersonal room – a private office or a living room. We do not know in which building he lives. Remember the important scene when the young Stonemans leave for the war: only Elsie says goodbye to the boys and there is a quick visual separation between the two groups. Austin Stoneman never acts as a father: whereas Doctor Cameron fights when they want to take his daughter away, Stoneman does not. His relationship with his daughter Elsie is ambiguous, bordering on incest: now she caresses him like a husband, now takes care of him like a child.

There is only one family, one house – the Camerons'. The final marriage is not the association of two families but the reproduction of the existing family. On the battlefield Ted Stoneman and Duke Cameron are killed together, hand in hand, like two brothers. Later, two Camerons, a son and a daughter, are killed and replaced by a boy and a girl: the family has not changed. Phil integrates easily with the family: from the beginning we see him in the frame of the Cameron house; during the war he treats Ben as a brother and, in the final fight he takes the place that a Cameron should have taken. The integration of Elsie is less obvious and it is achieved in three different ways: with the portrait that ties the young lady to the Camerons, without her knowing it;[19] through the coming and going of letters in which Phil participates from the beginning and in which he involves his sister; through the close ties the film creates between Elsie and the young Cameron daughter. At the end of the film, in the final parade, we can clearly distinguish the Cameron parents and the four children parading side by side. Stoneman has long since disappeared.

What the film shows is the endogamic family, the unique family, the departure point and the issue: the family house. In 1914 it is impossible for brothers to marry their sisters openly and subterfuges have to be invented. If we ignore the names, if we only think about the relationships between the characters, we find out that the Camerons marry each other. The film does not endorse the old rural slave society; it even refuses to consider its economic bases: its dream is a sort of American family, complete in itself, refusing any outside interference. The drama of the black invasion originates in this fact: marrying a black would be like marrying a complete stranger, someone who would never be a brother, never enter the family. The only genuine unity is the unity of the family, of the clan and they have to protect it by all means.

A scandalous film

The Birth of a Nation was a very successful film. It was presented simultaneously in Los Angeles and in New York and was retained for six months in the first city and eleven in the second. The first year it was shown, it was seen by several million people; no film had ever had so large an audience and its release marked a turning point in the cinematographic industry. In 1910, the industry was producing mostly short films lasting for five to ten minutes; the films were screened in small cinemas, cost little money and the programme changed every day; produced very cheaply, the strips had short lives. The size of the audience determined whether or not there would be any profit. From 1908, the main producers had joined together in what was called the 'Edison Trust'; it was not a trust but an agreement guaranteeing each of the subscribers exclusive rights to the use of equipment manufactured by Edison. Members of the trust created a distribution company, General Film, which supplied 60 per cent of the cinemas, but the conditions of sale were rigorous and many cinema owners refused to sign the contract offered – and found themselves with no films to show. To supply their demands, small companies started producing films using other equipment. These 'independent' producers had difficulty in replacing their equipment, however, and were forced to choose between being absorbed by the trust or finding an alternative solution.

The industry in Europe suggested one possibility. European film-makers were already producing big-budget feature films, lasting more than an hour, and with a proper scenario, film 'stars' and a host of extras. In 1912 some US independents decided to emulate this example, and branched out into feature film production, only to confront further difficulties: the distribution network was virtually non-existent, the cinemas were too small and the public unenthusiastic. The first one-hour American film, *The Life of Moses*, had to be cut into four episodes, which were then shown on four consecutive days in the nickelodeons. Firms that had branched out into feature films found capital hard to come by: in 1916, the most important of the independent companies, the Famous Players, had only $100,000 capital, and most of the companies had nearer $20,000. As the average cost of a feature film was roughly $20,000, the independent producers operated on very tight margins. If expensive ticket prices and longer runs failed to realize a profit, the only alternative was bankruptcy – which is just what happened most of the time.

In this context, *The Birth of a Nation* appeared at just the right moment. Businessmen, cameramen and actors worked together on a project for which they had no precedent: a two-hour film with a budget in excess of $100,000.[20] In Europe, productions on this scale had been accepted by the public for many years, but in the United States it was the first of its kind.

106   Originally, the film was nothing more than a speculative

venture, although it is not possible to discover the source of the funds provided. Anyone hoping to learn more about film investment of any sort must expect to meet with a stony silence on matters of total investment and final profit. We know the actors, the studios, but as far as the money is concerned we have to be content with vague details. In 1910, investments were small – roughly $2,000 to $3,000 per film. By 1920, costs had risen by 100 per cent, but by this time, the larger companies, with support from their bankers, had total control of production. Between 1910 and 1920, the finance involved in the production of a feature film could still be raised from a few private sources.

The triumph of *The Birth of a Nation*, which paid back the initial investment 120 times, marks a turning point in film production.[21] By 1916, financiers were already investing in the cinema, and in discussing this development I think we should recall some of the theories on the relationship between film and society that we have already mentioned – in particular, the theory proposed by the group of Danish historians. If we examine only particular aspects of the film, we note a remarkable co-incidence between the role of the producer and the mechanism brought into play in the film: the film insists upon the value of individual initiative and on the role men can play in re-ordering their lives. Certainly, at this stage in the development of the industry, a few individuals did try to succeed in big business. Their success accelerated the disappearance of the Edison cinema and hastened the monopoly of Hollywood. But we must admit that the opposite is also the case: these same producers were businessmen, adventurers swimming with the prevailing current – and yet their films celebrate the 'golden age' of the patriarchal family, endogamous, alien to economic growth. This is why the assumption that there is a necessary link between the social background of the film-makers and the social relations described in their films seems to me to be a worthless one. Sometimes it is true, sometimes not, and a theory that applies only occasionally is of very little use.

The Birth of a Nation sounds a warning note, in the call to defend the unity of the American people. The United States in 1914 faced two very different problems: labour agitation, rife since the turn of the century, had prompted large-scale strikes;

and foreign policy had divided public opinion on two issues – US intervention in Mexico and the Antilles, and the need to take sides in the European conflict. And yet neither of these problems was really acute. A domestic crisis was not immediately apparent, and the alarmist tone of the film is therefore somewhat surprising, particularly as the central danger – the black problem – was one on which the American people were apparently prepared to keep silent, as if everything had been settled. The film – certainly an alarming and shocking one – did not come out during a depression, when the future was uncertain and people were glad to escape in nostalgia for the good old days. It appeared when expansion and growth seemed to have no limits, when anyone could hope for success. How then can we explain the public enthusiasm for the film? We should be circumspect about this: there is no evidence that audiences were attracted by the film's message. In 1915, the feature film was still a novelty, and that could have been the main attraction: audiences were not yet bored with them. We shall never know what prompted audiences to see *The Birth of a Nation*. We can only assume that an interest in American history entered into it. *The Battle of Gettysburg* was also a popular success, although less spectacularly so than *The Birth of a Nation*, but the following year, *Intolerance*, dealing mostly with ancient and European history, was a dismal failure. *The Battle of Gettysburg* and *The Birth of a Nation* introduced an heroic version of American military history, and it would be interesting to pursue this point a little further and undertake a systematic study of the image of the American army in the cinema prior to 1917.

The slogan of the film could be: keep American WASP – White, Anglo-Saxon, Protestant. Fear of immigrants was already strong in those years although no one had yet spoken of limiting entry to the country. The film does not denounce foreigners, but it shows that the fate of the United States depends on the American people only; it praises the 'primitive family', free from any racial contamination and insidiously reinforces a covert distrust of the outside.

Drawing a hostile picture of the blacks, *The Birth of a Nation* is audacious; it shows with violence images the Southerners desire and the Abolitionists fear; the taboo was so strong that any critical presentation of the blacks aroused interest: the film provoked a scandal – but a limited one. It presents the obvious points – military pride, fear of the immigrants, fear of seeing the black problem arise again, the dream of a pre-industrial America – in such a narrow way that no crisis can result from it. Taking that into consideration, we may put forward an hypothesis: have not some apparently provocative films channelled potentially explosive fears or desires which consumed a society at particular moments in its history?

The inherited framework

The Birth of a Nation is both a western and an historical movie. Around 1915, westerns had not ousted other cinematographic styles and the Civil War was at the film-makers' disposal. In fact, although it has been the subject or the setting for many pictures the war has not given rise to any filmic tradition. It would be necessary to synthesize the various aspects of this period in American films, to draw a parallel with problems current at the time of the production, to determine if editing changes according to the conceptions of historiography or according to the dates. I do not intend to treat this question. I shall merely summarize how it is possible to consider the influence of *The Birth of a Nation* upon subsequent film descriptions of the war.

Historiography is a way of determining, among the numberless 'events' which 'happened' in the past, the ones which are important, and of defining connections between these events; it is a conventional setting of some social relations and it would be very interesting for historians to know how these conventions are established, how long they last, when they are transformed. Of course, facts are not clear; we cannot suppose that forms, values and themes emerge, endure and disappear, we guess that accepted formulas are gradually challenged by new forms until they are rejected. In this book, where we are not concerned with 'official' historiography, we are lucky enough to deal with rather simple things. As *The Birth of a Nation* had been a fantastic success and had at the same time created a scandal, film-makers were tempted to imitate it and at the same time, to avoid anything that might be contentious. In

109

this narrow field – the cinematographic versions of the Civil War – we observe a noteworthy continuity; we see, in film after film, the same omissions and the same predictable configurations.

Let us look at a film which is probably as well known as *The Birth of a Nation – Gone with the Wind* (1939). I suggest that we ignore the romantic plot (the story of an ambitious woman, Scarlett O'Hara, who experiences different crises, public and private, guards against them as best she can and constantly works towards her destiny) but look at the Civil War and the Reconstruction, which serve as a background in the first part and the beginning of the second part. The list of 'historical circumstances' seems to have been borrowed from *The Birth of a Nation:* quiet life in a Southern family; blacks working in the cotton fields; the call for volunteers in the North; excitement in the South and the departure of the young men to war; war misfortunes (plate III), hunger, fear, death; Atlanta besieged; the Confederates' surrender; repairing of houses and cultures; invasion of carpet-baggers and the self-defence of the Southerners. Numerous shots of *Gone with the Wind* were drawn from *The Birth of a Nation* but, rather than listing them, I shall insist upon more important likenesses.[22] We have strongly underlined the importance of evidence in *The Birth of a Nation* and the care taken in proving the historical value of the film. The same regard for historical truth is obvious in *Gone with the Wind.* Captions, voices over, giving general information, act as 'narrative voice' – the voice of history.[23] The end of the siege of Atlanta is particularly memorable in the overlapping of Scarlett's point of view and 'narrator's' point of view; starting from Scarlett's experiences, the film briefly abandons the young lady and gives a wider and more detailed over-view of the situation before returning to the heroine. From Ashley's return to the front line till Scarlett's flight through burning Atlanta, the film is punctuated by a constant swing from characters to narrator. In a famous passage, Scarlett, looking for the doctor, arrives at the station; we have her photographed in medium shot and, while running, back turned to us, she passes corpses, wounded men, stretchers; as we are looking at the scene from her point of view, we do not focus on the dead bodies; one of the effects of the editing technique is to restrict the spectator's attention to only one of the many potential views encompassed in every shot; we ignore the wounded, for we are following Scarlett as she moves forward, seen from slightly different angles. Suddenly we are looking from another perspective; Scarlett is outside, and a bird's-eye view shows the square filled with the wounded (plate III). The camera, moving slowly off, reveals a huge expanse covered with thousands of bodies, laid everywhere, even on the rails; now we hear moans and calls, whereas earlier the soundtrack had been muffled and indistinct. The shot ends with a Confederate flag half obscuring the screen. Shortly after, Scarlett finds the doctor. In the same sequence, then, we have watched the difficulties of the heroine and we have been told of the atrocities of the war. Authenticity, constantly reaffirmed, is drawn from general and individual behaviour. I am not claiming that Scarlett's story is given as a 'true story', but that 'the true history' of the war is presented as a mixture of general massacre and individual suffering. The Civil War is an accumulation of private misfortunes and disasters – all of them gathered together in a general overthrow. War – by which I mean war on film – implies death and slaughter. To say that war is intrinsically cruel is to miss the point, for we are not looking at 'war in itself' but at images of war. Brutal though they are, American screen battles are rarely fierce in films made before 1914, and if we look at the French cinema, we realize that the terrible battles of the Revolution of the Napoleonic era never appear on screen. Violence is not a necessary characteristic of war in films; it is specific to certain films, particularly films dealing with the Civil War.

We are in fact discussing a type of film that is both individual and sentimental; the second of these two adjectives is not meant to be disparaging – it gives a succinct definition of the framework within which these films are enclosed. I suggest that we consider Civil War films as 'family stories' dropped in to a bloody nightmare. But we must ask another question. To what extent does 'realism', 'realistic' description of individual suffering, insistence upon family ties, limit the war to simple, straightforward issues and how far does it evade the possibility that there might be other interpretations?

The similarities between *The Birth of a Nation* and *Gone with the Wind* stop when the Southerners secretly take up arms.

Kennedy, Scarlett's second husband, is killed: his murder should lead to retaliation, but we hastily step out of history and the film finishes with the domestic quarrels of Rhett Butler and Scarlett. The uprising of the South has no place in a film which is intended to win ten Oscars. Kennedy's death is dismissed as if it had been the private revenge of a jealous husband; yet Scarlett had been assaulted by black prowlers; after the first reaction of the Southerners, everybody admits that the heroine had incited the blacks to aggression and the blame for Kennedy's death lies with her. Such circumspection ties in with the film's deliberate silence on the black problem. Until 1960 the American cinema avoided showing black characters altogether – in a favourable or critical light. The black servants in *Gone with the Wind* are pets, as the ones in *The Birth of a Nation* had been; but the 'faithful souls' in the latter film rescued the Camerons persecuted by the 'devils', whereas the blacks who live with Scarlett are shadows at the margin of the film. Carpet-baggers alone are liable for the upset of the South.

Evidence for the conformity to a pattern is limited to one film and will need to be increased by further researches on other films; many films do not conform to the model, which does not mean that they have departed from the tradition. Without trying to carry the analysis through, I would like to open the debate with a comment on another film that apparently departs from the traditional pattern. *The Horse Soldiers* is an unremarkable film, released in 1959 when the US cinema was beginning to stage black heroes; the plot concerns a column of Northerners which dives far into the South and destroys warehouses. The picture is enclosed in the achievement of the mission and has nothing in common with our 'model'. If we scrutinize the sequences we realize very soon that they correspond to several of the issues that delimited the possibilities of screening the Civil War before 1915:

1. Spying (Northerners are like spies in Southern territory; they are spied by a young woman and then by an officer; the episode of the Southerner welcoming the enemies in order to allay suspicion and disclose military information is an exact reminder of some films made in the 1910s).

2. Betrayal and punishment (traitors of the Confederate army punished by the Unionists).
3. Love stronger than war (the spying woman is obliged to go with the column; romance between her and the Unionist officer).

But all the elements which, taken separately, refer to the old cinematographic version of the war are shaped in a framework similar to the one we defined earlier. It is not the exact 'pattern' but we find the same omissions; events and characters are confined to the same limited sphere of relationships:

1. Blacks kept in the background (once again in the margin, in poor villages where they live apart; the only black character, a servant, is killed without our knowing why).
2. Mixture of private life (in the lives of the two main characters) and war;
3. Horrors and atrocities of war.

Thus we wonder whether there is not, from the 1920s to the 1960s, an intersection between the old pattern, as described in a previous chapter, and the new pattern carried by *The Birth of a Nation*, with various arrangements and groupings. If that is the case we have the opportunity of investigating how two traditions of historiography coexist in a film production. Of course, our hypothesis cannot be taken for granted and we shall not be able to confirm or invalidate it until we have completed a thorough survey of the Civil War on film.

Notes

1. See above, p. 29.
2. We already know (see p. 23) that, in 1930, Griffith issued a new shortened sound version; he suppressed every mention of the Ku Klux Klan. The expression: 'Invisible Empire of the South' was borrowed from Wilson's *History of the American People*, vol. V, p. 60.
3. For instance, caption 61; Duke Cameron asks Ted Stoneman: 'Where did you get that hat?'

4. For example, caption 13: 'Elsie with her brothers at the Stoneman country home, Pennsylvania'.

5. Caption 27: 'The home of the Camerons where life runs in a quaint way that is to be no more'.

6. Caption 53: 'The visit of the Stoneman boys to their Southern friends'. Caption 59: 'Chums – the younger sons. North and South'. Caption 103: 'If the North carries the election, the South will secede'. The sound version adds a further subtitle after shot 104: 'The South will never submit to the North's dictation'.

7. See pp. 60–64.

8. Notice that references are often wrong. Lincoln is presented in his study, restaged 'according to Nicholay and Hey' but these writers, in their book: *Lincoln. A History, 1901–1910*, do not give any picture of Lincoln's study. Sentences taken from Wilson are falsified by cuts. But, for spectators, the only important thing is that the film is based on well-known historical books.

9. See above, p. 61 and 63.

10. For Senator Sumner and his relation to Stoneman, see above, pp. 32–33.

11. The audience was struck by such a detail. The day after the first show in New York, *The New York Sun* writes that the assassination of Lincoln, 'with the play *Our American Cousin* going forward on the stage is shown in careful accordance with the historical accounts of it. How Lincoln's guard left his post to get a view of the play; how Booth, waiting in the rear of another box, slipped through the door in the interval and fired at the President as he watched the play, all are seen'. (See plate III.)

12. See above, p. 57.

13. Subtitle 94: 'In the slave quarter. The two-hour interval given for dinner, out of their working day from six till six'.

14. 'Election day. All blacks are given the ballot while the leading whites are disfranchised.'

15. In the early days of the film industry, negroes, when they appeared on screen, were played by white actors; negro actors began to play only in 1914 and, in *The Birth of a Nation*, all the negroes, but an old woman, are whites. Negroes were always stupid men, like Stoneman's servants or devoted slaves, like the Camerons' 'faithful souls'. The bad negro marked his first appearance with Silas Lynch. See: Peter Noble, *The Negro in Films*, London, 1948 and Jim Pines, *Blacks in Films, A Survey of Racial Themes and Images in the American Film*, London, 1975.

16. 'You see, I'm a captain now – and I want to marry.' Notice that, in Dixon's novel, Flora is raped by Gus; her mother thinks the

only outcome is suicide; they both throw themselves from the cliff into the ravine. As a rape was screened, the following year, in *Intolerance*, it is impossible to say that the producers were afraid of showing a raped girl.

17. Lynch to Stoneman: 'I want to marry a white woman ... The lady I want to marry is your daughter'.

18. Lynch is said to hope 'to wreak vengeance on Cameron House'.

19. 'Though we have never met I have carried you about with me for a long, long time.'

20. The first producer, the Mutual Film Corporation, gave two commitments of $40,000 and $20,000 which were promptly used. Harry Aitken, one of the largest buyers of movies in America, organized his own company. the Epoch Producing Corporation, to take over the film. Aitken and William Clune, director of the Los Angeles Auditorium gave the main part of the budget; small amounts were given by friends, actors, technicians. The final budget is said to have reached $110,000.

21. 'Through the success of *The Birth of a Nation* the two-dollar movie was born. The sole habitat of the movies was no longer Eighth Avenue, Sixth Avenue and Fourteenth Street; the movies had reached Broadway to stay', Linda Arvidson, *When the Movies were Young*, New York, 1925, p. 255. In *D. W. Griffith. His Life and Work*, New York, 1972, R. M. Henderson writes (p. 161): 'It has been estimated that the film's gross receipts topped $48,000,000'.

22. The objection will be raised that *Gone with the Wind* was first a novel which was adapted for the screen. We might answer that the writer, Margaret Mitchel, born in Atlanta in 1900, had certainly seen *The Birth of a Nation* and was influenced by the film but that would miss the point. The novel was screened with constant reference to *The Birth of a Nation;* some pictures, like the blacks working in cotton fields, the young people in front of the Southern house, Atlanta on fire are quotations of that film. As a great many people, including three directors and several cameramen, were involved in the shooting, nobody was 'the author' and the 'inspiration' taken from *The Birth of a Nation* arose from a general consensus. For an history of *Gone with the Wind*, see R. Flamini, *Scarlet, Rhett and a Cast of Thousands*, Montreal, 1977.

23. For the narrative voice and the characters' point of view, see above, pp. 52–55.

5
The Italian Risorgimento

It is difficult to agree on a date for the start of the Risorgimento. In *Condottieri*, a film produced in 1937, the young ring-leader, John of the black bands,[1] devotes all his energies to the fight against separatism and to unite the small medieval principalities. In this film, unity dates from the Renaissance. Depending on our interest, we could go back to the end of the eighteenth century, or to the fourteenth century or even further back to the Roman Empire, for once we concede that Italy had to 'revive', any point in the history of the peninsula may be seen as a move away from or towards unity. Cinema answers the question by selecting some periods or problems in preference to others: as we have already looked at films from the silent era, we are going to study the talkies in this chapter. In more than forty films produced from 1930 onwards, the majority deal with two periods: the 1848 upheavals, paying particular attention to the Republic in Rome; and the liberation of the South from Bourbon rule. If we omit vague allusions, such as the ones we find in *Condottieri*, the screen versions of the Risorgimento are always confined to the nineteenth century, coinciding with a particular series of events. The episodes take place in a period of a few days, or more usually, over several weeks, five or six months: thus, we have no general survey, as we had in *The Birth of a Nation*. Many of the films are romantic stories with an 'historical' background: these films are not without interest, and we have learnt a great deal from our study of *Gone with the Wind*, for the image of history given in films in which history is only a setting often reveals how the past is popularly conceived. But if we do not want to confine ourselves to generalities, we will have to be selective, and we will therefore look at those films in which the Risorgimento is brought to the fore.

We are immediately faced with a problem: with the exception of two films produced in 1933, the fascist era was an unproductive one. Starting from a positive question: 'How is the Risorgimento filmed?', we move immediately to a negative question: 'Why was it so rarely filmed under Mussolini?' The two films that did appear are not of equal interest. *Villafranca* deals with the negotiations that stopped the war against Austria in 1859 and, under French pressures, delayed the liberation of the North-East of the Peninsula; it repeats the Mussolinian theme of a 'mutilated victory', a victory won by the Italians and negated by the European powers.

The second film, *1860*, is more complex and it would be impossible to classify it: is it an evocation of the expedition of Garibaldi's Thousands, or a journey throughout Italy, or the tale of a rescue? I could suggest a number of other possibilities. The general structure is clearly divided into three separate parts – Sicily under Bourbon tyranny, the call for help sent to Garibaldi, and the victory of the Thousand – but this tells us nothing about the film. In order to analyse it more fully, we shall examine the 'prologue' – more specifically, the opening shots of the film.

An example of consonance

We first see a tree silhouetted against the horizon, the iron gate of a jail – in other words, inside/outside, liberty/oppression. These two shots, immediately after the credits and before the caption which starts the narrative, convey at once a general interpretation of the film. The prologue, a medley of shots taken in slow motion, with a soundtrack combining crunching, rumbling, gun-shots. reveals charred houses, ruins, horse soldiers emerging from the smoke, dragging behind them prisoners in chains – all showing Italians under foreign rule. The first part of the picture sets out the eviction of the Sicilians by the Bourbons. We are facing a classical problem: how abstract sensations such as distress, helplessness, are felt at a certain

117

time. *1860*, in its predominantly emotional editing, is a good example of the problem.

After the dramatic opening, we linger over a small group of awakening countrymen: but immediately, drum rolls drown out any other noise; strong, rhythmic, the same sound will be heard again throughout the film, marching before the columns of Swiss soldiers which criss-cross the countryside. Free, unstructured shots showing the rural community are intercut with well-centred long-distance shots of the countryside through which moves the long black column of infantry. Unrelenting, the army moves on, overwhelming villages, putting down the resistance, exposing hiding places. The contrast between weakness and strength is evoked almost entirely through the opposition of shape and colour.

But the editing does not only intend to create an image of Bourbon despotism; simultaneously, it reveals the origins of rural society. In summer 1860, the expedition of The Thousand liberated the towns – and consequently the villages – of Sicily: although Palermo is mentioned a few times, *1860* ignores the cities and centres upon a small crew of inland shepherds. Here, people, clothed in sheep-skins, used to sleeping on earth, have a difficult life, but poverty is not extreme and there are no complaints for the countrymen accept their style of existence. The film does not present this romantic picture all at once: rural society is slowly drawn and, every time we begin to go deeper into the description, the group is repressed and scattered by the Swiss. By following the countrymen, by travelling with them, the film suggests that knowing them and their way of life needs patience. The soldiers, on the contrary, are all in a piece: overrunning the screen, as well as the villages, always with the same mechanical step, they obliterate what had been learnt about the inhabitants and we must wait to learn more of the countrymen until the following sequence.

Insidiously, a picture of the countryside – in a wider sense, of any Italian countryside – compels recognition. The village is seen as a whole, whose elements are indistinguishable; focusing first on one group, then on another, the camera never individualizes any of the villagers; even during the most dramatic scenes, when hostages are taken from the crowd and shot, anonymity is preserved. Only two characters stand out from the crowd: the

'Father' or priest who is in charge of the parish church and Carmenidu, the young shepherd who will be sent to Garibaldi; as a go-between, Carmenidu asserts himself when he is outside Sicily and we shall return to him later. The function of the priest is revealed at once: he is, at the same time, a leader and the example that everybody should follow; while the soldiers ransack the village and shoot the hostages, he comforts and heartens the villagers; as soon as the Swiss have left – they have been called to the coast to face Garibaldi and his troops – he harangues the villagers, telling them that 'the day of our liberty in Christ is at hand' and arranges a triumphal procession; later, always dragging the crowd behind him, he will meet The Thousand, before the battle. Religion and fatherland: the exact picture of what every priest should be. We must remember we are in 1933; two years before, there had been a clash between Catholic Church and Fascism over youth organizations; by the time the film appeared, the two parties had resolved their differences, and had agreed that the priesthood should be committed to the basic teaching of patriotism. But we must go further: the film not only praises the priest, it also gives a pleasant description of the life in a traditional Catholic village. For five years, Italy had been trying to stop the migration from countryside to towns.[2] A vision of the Sicilian – of the Italian – peasantry always standing up to work, never complaining, ready to obey its natural leaders and, first of all, its priests, is in absolute agreement with the general lines of the fascist policy.

Another contemporary reference is to the disastrous influence of the European powers. The countrymen never speak – they are the symbol of an Italy reduced to silence. When the soldiers take possession of the village, they seize the tongue of the bell, which is not a necessity (all villagers are kept in confinement) but a way of saying that the village no longer has a voice. The Swiss do not know Sicilian; the officer who has to inform the villagers of the king's orders, speaks in German although he cannot be understood. Things are no different on the mainland; Carmenidu, while travelling from the papal state to Genoa, hears every language of Europe, spoken by people who believe they are at home in Italy.

Historians often complain that it is hard to determine

whether official propaganda has an effect upon opinion or not. *1860*, produced without government aid, by independent film-makers, provides us with a possible, if partial answer; the movie does not aim at diffusing Mussolini's ideas but it complies with them. The distrustful eye cast at the foreigners is important for it suggests a concealed xenophobia. The film-makers do not suffer the linguistic colonization of their country and think that Italians should set their affairs in order themselves. This is exactly what we refer to when we speak of 'cognitive consonance'. It would of course be impossible to affirm that Italian opinion was impressed by fascist slogans but we cannot help calling attention to the congruence of the themes developed in the film with the official propaganda. Italians saw nothing remarkable in the priest, or the primitive life of the Sicilians. For them, it was 'natural' for a Sicilian priest of the nineteenth century to lead the countrymen, 'normal' for Sicilians of the past century to be impoverished and to accept it and it stood to reason that European powers had opposed Italian unity. The majority of the spectators were not aware of the attitude of the priesthood or of the powers in spring 1860 – but what they saw was 'consonant' with their expectations; priest, peasantry and foreigners were pictured as they were supposed to have been at that time.

Unity of opposed behaviours

Sicilians are mute because they are forbidden to speak – but silence has become a way of life, the only possible way to resist oppression; countrymen do not speak a lot and, when they are very affected, they become completely silent; Carmenidu says goodbye to his wife almost without a word; when soldiers kill a child there is no complaint, not even from the mother; the first hostages are shot without a whisper, with only the orders of the officer and the detonations heard on the soundtrack; later, soldiers choose new hostages: the strong emotions of this passage are expressed only by the movement of the camera which seems to jump, as if panic-stricken, from one villager to another.

120   Leaving the silence of the country, Carmenidu falls, on the

mainland, into the kingdom of speech; everywhere, in the pubs, at street corners, in the train, people speak; endlessly debating, asking questions and giving answers, they make Carmenidu dizzy.

I insist upon this parallel of silence and talk, because it introduces one of the most important features of the film, the contrast between North and South. Sicily is entirely white, with its long chalky plateau, its stone-built villages, its perpetually glaring sun. The North is, on the contrary, the country of blackness: dark clothes, shadows in alleys, pubs, houses. Most of the Northern sequences were photographed at night, or indoors and we find here another series of oppositions: Sicilians live with the sun, wake up at dawn, go to sleep early; Northerners live night and day. Sicilians are always outdoors, they work and have their meetings in the open air; Northerners prefer a man-made environment, found in pubs, clubs and other buildings. We could add many other characteristics but I shall be content with the most important, the political comparison. As we already know, everything is simple in Sicily: a faith, Christianity; an expectation, the end of tyranny. In the North, the controversies regarding the future never stop; while travelling to Genoa, Carmenidu is told of hundreds of conflicting solutions; one of the speakers suggests that the Pope should preside over an Italian confederation, not because he is himself a good Catholic but because that would be a clever solution: here, Catholicism is not the absolute faith and there are no precise expectations.

Between North and South, which look so different, there is at least one common factor: foreign domination. Sicilians, who are not even allowed to speak, would like to fight and need an ally: Northerners, who have the resources, waste time in arguing. In this respect, unity is an association between two opposed but complementary countries; they join forces because a decision is taken and because the two groups act together – in other words, because Garibaldi seizes the initiative, and Sicily and the North are led to fight together. Garibaldi's leadership, although referred to constantly, is not over-estimated. We cannot describe it as hero worship: Garibaldi is not seen as Mussolini's forerunner. The battle itself forms a large part of the film: exactly a quarter of the projection time. The Swiss, who were conspicuous in the first part of the film, have almost disappeared; we hear only their drums and see them only in the distance. The point is less the encounter of the two armies than the Italians' struggle to act together in their joint interests. At their first meeting, the Garibaldini and the countrymen, singing patriotic songs and canticles, form an unruly mob. As soon as they face the Swiss, they agree tactics, set a bugle call against the Swiss drums, and raise a flag; the sequence is timed in what we have called undetermined duration. We do not follow any specific action, we are simply aware of the motions, of the convergences which slowly propel the Garibaldini in the same direction: we realize that the film is going to end when the Sicilians, having regained the power of speech, cry: 'Garibaldi says we made Italy'.

Historical films and politics

Some readers may now feel that we are entering familiar territory: the philosophy of history. *1860* tells us that historic events result from the possibility of combining complementary factors, from a decision opportunely taken and from a test. Since Hegel, this point has been made hundreds of times, and the film adds nothing to the debate – except that it uses pictures and sounds rather than words.

We are actually mixing three different questions: (i) the philosophy of history; (ii) the application of this philosophy to the Risorgimento; (iii) the staging of this application. It is difficult to distinguish between the three questions. The philosophy of history is not actuality – it exists only through examples. Films about the Risorgimento, however, exist as particular, concrete phenomena. Films often contain a philosophy of history but it is generally hidden and vague as, for instance, in *The Birth of a Nation*. Why is it so precise in *1860*? Because the film deals with the Risorgimento and was produced during the fascist era. Fascists always felt uneasy with the Risorgimento: nationalism began with unification, but the major leaders of the Risorgimento were democrats and even republicans. In June 1932, for the first time, Mussolini credited the Risorgimento with having begun the revival of Italy – a revival that Fascism would of course carry through[3] – and inaugurated a re-evaluation which could never be brought to a successful conclusion.[4] It is not by chance that: (i) the production of films on the Risorgimento, which stopped in 1927, recommenced in 1933; (ii) the only two films dealing with politics were issued in 1933; (iii) the thirteen films produced from 1934 to the fall of Fascism are romantic stories with an historical background. The film-makers of *1860*, who were not fascist, tried to play their part in reconciling Fascism and the Risorgimento; in the original print, which was shortened in 1945, the movie ended with a double exposure of Garibaldi's 'Red Shirts' and fascist 'Black Shirts'. The inclusion of the themes we have mentioned above in a theoretical framework consistent with the fascist 'tenet' was an attempt to break the silence about the Risorgimento and to introduce a political dimension into the films dealing with unity. With *1860*, we light upon a film which ranks as one of the political events of the 1930s in Italy – although it has never been considered as such.

In our general survey, we have already found three completely different sorts of relation between historical films and politics and this helps us in clarifying the statements that we began with in Chapter 2. References to contemporary problems are found in all of our three examples, but they are not integrated in the same manner. The contemporary issues dealt with in *Napoleon Bonaparte* or *La Marseillaise* are urgent, dramatic ones; different though they are, the two pictures adopt a definite position on important matters; it is because the disagreements about the Revolution are very marked in France, that it is possible to use events of the year 1792 as a pretext to warn against impending dangers; in this case, an existing conflict, familiar to everyone, inspired a small number of pictures which were moments in the political struggle. *The Birth of a Nation* discloses a concealed possibility of discord; the political implications are extremely vague in the film and we cannot transpose directly the facts, the themes of the screened past into the facts or issues of 1915; the picture does not square with the major controversies of the day; however, it is highly political for it anticipates future conflicts. As far as *1860* is concerned, I do not think it is necessary to

123

repeat what we have just said. We have already noticed that the function of historical films is subordinated to the concerns of the day; we may add it is connected with the variations in conflict or agreement which appear throughout the debates on the reference period.

An 'objective' film

We have situated *1860* in the political evolution of fascist Italy but we have not yet spoken of the style of historiography implemented in this film. As usual, we shall use a shot-by-shot analysis. Let us start with a sequence chosen because it is a particularly short one. The countrymen, who want to resist the soldiers, have taken refuge in a remote village but the Swiss have spotted them. The sequence begins with a long shot of the countrymen, running back from the foreground. The camera, panning to the right, discloses a line of soldiers. This is followed by a medium shot of the officers, walking towards the background; soldiers, entering from the right, hide the officers. There is another medium shot of countrymen. Panning again to the right, the camera discloses another line of Swiss. Next, a distant shot of soldiers, followed by a medium shot of a villager, armed with a gun and dropping it at the end of the shot. Dissolve, into a shot of the same man, whose hands are being bound by a soldier. Finally, a medium shot of a group of countrymen, with bound hands, moving away towards the background.

The sequence is enclosed by two symmetrical shots, with the countrymen still free in the first, vanquished without a struggle and prisoners in the last. At the outset, we suppose that we are with the villagers and that we see from their point of view the preparations for the defence. But the camera, by panning, tells us that the actual point of view is the one of the soldiers; the countrymen are seen (which means nearly captured) by the army – more accurately, by the officers who immediately follow the soldiers; the same camera motion, repeated, points out that the repression is seen through the eyes of the Swiss – and not through the eyes of the sufferers. But the first part of the film is not presented entirely from the same point of view. We have already mentioned the opening, with the different pictures of oppression and the caption giving information on the situation in 1860; we have no difficulty in identifying this with the narrative voice. Thus, in this part of the film, there is no character (in the current meaning of the word 'character'); the predominant point of view, which is the one of a mechanism, of a soulless apparatus (the army) is intercut with interpolations of the narrative voice, which, as we have noted,[5] is supposed to be 'objective'; we never 'participate' in the events, we do not identify with any of the people who move on the screen; the picture aims at being an 'external' statement – and so, we are led to the conclusion that Sicilians are totally oppressed and have lost any kind of individuality. We noted at the beginning of the chapter the constant silence of the countrymen, a point which can be confirmed simply by looking at the dialogue; if we analyse the editing, we make the same inference: Sicilians have no voice left. I suppose that the excellence of this film, which in my opinion is one of the best historical films ever produced, is partially owing to the coincidence between the impressions resulting from the narration and the ones which are produced by the editing process – but this is no more than a subjective, incidental suggestion. Let us compare *1860* with *Napoleon Bonaparte:* both films do not simply narrate an episode or a series of events; both aim at getting the spectators to 'feel' rather than to understand a situation, and yet the way in which this is done is entirely different. As spectators, we are involved in *Napoleon Bonaparte* as if we were members of the cast, whereas we are kept in the background of *1860*.

In the second part of the film, we find a central character, Carmenidu, and we follow him as he travels throughout the Peninsula. But the shepherd is not always a character in so far as he does not play a part in the controversies, meetings, discussions that occur on the mainland. In some scenes, Carmenidu, moving from one place to another, asking questions, causes changes; he is then the main character and everything is seen in terms of his actions. But, more often, he only witnesses the debates. Take, for instance, the shepherd listening to the talk in the streets of Genoa: the shots are carefully drawn, with three men making a triangle on the screen. But Carmenidu is in

125

the background and the people who are chattering turn their back on him, thus concentrating what is most important for the spectators – motion and speech – in the middle of the screen. In this case, the shepherd is no more than one of the properties; he is the trick that directors use when they make different actors play in the front of the same building to inform the audience there is a relationship between these actors. The scenes that we are speaking of here are the political ones, and the most hackneyed; people with conventional faces and clothes (the republican with a felt hat and a sedate manner, the plump, oily supporter of the Pope, etc.) say what they are expected to say and what the well-informed spectators want them to say. In this section of the film, we have to note a difference between *1860* and *La Marseillaise*. Bomier, one of the two main characters of the latter film, looks, in more ways than one, like Carmenidu: both are uneducated, brave men of the common people who seldom speak and are never seen as stars. But we noticed that in *La Marseillaise*, time is divided into narrative time (adventures of Bomier) and symbolical time (the time of history). In *1860*, the presence of Carmenidu connects the scenes: the shepherd is what mathematicians would call a 'constant'; owing to him, the separation between two viewpoints is less obvious than in the French movie.

With the third part of *1860*, we find, again, short scenes seen from Carmenidu's point of view and hackneyed scenes, this time with The Thousand and the Sicilians fighting side by side: and we have another type of shot, taken in long distance, 'from outside', showing both the Swiss and the Italians. These shots, which are like external glimpses, re-introduce the narrative voice into the film. If we take the whole of the film, we notice a combination of three systems: we are at first entirely 'outside'; we are then, in turn, looking from the point of view of the character and looking with him at other people; eventually, the various points of view, mixed together, are framed by 'external' shots which aim at an 'objective' view. Can we repeat that *1860* is no more 'genuine', 'exact' than any other film? Here, we are only studying a model of historiography which, in giving none of the characters a dominant point of view, diversifies the vision and conveys the idea that all problems are solved and that unity is entirely successful.

126

Blood and suffering

1860 is probably the most optimistic screen portrayal of the Risorgimento; as we wanted to make clear why it was so enthusiastic and how it managed to glorify unity, we have looked closely at the period during which it was made and at the structure of the film itself. It is the fourth film we have examined, and now that my readers are (I hope) familiar with my methods, we are in a position to study a series of films. The Risorgimento is still a good example, for we find no fewer than twelve films on the subject from 1949 to 1954, with a seven-year gap before (nothing on the topic from 1942 to 1949) and a six-year gap after (nothing from 1954 until *Long Live Italy* in 1960). Three of these films are biographies (of Verdi, Ricordi and the countess of Castiglione), which deal with the Risorgimento only indirectly; four are romances in which the Risorgimento appears as a backdrop. I will ignore these films, and concentrate instead on the five remaining pictures: *Cavalcade of Heroes* (1949); *The Red Shirts* (1952); *The Brigand of the Wolf Cave* (1952); *The Lost Patrol* (1953);[6] *The Wanton Countess* (1954). Certain similarities between the five films are immediately apparent: none of them deal with the Liberation of Sicily – in other words, with the only period in the Risorgimento in which Italians fought successfully without foreign aid. Three films deal with the events of 1848–9, one with the 'Pacification' of Southern Italy,[7] one with the Liberation of Venice in 1866. Thus, four of our films refer to disasters: in 1849, Piedmont attacks Austria and is defeated at Novara (*The Lost Patrol*); in the same year, the Republic set up in Rome in 1848 is overthrown by the French Army (*Cavalcade of Heroes*), and Garibaldi, pursued by the Austrians, is forced to leave Italy (*The Red Shirts*); in 1866, while Austria is at war with Prussia, Italy attacks and is defeated at Custozza (*The Wanton Countess*); eventually Austria, although victorious, surrenders Venice.[8]

The Italians are successful only in *The Brigand*, but there they fight against fellow Italians – more precisely, against poor country people and against a gang of thieves.

In all of the films, we find a dramatic vision of war and a critical view of the army. We noticed that the horrors of war are a stage in the most common filmic 'pattern' of the Civil War in

127

the United States, but that they are described briefly, without being insisted on. Fear and death are a constant theme in the majority of Italian films; taking a general view of the series, we can suggest a model: the films are a succession of bloody episodes and dramatic situations intercut with more relaxed scenes. Of course, there is development in all of the films: they move from one point to another and we shall return to this evolution. But here, I want to emphasize the fact that every dramatic episode is self-contained. Take *The Brigand* as an example. In the first sequence, the brigand, who supports the Bourbons against 'the king of Savoy', arrives in a small town; the supporters of Piedmont are hung. A number of sequences follow, in which the army prepares to depart and sets off. In sequence 8, soldiers halt in a village; there is a thorough enquiry; those found guilty of supporting the Bourbons are shot.

Hanging, shooting are of no consequence, with only one or two exceptions; we know nothing of these men, who are unimportant in themselves; each episode, which exists in-independently of the others, tends to create a feeling of repulsion, and could be conveniently inserted at any other point in the filmic chain. We are presented with what we have called a 'sentimental' series;[9] our purpose is not to criticize the sentimentalism but to 'evaluate' it, to understand what devices are used to lead an audience in the 1950s to sympathize with men of the 1850s or, to put it another way, how the audience is moved to pity. There seem to be three main techniques:

1. The camera focuses on dead bodies, wounded, ruins. We saw the same thing in films conforming to the 'pattern' of the Civil War but, if the shooting is more or less identical, the connection between the scenes of carnage is completely different. We saw how Scarlett's vision and narrative point of view are separated. In the Italian series, there is a connection between the scenes of horror and the scenes preceding or following them. At the end of *The Lost Patrol* the four survivors of the massacred patrol cross the battlefield of Novara and we see the disaster through their eyes (whereas the battlefield of Petersburg is seen through the eyes of the narrator). At the beginning of *The Red Shirts*,[10] we are in a large palace: we wander through various rooms, follow a

staircase and eventually come across Garibaldi talking with his officers: while the camera moves, following the people who are looking for Garibaldi, we see dead bodies, horse carcasses, the wounded, suffering men lying on the ground. As Scarlett has a precise objective, we do not really pay attention to the wounded; in *The Red Shirts*, we do not know, on starting, why people are searching for Garibaldi, and we do not see the scene according to the interests of one of the characters; thus, we pay attention to the gruesome sight.

2. Extreme importance is attached to a distressing scene. After several battles with the Austrians, the Red Shirts are exhausted when they reach the sea – their only hope of escape. The camera takes one of the Garibaldini in medium shot, trying desperately to help a wounded comrade, dragging him along and, finally, abandoning him. The scene is, of course, terrifying by itself but I want to point out the specificity of the editing, which is characteristic of our series. A soldier, in *The Birth of a Nation*, drives his bayonet into his enemy's belly; it is horrible and quick, but we see only what is necessary to understand and the shot is intercut with other shots showing aspects of the war. With the Italian film, however, we linger and the film does not spare us the details. In both pictures we find a condemnation of war but, because this condemnation is screened in a different way in each case, it does not involve the audience to the same extent.

3. Opposition between before and after. Three soldiers on patrol halt at a farm (*The Brigand*); farmers and soldiers go to bed. The following day, we are with the rest of the army; we arrive at the farm: soldiers and farmers have been killed, the farm has been set on fire. The most impressive use of this trick is probably to be found in *The Wanton Countess;* Italian battalions get ready for the fight, flags are raised, soldiers proudly fall into line. We see nothing of the battle at Custozza, but shortly after we are shown fugitives and wounded attempting to run away.

Our films do not simply use one of the above described devices: by adding or combining them, they maintain a certain 'atmosphere' throughout. Before examining how this portrayal of violence affects the conception of historiography, I would like to draw attention to an interesting, though secondary characteristic of our series – the pessimistic view of the army. Many other films, which have nothing to do with history, give similar illustration of the military life and the question is, in one sense, outside our subject; however, it is important to insist upon the army's inefficiency. I will give only two examples. The army vainly searches for the 'Brigand' and only succeeds in killing countrymen or releasing a few soldiers; it is a civilian who spots him and leads the soldiers to 'the Wolf Cave'. *The Wanton Countess* is filled with brilliant young officers and splendid battalions, Austrian as well as Italian: after Custozza, both armies, the defeated and the victorious, break into a rout. We have already explained how the Italians were put to flight: when the countess arrives in Verona, a town in the hands of Austrians, she comes upon drunken, dishevelled soldiers; the imperial troops have fallen into confusion for they were unable to do anything well but to go on parade; the last sequence is a cross-cutting of scenes of rout and confusion with the execution of an officer carried out to perfection and with due decorum.

Selling off the past

The various afflictions which are more or less self-explanatory are distributed along the filmic chain; they are bound by the same pretext: a journey from one point to another, from Rome to the sea, from the town to the 'Wolf Cave', from Venice to Verona (*The Wanton Countess*), and so on. Journeys are common in Italian films of the 1950s, and the pictures dealing with the Risorgimento are specific only because the journey causes new problems: the patrol is lost, the Garibaldini lose many men, the countess renounces her honour.[11] At the end of the journey, the survivors stop briefly and meditate upon the disaster: the patrol has been reduced to nothing whilst the Italian Army was destroyed, Anita Garibaldi and most of the Red Shirts have been killed, Livia has lost husband, lover and friends. *The Brigand* is, of course, an exception – although many soldiers

130

died and the survivors are told they have to keep on walking in an unfriendly countryside;[12] 'We did not achieve our end', Garibaldi says at the end of *The Red Shirts*, 'maybe our sacrifice was useless.'

Throughout the series, we cannot avoid thinking that it is an evasion; we are not shown the whole of the process but only the borders, the footnotes of history, or the final moments, what happens when everything is settled. Consider the symbolical situation of the patrol: it should get information and, by inference, know the situation rather well; in fact, it is unaware of its own position. The other characters are equally ignorant of what is happening (where are the Austrians? Where is the Brigand? How is war going on around Venice?). This ignorance of particular, limited questions is part of a wider ignorance: spectators, unless they are very well informed of current historiography, are misled; they are given the details necessary to follow the journey, but they get no general sense of the 'moment'. In the other films, we are frequently told of 'the historic conjuncture' by captions, voices over, dialogue. The 1950 series uses tokens that identify history – we cannot forget we are in 1849 or in 1863 – but these marks do not intentionally explain the interests at stake. Once again, *The Wanton Countess* is the most noteworthy example, for there matters are taken to extremes: things are upside down, the victors (Austrians) are defeated, the defeated Italians are the vanquishers. The characters are not involved in the events (Novara, Custozza), although they are influenced by them; similarly, the decisions are not really taken on the battlefield, but elsewhere, not shown on the screen. The films separate the historical data (dates, partition of countries, treaties) from the particular destinies; the individuals are swept along by circumstances they do not understand, moving in the opposite direction to the one they intended; the coward returns to fight, the ordinary man becomes a traitor. Remember *The Wanton Countess:* Livia, who supported Italian unity with all her energies, betrays Italians, whereas her husband, a loyal subject of Austria, comes to the aid of Italians.

This pessimistic conception of human life is not particularly novel but it is interesting to speculate why it inspired a small group of films produced in a brief space of time. The reader should know that there were lengthy debates in Italy at the

131

end of the 1940s, on the subject of the Risorgimento. The fascist era was seen as a parenthesis, twenty years that were to be forgotten: it seemed important to go back to the beginning, to scrutinize what had not been done during the period of unification and immediately after.[13] Our films join in the debate, and they deal with it in a specific way; books or articles dealing with the debate on the Risorgimento ignore the films; thus, it is important to realize that people who never read magazine articles or political journals were introduced to the debate through these films. The film-makers did not argue about the mistakes of the ruling classes or about the deficiencies of unitarian policy: they took their place outside the events; if the politicians were able to polemicize over the nineteenth century, popular opinion was not yet disposed to take an interest in the topic. The films transposed present-day issues to a setting in the past. A few years after the end of the war, many Italians thought that their country had been completely passive during the conflict: it went to war almost by accident, its troops were defeated most of the time and, in autumn 1943, its former ally (Germany) suddenly became a fierce enemy. Suddenly, soldiers were asked to fight alongside their former enemy. The North of the country suffered two years of German occupation – but Italy was treated as an adversary at the end of the war. There is no need to emphasize the connection between the bitterness of the Italians and the themes developed in historical films; it produced a form of historiography we have not so far encountered. The films ignore causality or at least use an indefinite, external causality. If we look at other films, for example the US films on the Civil War, we find that things hang together: blacks prevail on whites; the whites react; the blacks begin to slaughter whites; and so on. Here causality is, to a large extent, co-extensive with the succession of actions. Turning to the Italian films, we find a general cause, which is usually distressful; in this framework, each sequence looks self-contained; it is as if, given a main theme (the deaths of many people), the distance from start to finish could be filled with a medley of apparently unimportant events. *1860* provided us with a 'model' of historic events; the films of the 1950s bring a change of approach which includes the rejection of any pre-existing form. The dispute of the 1950s was dominated by a Marxist analysis and could be summarized in a short sentence: 'What was the sense of the "unrolling" of events from the first attempts at Unity until the First World War?' We should not restrict our discussion to the Marxist debate, on the pretext that it was prevalent in Italian intellectual circles in 1950; fascism, in a disordered way and with no reference to the class war, had also tried to define the conditions which fixed the causes of historical evolution. Thus, the films we are discussing here are a reaction against any kind of evolutionism – conceived as the development of a society according to its inherent tendencies and according to the decisions taken by its leaders. This opposition to the systems that specify history as a continuous, connected process escaped notice for many reasons: partly because no one felt that these films deserved serious attention (film-makers were not supposed to interfere in a philosophical debate) and partly because the criticisms of the army, social institutions, governments and the ruling classes were interpreted as proof that these films were imbued with the spirit of the left.[14] Critical though they are, the films cannot be labelled as 'left-wing productions'. A wider, more thorough examination would be necessary to determine where Italian opinion stood on the major issues of the 1950s – but we can safely assume that the films concerned with the Risorgimento, far from being simple tales of the fight for unity, took issue both with the disputes over the significance of the Risorgimento and the tendency to insist that the past, still active in the present, will shape the future.

Garibaldi questioned

We have noted a six-year break after 1954 in the production of films dealing with the Risorgimento. 1960 was an anniversary year – the kingdom of Italy had been founded in 1860, after Garibaldi had liberated the South and after Piedmont had occupied the Papal States (excluding Rome). Although *Long Live Italy* was commissioned to celebrate unity, the anniversary was of little importance and did not inspire a new wave of films on the subject. *The Leopard*, produced in 1962, was to some degree an opposite view, a reply to *Long Live Italy*.

133

The two films, which have to be analysed together, coincide with the temporary closure of the post-war debates. Two answers had been given to the question, 'What ought to have been done?' Some felt that there had been no option: a poor, predominantly agricultural peninsula, surrounded by powerful, industrial, suspicious nations, had to grow stronger to amass money before beginning to change its social structure. Others felt that the middle class, which achieved unification, should have formed an alliance with the peasantry against the Southern landlords and the Northern capitalists: instead, the middle class abandoned the struggle, and the new ruling class, having made some apparent concessions, had freedom to act as it chose.[15] Needless to say, both interpretations, under the pretext of history, dealt with contemporary questions: Italy had entered the EEC and started the period of growth often described as the 'Italian miracle'; the parties in power claimed that it was essential to strengthen the national economy, if Italy was not to become a colony for the five other countries in the EEC. The left opposition retorted that, once more, depressed areas – Sicily, the Southern provinces – were to be sacrificed for the benefit of international business. The films we are dealing with intervened midway in the controversy: they are not simply propaganda leaflets; they are films with all the qualities of audiovisual products – later, we will insist upon their cinematographic characteristics. But we will treat them first, as two stages in a political debate.

Notice that they illustrate the Southern period of the Risorgimento. The South had become (and still is) a problem for Italy. Whereas the North was able to compete with Western countries, the South was still weak and undeveloped; in the press, novels, and in sociological and parliamentary proceedings, we see the same concern over the question of the islands and the Southern provinces; our films demarcate a small district in the dispute; despite important differences, it is easy to draw a parallel between them: both have a main character, whose point of view we follow most of the time; both start with Garibaldi's expedition and deal with fights in the countryside or in Palermo; both adopt a definite position on the situation at the end of the Bourbon monarchy; both give a general view of Sicily.[16]

134   By focusing on Garibaldi and his Red Shirts, their journey

into Sicily (plate IV), their discovery of the island, *Long Live Italy* tends to suggest the men who came from the mainland regarded the Sicilians as Italians, and saw Sicily as an Italian territory. When Garibaldi decides to leave Genoa, the rising of Palermo has been put down; the Garibaldini stand alone against the Bourbon army and they have to withstand violent attacks from the enemy.[17] (See plate IV.) After the victory, we visit some villages with Garibaldi; we see him encouraging the villagers, promising to discharge the prisoners,[18] shielding the wounded Bourbons. In a highly symbolical scene, the Garibaldini, realizing they pass near the ancient temple of Segestum, climb the mountain to contemplate ruins which are now the common property of the Italian people. Thus, in this film, the North, and especially Garibaldi acting for it, brings to Sicily hope, peace, equality with the other provinces of the kingdom.

The Leopard is focused upon Prince Salina (plate V), his nephew Tancredo and some of his followers; from the very first day, Salina has given the Bourbons up; the fights, cruel though they are, are not serious. Tancredo and his friends rejoin Garibaldi and enjoy themselves taking pot-shots at the enemy. After the Bourbons have left, three men come from the North: a ludicrous young general who bores the Salinas with his songs,[19] a pale shy officer and a fat middle-aged government agent (plate V) commissioned to offer Salina a seat in the Parliament. Salina refuses the proposal: 'sleeping: that is all that Sicilians wish for. I doubt whether the new kingdom has many gifts for us. . . . Sicilians will never improve for they think they are faultless.'

Sicilians treated as equal by Italians or Sicilians in a closed world of their own? Obviously, both films primarily aim at demonstrating a pre-established theory; both distort political dialogue; closeted with a friend in a well-furnished room (the furniture suggests the middle of the nineteenth century) or walking in countryside, Garibaldi and Salina give lectures which are inspired by the two prevailing interpretations of the Risorgimento. Garibaldi explains why he is obliged to give up the Republic and to appeal to the king of Savoy. Salina reveals how he intends to maintain the privileges of his class: 'Do you know what is happening in our country? Nothing. Nothing but a trifling swing of class almost on the spot (plate V). The middle class does not mean to destroy us. . . . At bottom, everything is going to remain in the same place.' Tancredo has become an officer in the Italian Army and is going to marry the daughter of a rich farmer; tomorrow, he will be an ambassador of the king of Italy; his sons will inherit his name together with the fortune of their mother. Salina again: 'We had to change something in order to leave things as they stand' – in other words: 'We will support the northern middle class on condition that government keeps order in Sicily.'

In their spoken scenes (by which I mean scenes in which people speak of political topics while the camera slowly pans around them), neither film adds anything new to the debate of the preceding years. If we compare them with the films we discussed earlier, only *La Marseillaise* is as verbose. In this film, Arnaud tells his comrades in arms what they ought to do. Garibaldi and Salina are much more than Arnaud: they take the part of 'the bourgeoisie' or 'the aristocracy'; when delivering their speeches, they tell the audience their view of the situation. The opposition between two incompatible interpretations of the Risorgimento entails a re-examination of Garibaldi's role in the Risorgimento. Saying the right word at the right moment, juggling people who want too much and people who do not want to do anything, the Garibaldi of *Long Live Italy* is less a character than an ideal (plate IV). In *The Leopard*, he is constantly in the background: people never stop speaking of him and, slowly, without anybody laying any charge against him, we suspect something is changing. Has Garibaldi himself altered? Have people stopped fearing him? It is up to the audience to answer the question.[20]

I believe it is impossible to interpret the 'ambiguity' of Garibaldi only by referring to the Risorgimento. May I put forward an hypothesis? The Italians read and heard more about the South in the 1960s than they had done ten or twenty years earlier; if we want to discover their 'image' of the islands, the films provide us with useful evidence. What is Sicily supposed to have been like, in the years of unity? On this, both films supply similar information. First of all, the palaces, then, the villages; the country palace of the Salinas is in a small village; the Garibaldini, marching towards Palermo, pass through a village;

in both cases, we see a church, a square, a few houses, we meet the priest, the mayor with his municipal sash, a small group of countrymen. We enter Palermo when the Garibaldini assault the town and we see narrow streets, tumble-down houses, weeping women. Add green hills, trees coming into leaf, spring-like sun over the island – and the dust, the wind, the hot weather of summer. The scenery has been rapidly set up: it is no more than a setting, the framework that makes the audience constantly aware that it is in Sicily (plate IV). But this is precisely what we are looking for: the minimum visual information common to the majority of Italians and, for them, typical of Sicily.

Surely, with the films of the 1960s, we see a change in film form and in historiography? The centre of interest in a 'classical' film was the main character – Scarlett or Livia Serpieri – who comes to grips with various problems. After 1960, the conflict of the individual with the surroundings is less important: instead of individuals, the characters are, very often, the spokesmen of a group or a class; at once, historiography is conceived of as external to the films, and applied to them.

More on method

We have seen that Italian talkies interpreted the same historical topic in three different ways, with three systems of historiography; we can now be more precise. We return to the problem we mentioned at the beginning of our survey of films dealing with the nineteenth century: what is the relation between an historical film and its social context? There is an obvious link: films constantly evolve, and their changes are profoundly affected by the 'march of time'; we do not find a film produced in 1960 according to the pattern of 1950. Would it have been possible to produce *The Red Shirts* in 1962? Of course, we are not in a position to answer the question, but it is unlikely that *1860*, for example, could have been shot in 1930 or in 1935 – two years before or after it was actually made. Films are rooted in a precise period and we can easily detect differences between the films of 1933, 1949–54 and 1960–2.

We have already established that the two films made in 1960 are strictly related to the disputes of that year; in this case, the means of communication (manner of addressing the public, of delivering a pre-existent message) are shaped in order to fit historical films to the prevailing pattern of historiography. With the 1950 series, correlations are simultaneously positive and negative: the pessimistic view of Italy and of its political destiny was widely diffused in literature, the press, political speeches, the cinema – but the conception of historiography is typical of the series; here, the films constitute a separate category, linked to the debates and disillusions of the day and, at the same time, containing a specific model of the relations between the individuals and the society. I would describe the 1950 series, by itself, as an autonomous social process: the films are not representative of contemporary problems but neither are they exterior to these problems; they are independent of them. We might call 'autonomy' this kind of relation. As regards *1860*, this picture is a political act, an attempt to influence the reassessment of the Risorgimento. Film and society? A constant interaction rather than a mere correlation.[21]

Notes

1. Is it necessary to emphasize the name of the bands? The Mussolinian Black Shirts were quick to identify their forerunners.
2. See for instance Mussolini's article in *Popolo d'Italia*, 4 July 1933 – an article written just as the film was going to be presented to the public.
3. From 1922 till 1929, Mussolini does not say a word about the Risorgimento; his only important speech on this topic is delivered for the unveiling of Anita Garibaldi's statue, in June 1932. The most important fascist book on contemporary Italian history, *Italy on the Way* by Volpe (1927) assigns less than thirty pages to the Risorgimento and begins the 'prehistory' of fascism in 1870 (Rome, capital of the kingdom).
4. The first mention is to be found in Mussolini's speech of 14 March 1929; shortly after Gentile, official theoritician of fascism, and Volpe laid stress upon the importance of the Risorgimento; in 1932 the government founded a 'National Society for the History of the Risorgimento'. To elucidate the significance of this revival is beside the point and I shall be content with two remarks: (i) Mussolini's speech of 14 March 1929 is devoted to the agreement between the

Vatican and the Italian kingdom; to insist upon the Risorgimento might be a concession to the anti-clerical group of the fascist party and a concealed warning to the Vatican; we have mentioned the clash of 1931 and the subsequent reconciliation: did the reassessment of the Risorgimento stop after that reconciliation had been transformed into collaboration? (ii) In 1928, Croce published his *History of Italy from 1871 to 1915* which quickly became a best-seller; he taxed fascism with having broken the Italian traditions; the fascists reacted by trying to appropriate the Risorgimento but they eventually gave up.

5. See pp. 52–53.

6. Not to be confused with the English film of 1936 with the same title.

7. For a short account of this film, see above, pp. 55–56.

8. The fiction is especially important in this film and it might be useful to give an account of the story. The young Livia, who married the old count Serpieri, lives in Venice; with her cousin, Roberto Ussoni, she supports Italian 'patriots' against Austria. Ussoni having challenged an Austrian officer, Lieutenant Franz Malher, to a duel, Livia meets Malher and falls in love with him; she does not try to hide it and everybody but her husband knows all about her intimacy. Livia and Serpieri go to their country house in Aldeno; Austria is at war with Italy and Ussoni asks Livia to keep the money that he will use to buy arms; Livia pretends to forget Malher but, when he arrives in Aldeno, after having deserted, she gives him Ussoni's treasure to pay the doctors. Learning that Malher is in Verona, Livia abandons Serpieri, crosses the battlefield, finds Malher with prostitutes, denounces him to the authorities; Malher is shot as a deserter.

9. See above, pp. 77–78.

10. It is not the absolute beginning. The film is constructed as an extended flash-back. At the outset, we are with Garibaldi who is told to leave immediately, for the Austrians are nearing his refuge; then we are in Rome and a voice-over tells us we are going to see an episode of Garibaldi's life, the flight from Rome to exile. At the end of the film, we are back in the refuge and Garibaldi leaves.

11. In Venice she renounces her womanly honour by becoming the mistress of an Austrian officer; in Aldeno she loses her honour as an Italian when she gives an Austrian the money saved by Italians to buy guns; in Verona she renounces her status as a human being by informing against Malher who is sentenced to death.

12. More precisely, the officer and a few soldiers spot the cavern but they are besieged by the brigands and are on the point of being killed when a fresh supply of troops arrives.

139

13. On the re-examination of the Risorgimento, see Walter Maturi, *Interpretazioni del Risorgimento*, Torino, 1962.

14. We must add another remark. Four of our films were well received, but *The Wanton Countess* was a tremendous success; shot with a crowd of many thousands, this film lasts two hours; film critics say it is a masterpiece; as historians, we are less interested in its peculiarities than in the concordance with the contemporary films.

15. This interpretation, suggested first by Gramsci, became extremely popular when the writings of the Italian Communist leader were 'rediscovered', particularly in the 1950s.

16. The films do not end with the same events; in *Long Live Italy*, Garibaldi, after having liberated the island, crosses the channel, liberates the kingdom of Naples and gives way to the king of Savoy; in *The Leopard* we see the liberation of Naples, the plebiscite which sanctions the unity with Italy, the slight changes in the administrations; during the last sequence we are told of the battle of Aspromonte in which Red Shirts are defeated by the Italian Army.

17. In *1860* Carmenidu, in the name of Sicilians, asks Garibaldi to come; the countrymen join the Red Shirts and fight arm in arm with them.

18. In *1860*, Bourbon soldiers are Swiss; in *Long Live Italy* they are Italians.

19. Once again Sicilians are silent, Northerners noisy!

20. At the outset, his name terrifies women, but Tancredo very soon enlists among the Red Shirts; a few days after the victory, officers no longer comply with Garibaldi's orders; at the time of the plebiscite which sanctions the unity with Italy he is seen as a mere troublemaker; during the ball which celebrates the upholding of traditional order Garibaldi is said to have admitted he had been misled by unscrupulous people.

21. For an extended study of Italian history in Italian films, see *Momenti di storia italiana nel cinema*, Siena, 1979.

III
The History of Yesterday

The Twentieth Century
Portraying Itself

For many people who are not interested in historical research, history is no more than an attempt to establish some 'facts' and to locate them in a setting. In the films we have seen so far, the spectators are told they are looking at an historical film by three kinds of information: the men, the events, the dates. All these data assert an intrinsic meaning which arises from a pre-determined cultural consensus and here we reach a preliminary stage of our study of history in film: what is the minimum information required by the audience to be able to define the characters, the place, the time or, to put it in another form, how long does it take people to know that they are looking at the American Civil War or at the Italian Risorgimento?

But an historical film cannot be reduced to a linear unfolding of recognizable elements; it is not a description of events but rather a construction, a system of relations. In previous chapters we have particularly insisted upon two of these relations: the present, which constantly implicates the past; and historiography conceived of as the various ways of retrieving and ordering the past. Given these characteristics, an historical film is not necessarily a film dealing with a remote past: events of yesterday, events we witnessed, can be filmed in an 'historical manner'. The difficulty is that we generally lack the very elements that designate a film as 'historical': there is some presumptive evidence, the most important being the moment, the juncture in which the story takes place. The two world wars, the world economic depression, the revolutions are, by common con-sensus, classified as 'historic' periods. However, we cannot assume that every film referring to the world wars or to the revolutions is an historical one. If matters are so imprecise, is it useful to look for present history in films? Our purpose is less to study history as it is restaged in the films than to under-stand how history is conceived, in what framework of knowledge it is defined at a certain time. The films we studied in Part II of this book were a good beginning but we cannot go further without comparing them to other films. In the third section, therefore, we will tackle the questions we had no opportunity to grapple with earlier. We might summarize these questions as follows:

1. Knowing that audiovisual media influence us we should 143

determine what, in our evaluative framework, is entirely correlated with stereotypes or typifications embedded in what we could call the standard 'imagery'. I will try to summarize this point by looking at the portrayal of Germans and foreigners in La Grande Illusion.

2. We have insisted upon the contemporary references and established how the present is often concealed by the past. We might turn the question around: are there circumstances in which the past is used to conceal completely the present? La Grande Illusion will provide us with a good example of 'historical diversion'.

3. We have often paralleled two or more films on the same topic, produced at the same time and with politically conflicting or at least divergent views. Can we imagine two politically convergent films in which the same events are shot, edited and staged in a completely different way? This is the question we shall try to answer with regard to the Russian Revolution.

4. We have mentioned several films made in agreement with pre-existent political theories. We shall now investigate another assumption – that films can play a part in the definition of new political positions – and we shall test this hypothesis by looking at the resistance as it was staged in the Italian cinema.

The questions we are dealing with are only a part of the analysis; by studying them, I intend to supplement my earlier discussion.

6

Escaping the Present

When I say that *La Grande Illusion* was one of the greatest successes of the cinema in the 1930s, I am in no danger of repeating what I have said about *The Birth of a Nation*. Film distribution and the political context changed so rapidly during this period that the same word – success – can mean two completely different things. *The Birth of a Nation* was shown commercially only in the American market and the few copies that circulated in Europe were seen only by members of film societies. From the end of the First World War, the recession among the European companies, who were unable to supply their own networks, enabled the Americans to get a foothold in Europe; only those companies which had managed to take advantage of the rise of feature films in time survived, while the others disappeared. The arrival of talking films speeded up the concentration, as the strongest companies monopolized the expensive equipment needed for sound recording and projection. After 1930, five companies, known as the 'majors', controlled most of the cinemas in the United States and, through shareholdings in or agreements with the European companies, dominated a large part of the programmes in Europe. In European countries, at least a third of the films shown came from America. Only a minority of European films, on the other hand, had an international career; this was the case with *La Grande Illusion*, which was shown in every Western country except Germany, where it was banned.

1937: the coming war

The Birth of a Nation came out at a time when American opinion was not divided by any serious conflicts; the film itself caused – or exposed – certain dissensions. In 1937, opinion was deeply divided everywhere; the crisis was still going on, fostering permanent unrest that was extinguished only by the war. In central Europe, social strife was crushed by dictatorship, which partly corrected the disordered state of capitalism. The arms race used by the dictatorships to revive their economies threatened the international balance of power. The dual opposition between democracy and dictatorship, and between the defence of peace and all-out re-armament, caused tensions in Europe and America whose violence we have difficulty in imagining today. In this climate, a film dealing with essential questions like war or patriotism was an occasion for renewed controversy. Earlier political divisions were fully reflected in the reception given to *La Grande Illusion*. I will give two brief examples. In France, the right wing saw the film as a defence of patriotism and a glorification of war, which makes each individual sacrifice himself for his country; the illusion condemned in the title is that of the pacifists: in the face of the enemy, men who thought they were different discover that they are French before all else. The left wing, on the other hand, thought that the film served the cause of peace by making a clear distinction between the aristocrats, professional soldiers living for war, and all other men, dragged into the struggle in spite of themselves. The illusion is that of national unity, and in fact social divisions are stronger than the apparent cohesion born of patriotism. In Italy too the film stimulated widespread controversy. Here the distinction cannot be made between right and left but opinions on the film were more or less the same. Some people saw *La Grande Illusion* as a contemptible defence of pacifism: fascism was developing its nationalistic aspect to the full at that time. Others interpreted the film as an apologia for patriotism and fully approved of it as such. If we simply count audiences and total takings, we cannot compare *The Birth of a Nation* and *La Grande Illusion*: both films were very successful but the circumstances were completely different. *The Birth of a Nation* caused a scandal and divided public

146

opinion; *La Grande Illusion* served as a pretext for re-awakening an old conflict – and we have to ask ourselves why this film, more than others, renewed the political conflict which divided Europe.

As the film is relatively complex, I will first give an account of the story.

The film opens in a French military bar, close to the front, during the First World War. A pilot, Lieutenant Marechal (Jean Gabin) is ordered to take Captain de Boîeldieu (Pierre Fresnay) in his plane. The second sequence begins in a German military bar. Major von Raufenstein (Eric von Stroheim), who has shot down the French plane, invites both of the French officers to lunch. Marechal and Boîeldieu arrive at a prison camp. They are put in a barrack-room where life is not too difficult. Lieutenant Rosenthal (Georges Dalio), whose parents are wealthy, receives many food parcels and feeds his comrades. At night the prisoners burrow a tunnel underground in order to escape and, during their daily walks, they carry the earth out of the barrack-room.

To amuse themselves the prisoners decide to give a show, in which English prisoners, dressed as girls, dance to 'It's a long way to Tipperary'. Lieutenant Marechal suddenly bursts on to the stage to announce a French military success. All the prisoners, English and French, sing 'La Marseillaise'. Marechal is thrown into prison. When he gets out, the tunnel is finished but the Germans transfer the prisoners to another camp.

Later, Marechal and Boîeldieu, who have tried many times to escape, are locked in a fortress where Major von Raufenstein, grievously wounded and no longer able to fly, is commanding officer. The French meet Rosenthal again. Raufenstein, who holds everybody but the aristocrats in contempt, spends the afternoon speaking with Boîeldieu. Marechal and Rosenthal still want to escape but it is extremely difficult due to the surveillance kept on them.

One day, the hungry Russian prisoners riot. The French realize they could escape if the fortress were thrown into confusion. Boîeldieu pretends to escape; while the Germans are looking for him, Marechal and Rosenthal run away. Raufenstein orders Boîeldieu to come back and, as the latter does not comply with his orders, he shoots him. Mortally wounded, Boîeldieu dies in Raufenstein's room.

147

Marechal and Rosenthal walk through mud and snow. Having twisted his ankle, Rosenthal slouches along; his friend leaves him but, after a short while, returns and helps him to hide in a farmhouse. The woman farmer, whose husband and brother have been killed, takes care of them; Marechal becomes her lover and works as if he were the farmer. When Rosenthal is fully recovered, the men cross the Swiss frontier.

Tokens of war

La Grande Illusion does not show any well-known episodes or characters; it does not deal with the First World War as a whole, but with a limited aspect of it. The first two sequences, the one showing the French setting off on a mission, and the other depicting their arrival as prisoners in the canteen of a German squadron, would be enough to define the period. The film nevertheless contains a very precise chronology. The starting point is the wreath which is the Germans' tribute to the enemy pilot who has just been shot down; the bulletin on the capture of Douaumont is dated February 1916. Later details are less clear for us, but they were obvious at the time of the film because the great majority of the audience had lived through the war: the recapture of Douaumont refers to March 1916. The escape takes place in December, because the French spend Christmas at the farm; this must be the winter of 1916, since just prior to this episode the Russian officers speak of tsarism. So the story covers a little less than two years.

Such details seem completely unnecessary; the anecdote could be set at any time during the war, and extend over six months or three years. The characters never refer to the passing of time, and there is nothing to show that they have changed or aged. Why are the historical references given so clearly, when they play no part in the story? The reasons we have given in the case of other films, in particular *The Birth of a Nation*, do not apply here: there is no need to make the story convincing at all costs and so is it unnecessary to set it in a strict chronological framework.

What events were taking place at the time? Essentially, fighting – individual encounters for the pilots, major battles for the land forces and, for all, waiting, hunger, cold, fear, death. The picture barely speaks of this. I use the word 'speaks' deliberately; details about the war are given indirectly, reported through speech or writing; we learn about the dog-fight in which the French are captured and one of them injured only through a description by a German; the battles for Douaumont are referred to in official bulletins or in newspapers. The men we see on screen, however, are not hungry, cold or afraid; they do not seem to suffer much from the circumstances, and the injury to one of them is so slight that we forget it after a few sequences.

The war leaves only two profound marks: the permanent disablement of the German officer, and the death of one of the Frenchmen. Both men stand completely apart from the others; the film isolates them not only through what they say (it is they who discuss their condition at the greatest length; as aristocrats, they think that their caste is condemned to disappear; as professional soldiers, they consider death as the normal end to their career), but also in the way in which they are presented. Remember the Frenchman's visit to the commandant of the fortress; the scene begins with shots of vertical objects – a crucifix, a statue, a mirror – which the editing assimilates with the stiff, motionless silhouettes of the two men; they go and stand in two opposite corners and the camera takes them one after the other, in reverse shots; their bodies, leaning backwards in two opposite directions, make two diagonal lines across the screen. This is an opposing montage which, through the use of symmetry, makes a contrast (the men are enemies) and a formal comparison between the antagonists: these regular army officers belong to the same category, that of people whose life is indistinguishable from the practice of war.

For professional soldiers, the historical event is also a personal event: their life is marked by history. The other prisoners are not affected; they seem to remain outside history, in a universe with no definite contours. You may have noticed that it is difficult to get an idea of the place where they are imprisoned; general views, showing the buildings in their surroundings, are extremely rare; we have a brief glimpse of the outside of the first camp but we are soon restricted to the barrack-room and the yard where the small group that the film

149

is about spend their time. We never see a complete picture of the fortress, either when the commandant is showing the men round it, or at the time of the escape. There are few exterior shots: I have counted sixteen, only one of which, the march across the countryside, is fairly long. So we have practically only interiors, filmed in medium shots or close-ups. In *The Birth of a Nation*, we showed the symbolic value of the house; with *La Grande Illusion*, except for the commandant's room, where everything bears the mark of the cult of the past, the rooms are neutral and indifferent. Those which are permanently occupied should be untidy, with personal objects and clothes lying about, but we see very few things, apart from a few nicely framed prints. The background is abstract, forming only an indifferent horizon which does not attract attention. Like time, space is neutralized; it seems to exist only in relation to the actions of those who occupy it. Think of the scene where the tunnel is dug: the camera first goes around the room, giving a glimpse of what each person is doing; then it moves in closer to show the preparations that each person is busy with; finally, there is a close-up of the person who is going down into the hole. The order of the montage is subordinated to the prisoners' plan, and the setting is included only indirectly, in so far as the scene needs a background.

Portrait of the Germans as automatons

Some men, set outside history, form a group which defines itself by the activities it performs. In order to define this group better, we will look first at those who do *not* belong to it, beginning with its enemies, the Germans. There is no need to emphasize the importance of this question in 1937: how are German soldiers depicted in a French film about war? I will omit the commandant of the fortress and I will be discussing the woman, whose part is important, at greater length below: here I will consider only the Germans who appear episodically. The first two sequences, before and after the capture, draw a very marked parallel between the French and the Germans. On both sides of the front, the men, the places and the duties are practically identical; the entrance of the French pilot in the first sequence and the German airman in the second are filmed in exactly the same way, with a fixed shot of the door opening, a movement towards the person coming in, and then a horizontal panning round the room. The Germans behave very politely; they receive the prisoners with courtesy, pay tribute to the French officer who has been shot down, and help the one who is wounded. Across the national barrier, contacts are made according to social class: the two aristocratic regular army officers join one another immediately, while the two engineers come together. The Germans are enemies, but in their behaviour and in their individual relationships with the French, they are no different from their opponents.

Several other episodes could be mentioned; for instance, the one where a guard comes to comfort the Frenchman sentenced to solitary confinement for creating an incident during the entertainment; in everything that forms the plot there is no variation in this matter. But we must also consider the pictures, independently of what is being told. At the beginning of the third sequence, the new prisoners arrive at the camp: we first see the German soldiers marching past like machines; then we have the prisoners, in cheerful confusion; another shot shows, in a perfectly regular triangle, the chief of the camp on the right, an NCO on the left, and a sentry at the back; after the movement of the prisoners, the montage immediately brings in a too-carefully constructed photograph, where the Germans seem enclosed in rigidity and immobility. After the French have dug their tunnel, they go into the yard to empty the earth from their pockets; they straggle across the screen, and wander about, followed by the camera which moves very freely from one to another. The scene is interrupted when a squad of Germans passes; the soldiers are first shown in a fixed shot, behind railings; then they march forward, always mechanically, and cross the yard with the same stiffness. The tour of the fortress, led by the commandant, brings out a strong contrast between the casualness of the French and the discipline imposed on the Germans. The clearest scene takes place just before the escape. First we are with the prisoners, making their disorganized preparations; suddenly there is a close-up of a clock, whose pendulum we see for a moment; is this a reminder that is is nearly time? The camera swings down to show two German

151

officers, standing rigidly on either side of the screen, speaking without moving and without looking at one another. With no comment needed, we have here a double shift: first from the prisoners' plot to the clock, by an association of ideas, and then, from the mechanical movement of the pendulum to the rigidity of the Germans, by an association of pictures. By a kind of implicit reversal, the prisoners seem freer than their guards.

The Germans are depicted in two different ways: sometimes they are like anyone else, but at other times they are the eternal Prussians, slaves of a discipline which drains them of all personality. Notice that no judgement is ever made on this point, and that no words are ever spoken comparing the Germans to robots. The two contradictory portraits are developed by two different methods of expression. The most favourable portrait appears in the dialogue and in the plot; these details were planned beforehand and decided when the scenario was written; they are the result of the deliberate intention of those who, when they were preparing the film, wanted to be impartial towards the enemy. A scenario is written, re-read, corrected. The shooting has to be much more improvized; the actors, extras and technicians are assembled for a limited time; sometimes unsuccessful scenes are shot a second time, but for most of the film the makers are content with what they take the first time. As they have to work fast, without stopping to think too much, habits of thought, reflexes and traditions have full play; without discussing the matter, it is agreed that the extras wearing German uniforms will behave like robots, and that everything concerning the enemy will be filmed in fixed shots, in an overconstructed setting.

Here we come to an important methodological problem that we have not had to deal with before. In silent films most of the information comes from the picture; the subtitles point out the meaning of shots over which we might hesitate, they add comments and dialogue, but they alone could not form the essential part of the film. With talking films, the dialogue may sometimes dominate. Perhaps you have seen the BBC television series on the six wives of Henry VIII; it could easily have been followed by ear, without looking at the screen. Whatever the value of this series may have been, from the point of view of the cinema it was a bad film. The importance of a film for the research that we are considering does not lie in the story, nor in the psychological richness of the characters, but in the way in which the different methods of expression available to the makers are used together. I find the story of *La Grande Illusion* third-rate and unconvincing, but the film nevertheless interests me enormously because, through the shots and the editing, it reveals attitudes and feelings that contradict the point of view expressed in the dialogue. It is in fact this kind of ambiguity that explains why contradictory opinions have been formed about the film, and why both the left and the right find in it what they want to find.

We will restrict ourselves to examining the case of the makers of the film. Without knowing it, they were imprisoned in an insoluble contradiction. They wanted to work for peace, and to avoid anything that might arouse a hostile reaction in the Germans; they were anxious to give an objective portrait of the enemy, and they show a German woman behaving in a way that is bound to find sympathy with French audiences. But in spite of themselves, by the mere fact of translating their impressions into pictures, they confirm the traditionally accepted ideas that the Germans are sticklers for discipline and that the French individualists are capable of preserving their freedom even in prison.

A comparison of the words and the pictures gives us a brief glimpse of the underlying nationalism. We will make the forms clearer by examing the way in which the prisoners who do not belong to the main group are shown. The arrival of the convoy in the third sequence, the roll call in the fortress, and other scenes, show that the film takes place in international camps containing French, English, Belgian and Russian prisoners. The group that is in the centre of the film has no contacts either with the French or with anyone else. The very brief appearances of the English and the Russians are nevertheless worthy of attention. During the search, in the first camp, an Englishman breaks his watch so that the Germans will not take it away from him; the gesture is spectacular; but the French do not seem to break anything nor to have anything taken from them, because at the time of the escape one of them uses his watch. On its own, the detail is negligible; taken together with the other scenes it becomes an interesting sign. Women's costumes

153

arrive for the entertainment, and a Frenchman puts one on. There is something uncomfortable about this passage, and an obvious sexual ambiguity; the French are strongly threatened with feminization. The film moves directly on to the performance, and only the English appear in women's costume. There is a single shot of the Frenchman in disguise, there are five of the English. The film has made a substitution, though nothing in the story calls for this, and the threat is transferred to the English. The last appearance of the British is when they change camps. You may have noticed something strange about this scene: the officer who tries to explain to the English that there is a tunnel all ready to escape through is the one who does not speak English, and the one who speaks English, and who is right next to him, says nothing. A psychological explanation could be found – perhaps this officer dislikes the British – but, as the film does not give the slightest indication of this, it remains a speculation. When we invent possible explanations we leave the film and we tell a different story. Within the logic of what the film has already shown, is there any reason why the French should not tell the British? My hypothesis is that the English are neutralized in advance, they are reduced to helplessness because they have inherited all that was negative – so that the French are rid of it. I base this idea on the scene where the Russians appear; they too are completely helpless; we were told so in the first camp, and this is repeated in the fortress: they have nothing to eat, and they have to rely on the presents that the French are willing to give them; a woman, the Empress, sends them a parcel which will enable them to restore the balance, but its ridiculous contents transform the gift into an additional weakness.

I emphasize the sexual aspect of the comparison between the French and their allies: the English are feminized, and the Russians are the victims of a woman, whereas a Frenchman wins the only woman in the film, who is an enemy. If you add that the Russians are dying of hunger and that the French eat well, that the English break their personal belongings and do not escape, while the French do the opposite, you will admit there is a systematic contrast, which operates as though the weakening of the allies were the price to be paid for the strength of the French. Of course, none of this is expressed in the dialogue, and there is not the slightest suggestion of suspicion towards the other prisoners; all this is outside the story. The nationalism of the makers of the film leads them to mark the superiority of the French, in an indirect and indefinite way, without realizing it.

The people round about, the others – enemies or allies – intervene mainly to enhance the originality of the central group; in fact, it would be better to say groups because there are three in succession, which vary slightly – in the first camp, in the fortress and at the farm. We know little about the members of these groups; most of them do not even have a name, and are referred to by their profession – the engineer, the actor, the teacher. The conversation they have together gives us little information, and the discussion they try to organize about their reasons for escaping leads only to vague comments. What are these groups based on and how are they held together?

The French out of the game

The groups are identified, first of all, by the actual technique of the film, in which the participants are strongly linked by the shots and the editing. Sequence 4 takes place in the mail office, where the prisoners collect their parcels, and sequence 5 in the barrack-room where they have their meals. In the mail office, the camera starts with one of the officers, travels quickly round the room, and comes to rest on the officers – who are shown for a long time, face to face, in a fixed view. In the barrack-room, the prisoners are first photographed in twos, chatting, and then grouped round the table; a circular panning encloses them in this position and the sequence stops. We have already examined the organization of the montage in sequence 7, the tunnel sequence, and we have made similar observations. The film shows the elements, the different parts of the group, then it shows the whole group, underlining its cohesion. In the terms that we have already used, we have a continuous descriptive montage which gradually builds up into a whole. The constant repetition of the same process should be emphasized: one of the essential operations performed by the treatment of the pictures is to assert the existence of the group.

155

The shots and editing also bring out the centres of interest round which the groups form. We will have another look at the three sequences that we have just mentioned. Sequence 4 ends with a food parcel, sequence 5 with a meal, and sequence 7 with the digging of a tunnel. We discover here two fixed points that are found throughout the film. First of all, food is very often mentioned: in a very brief scene, inserted between sequences 4 and 5, two Germans say that the French eat well while they and the Russians are continually short of food; in the farm where the escaping prisoners take refuge, there is constant talk of meals, and the trio meet at table. The escape is planned by the groups, and is the reason for their existence. In the fortress, apart from the discussion between the aristocrats, the only topic of conversation is escape. Until the French leave the fortress we see only fragments of it, corners of rooms, passages, doors; the only time all the prisoners come together is as the result of the escape; the flight of the French is developed like a theatrical production in which the principal actors bring the scenery and the crowd into existence round them. The point I want to make is that the successive groups are characterized by two permanent features. These two features are somewhat surprising; for the the moment, we will not try to explain them, we will restrict ourselves to pointing them out.

There are always several Frenchmen; at first sight, there is no main character, no hero. But here we must draw attention to an important methodological problem. A story is built round the fact of a lack: something has been lost and must be found, or the characters would like to have something that they do not possess. The basic structure of any story lies in defining the lack, finding someone (an individual or a group) to make good the lack, and performing the operation by which the lack is made good. Between these three essential stages the secondary episodes, which are variations on the three principal stages, provide the length needed – the ballast – to satisfy the public. The person who fills the lack may be conspicuous, or he may be part of the crowd. In the first case, which is the most common, the story is built round a hero, such as Ben in *The Birth of a Nation*: the white community has been harmed, and Ben repairs the harm. In the second case, which applies to *La Grande Illusion*, there is no appointed hero; in order to find out who is

156

the main character, we must decide what harm has been done, and who is qualified to put it right. Only one character goes through three successive ordeals, over which he triumphs: this is the engineer officer played by Gabin, who is in turn wounded, imprisoned and tempted to abandon his friend. There is a double lack: of women (remember the importance of the sexual element) and of freedom; he is the only officer to triumph over both.

Who is this character? If you look again at the scenes where he appears, you will notice that he speaks little, and says practically nothing about himself; he often appears with other members of the group, however; he is the common factor, the mean, the point at which the French converge. The only officer who has a heroic side, the one who sacrifices himself for the others, is not the main character in the structure of the story; the central character, on the other hand, is an ordinary individual, similar to all his fellow officers.

Let us begin again from the beginning. The film indicates its historical nature, but history is relegated to the background, the characters are not involved in it. A small group of men, closed in on itself, completely different from the others, whether they be enemies or allies, lives with a constant concern – food – and a single plan – escape. The film expresses a refusal of history, or at least a desire to remain apart from history, and this is in 1937, when everyone knows perfectly well that history, in the film's sense, is moving again.

The ideal of *La Grande Illusion* is an enclosed universe, protected from the outside, where a narrow and well-defined task is performed. The nationalism, of which we have noticed several signs, is primarily a wish not to get involved in world politics, and to keep to narrower and more familiar problems. It also expresses the conviction that the French, because they are clever, and because they know how to find the right solutions, overcome every problem. Examples of this rejection of history can no doubt be found in other films made in the West at this time. What is striking in this case is the coherence of the whole and its prophetic nature. The situation depicted in the film parallels exactly that of France after the defeat in 1940: the French are out of the game, history is taking place beyond their frontiers; the weight of the war is being borne by the

British and the Russians; the French are the prisoners of the Germans and, in the underground, are preparing to resume fighting, which has a symbolic value but no more effect than the return of one escaped prisoner to the front in a world war.

La Grande Illusion is evidence of the state of mind of certain French people, just before the war; we can see enormous contradictions, great uncertainty and an essentially negative nationalism, which does not assert itself against the enemy, but through ignorance of what is foreign. Confronted with the growing threat of Hitler, the makers of the film tried to develop a few general themes on the unity that is achieved in the face of great peril; behind their demonstration we can detect the hope that the crisis, which is felt to be very close, will pass them by and take place somewhere else. Munich is not far off, and a film like this helps us to understand the reactions of the public in September 1938. *La Grande Illusion* is neither defeatist, nor pacifist at any price; the most suitable word is no doubt isolationist.

7

The Russian Revolution

1927: another anniversary. Unable to challenge the American studios on their home ground – the fiction film – young Soviet film-makers tried to attract their audience by picturing the past of the Revolution: revolts against the Tsar in the nineteenth century, European uprisings such as the Paris commune, 1917 in Moscow, in Southern Russia and in Petrograd.[1] Two projects, assigned to the best directors and technicians of the time, were started together and resulted in two films, issued at about the same moment – *The End of St Petersburg* and *October*. Both are pieces of propaganda. I agree with those who say that we must not ignore the problem and that we have to look at the conditions in which the films were produced; *The End of St Petersburg* and *October* force us to deal with the question of the overlap between history, propaganda and films, which we did not fully consider in previous chapters. The way in which these films are constructed differs greatly from conventional film norms and confuses viewers familiar with Western cinema; we cannot look at them as easily as we did the films dealing with the nineteenth century, and we must take the film expression, film language, far more into account than we have done up to now. I am not going to comment on the films: such a task would take too much time; I only want to illuminate a different, non-narrative conception of screened historiography.

Signs and filmic expression

The similarities between our films are noticeable but, if we see other 'historical' films produced in the 1920s, we observe the same likenesses: many things, relations, facts are pictured in a constant, not to say unequivocal manner. These data are not only defined by their junctions and oppositions: each of them is represented by specific colours, shapes, objects which symbolize and designate them. Some of these designations are borrowed from a common, trite field of knowledge, such as the props representing the Church or the guns symbolizing the necessity of fighting against the government. Other symbols, created by the films themselves, require more attention.

An example would be the symbol of the middle class. The words 'middle class', 'bourgeoisie' are never mentioned but there is a certain convention which presents middle-class men as stupid, fat, well-dressed (plate VII). Our films make use of this convention, without describing the bourgeoisie; what we see are symbols – series of symbols – rather than portraits. *The End of St Petersburg* begins with the countrymen in their village; then come the workers in their factory and the bourgeios in the stock-market (in other words, everyone in his ordinary surroundings). Stockholders are agitated, chattering, plump men; catching glimpses of faces, hats, glasses, chins, we are led to conceive of the middle class as a collection of disordered objects, in a state of constant excitement. The second sequence of *October* is devoted to the middle class; it lasts for less than one hundred seconds, with fifty shots; thus, a third of the shots are less than one second long and some of them have only two or three frames: when working at the viewing-table we realize that we have seen only stupid fat people on the screen for the entire sequence – but, during the projection, we do not exactly know what we are looking at, we have insufficient time to identify the men and women, we only gain an impression: these people, different though they are, do exactly the same thing; they change, but the smiles, the shouting remain the same: this 'motionless motion' (not the fatness nor the clothes) is the symbol of the middle class.

We have noted that the other 'pairs' of films – the French and the Italian ones – illustrate the same events; the difference lies in the staging of these events. We find few events as such in the Russian films; to be precise, there is nothing, in *The End of St Petersburg*, which might be compared to the call for volunteers in the French Revolution or to Garibaldi's disembarkation in Sicily. As events are conceived in a different way in the two Soviet films, we shall return to this question, once we have cleared up some difficulties concerning the 'visual signs'. I take the word 'sign' in its classically-accepted sense: the bond between a signifier (a materialized manifestation which is supposed to impress any potential addressee) and a signified (the data that the signifier is supposed to evocate for both the emitter and the addressee). It has often been said that signs do not exist in films, for you can never determine a rigorous concordance between a signifier and a signified – but such a concordance does not exist in any other system of communication; even the words, which are the most precisely delimitated signs, never unilaterally stand for well-defined data. The signs communicate meaning not because they automatically provoke a reaction (the drawing of a large animal with a trunk making us think: 'elephant') but because they are included first in an homogeneous system (language, drawings, road warnings, and so on) which articulates the signs with other signs and secondly because they form part of the complex of relations, conflicts and connections which structures a society. Signs exist in so far as they can be inscribed in the messages that a group of human beings makes use of.

We might say that the few events which unequivocally point out the year 1792 for a Frenchman or the Liberation of Sicily for an Italian are signs – but general and vague ones; the sharp, precise signs of the Russian films lend themselves to various groupings. A chimney stands for 'factory', the statue of a tsar for 'monarchy', a fortress for 'repression'. This is the simplest degree, the sign fixed to the thing; but such signs are not transparent signals, devoid of quality; on the contrary, they are meaningful; around a specific, conventional significance (Pope = Church) they give way to a multitude of associations. The villagers of *The End of St Petersburg* arrive in a large town. The caption reads: 'Petersburg, capital of the tsars' and then we see the equestrian statue of Peter the First. At the beginning of *October*, we see the huge effigy of a king and, when we read his name on the plinth, we understand he is Tsar Alexander III. Peter the Great, Alexander III: we very soon remember Old Russia, tsarism, the Orthodox Church; what we see is not merely a statue, but many other things, depending on the

161

understanding that we bring to our perception of the film. When looking at a film, we cannot perceive 'everything' involved in every shot: we have to choose and, very often, the film helps by pointing out what is absolutely necessary to understand the plot. But at the same time, we notice things that are familiar to us. Pictures, or any other documents, are related to other documents, ancient or modern. Let me give you an example. In the first sequence of *October*, a running crowd climbs up the steps at the base of the statue; we might think that the crowd is stronger than the Tsar and is going to destroy him; but crowds on steps had already appeared in two previous films, *Battleship Potemkin* and *Metropolis*; the crowd on the steps in *October* recalls the themes already established in those earlier films. In *Potemkin* and *Metropolis* the crowd is overcome (or, at the end of *Metropolis*, forced to retreat with its enemy): if we had seen these films – and many people had seen them in Soviet Russia – we would expect the crowd to run to its defeat. Semiologists describe this overlapping of texts as 'intertextuality'.

We might take our films shot by shot and discover thousands of hints, allusions, references to other films or texts but it is enough for us to note that signs can either be debased and reduced to indicate a precise, limited signified or used as intersections of meanings. By accumulating redundant signs, many historical films communicate well-defined, precisely dated information; on the contrary, the Russian pictures enlarge the evocative power of the signs. Consider one of the most obvious references in *October*, the statue of Napoleon. Prime Minister Kerenski is becoming dictatorial: before entering Nicholas II's apartment, he stops for a short while and we see him, with his hand in his jacket, in a 'Napoleonic' posture. It is only a brief indication, and one that could be easily overlooked, if the film did not later show, when Kerenski is alone in his office, a small plaster-of-Paris Napoleon. The editing process thus far is rather simple: Kerenski dreams of being a new dictator but he is no more than a pale imitation of Napoleon. Now, we come to General Kornilov's putsch. Kornilov wants to take Kerenski's seat; he is shown on horseback and is immediately followed by a statue of Bonaparte on horseback. Bonaparte and a military putsch: we are at the end of the French Revolution, in the days of the *coup d'état*. Five shots later, we are back to the plaster

Napoleon and, shortly after, we see the British tanks coming to the assistance of Kornilov. We are far from Kerenski's dream; Bonaparte and Napoleon represent the end of the French Revolution and Napoleon's invasion of Russia. Another step forward and we see two plaster-of-Paris Napoleons: two novice dictators cancel out. At the same time, the pair of statues reminds us of another couple, a pair of rough wooden idols which appeared a little earlier in the sequence. Jumping from one substitution to another, we are forced to take various problems into account; the historical information illuminates Kerenski's and Kornilov's political aim (to take the dictatorship) and stresses the relationship between power and religion. The multivalence of the quotation establishes an uncertainty which leads to different readings of the sequence.

We have been speaking hitherto of isolated signs but signs, far from being individualized, are always included in a series of data, some of them other signs and some not. In the simplest situation, we have what Pudovkin, the director of *The End of St Petersburg* used to call 'linkage' of signs. Take the first scenes of this film – more precisely the ones which lead from the outset to the departure of two villagers to St Petersburg. The opening shots have no defined significance but they already orientate our mind in a certain direction: a windmill, a corn field, some sheep; we would assume that the film deals with countryside if the title did not suggest otherwise. The following shots corroborate our assumption: two men dressed in rustic clothes, 'isba'. Here, we better understand what signs are and how they work. In our experience (which is, in this case, a purely cultural one), Russian rustic clothing (plate VII) or isba are clearly defined and refer to rural life; the first shots of the film were suggestive, evocative pictures, directed by subsequent shots towards an unavoidable conclusion: we are in the countryside; other scenes, built in the same manner, then give the main characteristics of the old-Russian country life: hunger, pain, long-suffering resignation.

I am struck by the difference between this sequence and the few glimpses of the peasantry we found in films made in the West. In the French or Italian pictures, the countrymen are seen through their relations with the landlords or, at least, with the townsmen; they are, at the same time, inserted into a plot, they play their

163

trifling part in the story. In French and Italian films, the fiction is essential; the signs only give information on the period and on the social status of the characters; thus signs have little importance; they are often redundant and always subordinated to the plot. As we have said many times, when looking at films made in the West, we follow the main character – or a central group of characters – and see the events with him; *The End of St Petersburg* does not provide us with any guide and gets us to 'decode' a series of signs by ourselves.

I am not saying this is a better way of filming or of implicating the audience: one may assume that neither the filmmakers nor the audience are free to select their signs, for the signs which are defined and accepted in a society pre-date the people who use them; we cannot read the picture of an isba as pointing out 'sunset on a wood' or 'industrial building'. It is up to the reader to decide if the Russian silent film expression is better than the Western one, but it is not our concern here. Confronted with a film, we are in an ambiguous position. As spectators, we like or dislike: it is a matter of cultural background (and, incidentally, it is interesting and illuminating to question the reasons why we accept or reject a particular film). As historians, we see documents that inform us about the relationship between historiography, culture and politics at a given time; here, there are no value judgements to be made, we can make use of all films. The great majority of films belong to the type we described when studying the films dealing with the nineteenth century; the Russian films may appear as odd, especially if we try to situate them within the context of the whole of the cinema of the 1920s and 1930s. As we live in a 'Hollywood' world, as television gratifies its audience with prevalently narrative films, is it necessary to compare the prevailing pattern with the few Russian films of the 1920s; the reader may have found the previous pages too theoretical, too marked by a systematic research into definitions and means of classification; yet, they were useful for two reasons. First, since the 1960s, we have seen an ever-increasing number of attempts to bring about changes in the cinema, which, partly at least, refuses narration, finds its own language in the play of the image and, very often, refers to the Russians film-makers of the 1920s as its forerunners; since then, there have been several forms of cinematographic expression and it is of the utmost importance to reflect on the methods that enable us to study non-narrative films. On the other hand, the comparison has enabled us to define our earlier analysis of Western cinema more accurately. In this chapter, my purpose is only to persuade my readers to alter their approach when watching films that handle signs in such a different way.

The bases of the Revolution

The opening scenes of *The End of St Petersburg* have provided us with some feeling for Russian rural society, the most important point being the immobility of the life and the submissiveness of the countrymen. As there are too many people and too little food in the villages, two villagers go to St Petersburg to look for work. We do not know their names and we shall very soon lose sight of one of them. Their journey towards the city is not narrated but suggested by other signs (people walking through dust and wind; landscape seen from a train). New signs designate the town: huge buildings, factories, traffic in the streets; but here, the linkage of shots, which is still effective, is accompanied by another trick, the counterpoint between two series of signs which stand for 'factory workers' or for 'capitalists' respectively. In the sense we have given to the word,[2] we have a structure – that is, a system of opposition: work versus leisure, exhaustion versus well-being, fatness versus thinness. This structure is not a result to be described as such but a constant relationship between two terms through which each term is defined not in itself but in its relation with the other term: the structuration, which is an intellectual, purely conceptual model, helps us to identify the social powers which act and react in the film.

We cannot help noticing an asymmetry between the countryside and the town: the first, settled in motionlessness, seems to ignore any kind of contradiction, whereas the second is violently divided between two opposed classes; we are told that capitalists exploit the workers, but we are given no reason why the villagers feel hungry. That is not surprising. The Russian cinema was not protected against contemporary references, which are as perceptible as they used to be in the West. In 1927 Soviet Russia was still in the period of the New Economy Policy; the countrymen were expected to support the proletariat in its struggle to build socialism. A few years later, films like *The General Line* will show the poor peasantry dominated by wealthy farmers and we shall witness a class war, with Bolsheviks and Soviet engineers teaching the poor how to use tractors and inciting them to expel priests and 'kulaki'. At the time of *The End of St Petersburg*, there was no class division in villages; thus, nothing can happen in the countryside: the film corresponds with the official tenet when it links revolt and the town.

After we have discovered the conflictual aspects of the city, we enter the main part of the film, the course of the Revolution. The filming process changes; the characters become the representatives of the three classes which, according to the official view, played a part in the Revolution (bourgeoisie, proletariat and peasantry) and the story mingles with history. Let us examine both these points.

The signs are now used in a quite different way and I would like to suggest another word to describe them: we might call them 'symbols'. As there is no clear difference between a sign and a symbol, there is no reason for us not to draw our own distinction. Signs, although they do not have an obvious and unique significance, tend to indicate a precise signified; 'symbol' will be taken to be related to data which cannot be distinctly determined and, to a large extent, are purely intuitive. A few signs help us to identify a worker, a bourgeois, a villager (plates VI and VII); once the characters are on, *The End of St Petersburg* induces the spectator to infer some characteristics of their class from their behaviour and from their acts.

Take the villager as an example: unable to understand the problems of the factory workers, he denounces their leader to the police and blacklegs as soon as they start striking (plate VII) he then becomes angry (plate VII) and attacks some members of the bourgeoisie; thus, he is sent to jail (plate VII) and, when war breaks out, immediately enlists. This man has no identity (no name, no specified age, no family); he symbolizes the overexploited Russian peasantry, which colludes with the bourgeoisie and strengthens the bourgeois domination over the urban proletariat.

The other classes, being less unified, need 'multiplied' symbols. The bourgeoisie is represented by a prosperous manufacturer, Lebedev, and his director – in other words, by the capitalist and by the bureaucrat who gathers up the crumbs. The capitalist is the more interesting of the two: far from being anonymous, like the villagers or the workers, he bears a well-known name. A few illustrious men are responsible for exploiting the workers and for the war; the two sequences of the strike and of the war are intercut with shots of Lebedev, and the first consequence of the revolt against the war is the elimination of the manufacturer and his director.

The proletariat is also divided; its representatives are a man and his wife. The man, a factory worker, is said to be 'a communist': he is constantly agitating, in his shop, at home, in meetings with his comrades and, when he is apprehended after the villager denounces him, amid the soldiers. His wife at first criticizes him because she is afraid she will not be able to feed her children, but she then helps him against the police. The symbolical function of the woman is worth noticing; the first time she appears in the film, she is inside at home and keeps everything she owns for her family; in her final appearance, she is outside, in the street, helping strangers and giving them the food she intended to carry to her husband. The workers have no name but they have – more accurately, they are part of – families and they are constantly developing a class consciousness.

The people who represent the three classes are involved in a series of short scenes. As we have said before, no historic event is staged in the film and the audience is not provided with any kind of chronology. We are told of the war in an indirect way: guns standing out against the horizon, a man at the phone, a group of chattering capitalists, an enthusiastic crowd, some shots of soldiers filing off in the streets – and we translate this as 'hostilities'. We are then at the front: trenches, mud, explosions, dead bodies. A caption reads: 'three years!' Pictures of women crying, making a public demonstration; captions again: 'freedom, peace!' Now, middle-class men are congratulating each other and we guess it is the time of the Provisional government. The 'evocation' of history[3] is interrupted by the two narrative scenes we have already mentioned: the communist escaping the police; the communist bringing the soldiers over to the cause of the Revolution. Immediately after that we witness the attack on the Winter Palace and we are told that 'St Petersburg is no more'. It would be difficult to follow the film if we were unaware of the dates and events of the Russian Revolution; in fact, the history of 1917 is assumed to be known by the audience, for whom the film offers an interpretation.

The picture is built on the alternations between four types of editing:

1. Linkage of signs;
2. Linkage of signs + opposition between two series of signs;
3. Narration of fictional events, in full-length or in shortened time;
4. 'Evocation' of history.

If we consider the concatenation of the various film processes, we are in a position to give a general outline of the film:

FILMING-PROCESS	INFORMATION	INFERENCES
1	the countryside	the villagers are resigned to enduring their life
2	the town	social conflicts in town
3	the strike the communist arrested anger of the villager the villager in jail	the proletariat, divided between a conscious minority and a suffering majority is vanquished because the peasantry complies with the bourgeoisie

Table continued

4	breaking out of war three years of war the provisional government	
3	the communist haranguing the troops the villager helping him	alliance between the workers and the peasantry
3	the Winter Palace assaulted the woman in the street and among the wounded	the formerly ex-ploited classes united in their victory

A complex filming process succeeds in giving a rather sim-plified vision of the Revolution: traditional villages never change. Social conflicts arise in towns but the conscious minority is stopped by the enslaved silent majority. The war and the evils it brings about (in other words the eruption of history) result in the development of class consciousness, which leads the classes with similar interests to assume power.

History rebuilt

In *The End of St Petersburg*, history is given as 'another text', antecedent to the film, accepted but accorded a different status. In *October*, history is rebuilt by the film and included in its stream. The film includes some dates and numerous shots produced in accordance (Plate I) with existing documents (newspapers, leaflets, pictures, photographs) but it never presents them within quotation marks, it does not use them as pieces of evidence. For instance, if you have looked at illus-trated books on the Russian Revolution, you might think that

169

many of the photographs of crowds, streets, political demonstrations must have been reproduced from contemporary documents, but you are never sure that you see a reproduction; a still which could be a document is not presented as a proof; it is inserted, inscribed in the continuity of the film. Thus, history is not pre-existent to the film, it is produced by it.

An illustration will clarify this point. After General Kornilov's defeat, a short sequence is devoted to the mobilization of the Russian proletariat; this purely symbolic sequence is built on a shifting of objects and movement from frame to frame: we see rifle-bullets, then guns, then a few people with guns, then a large crowd of armed people, then the revolutionary staff; at the end of this progressive development, a caption tells us that 'everything is ready'; next, we see a printed document, a Bolshevik leaflet, photographed as it appeared on the very morning of 25 October; all the shots in the sequence are film studio material and the only document is not given as evidence but as a result of the sequence; if the sequence had begun with the document, instead of leading up to it, the impression would have been completely different. The leaflet tells us that the Bolsheviks put an end to Kerenski's government at ten o'clock, on the morning of 25 October – but the whole of the second part of the film shows that this statement was incorrect; at ten o'clock, the government was still in the Winter Palace; literally taken, the printed document is untrue.

History is not a reality used by the film; it has to be rebuilt and the result of the reconstruction is never reliable. *October* is constantly undermining the certainties. The multivalence of all the data is particularly apparent when the film uses symbols, and a comparison with *The Birth of a Nation* will help us to understand how symbols deal with history in the Soviet film. In both films, buildings appear – the Cameron house in *The Birth of a Nation*, the Winter Palace in *October*. At the beginning of its fourth sequence, *The Birth of a Nation* explores the house: we see the whole of the Cameron home and its residents. We could not be satisfied with saying that this is a description: as we have already said, it is much more, it is the symbol of the old American family – but this symbol is established as a reality, as a 'real' house. In *October* we never see the Winter Palace in full. After July we are, for the first time, in a building,

170

in a long corridor and then on a step; in this sequence, which is one of the most famous in the film, the symbol is not the Palace (nothing indicates we are in the Winter Palace) but the sequence itself, which represents Kerenski's helplessness: subtitles indicating regular ascending ranks climbing higher and higher are cut into shots of Kerenski climbing the stairs, all at exactly the same pace. The Palace re-appears after the middle of the film; we see its main gate but we do not pass beyond the doorstep (in 'classical pictures, the film, in showing the door, invites us to come into the house); Kerenski goes out and leaves; we have the opposite of ritualized formulas, the gate being used as a point of departure rather than a point of entry. Immediately after Kerenski leaves, his soldiers, junkers and women, enter the Palace; following them, the camera stops on details which are not symptomatic of the yet unknown inside; the Palace appears as a mosaic of rooms (a caption tells the audience 'there are more than 1,000 rooms in the Palace') that never succeeds in becoming a whole. We shall see later that the Palace offers a political vision of the monarchy and, generally speaking, of power, but here, I only point out the symbol: the Palace has no homogeneity, it does not exist as a building and everyone who deals with it is doomed to failure.

We have discovered two functions of symbols: they take the place of too precise, too realistic descriptions (the symbol of 'the bourgeois', of monarchy in general instead of a precisely defined middle class or a particular monarchy) and they suggest abstract, inexplicit ideas such as 'weakness', 'power', 'strength'. But we must never read them in a definite way, because they are made to be understood in various ways. A sequence like the one of the Gods, in Kornilov's putsch, is open to a wide range of interpretations; I mention two, given by Eisenstein.[4] Kornilov's march towards Petrograd was under the banner of 'God and Country'; the procession of the Gods suggests the religious significance of the putsch; a number of religious images, from a Christ to an Eskimo idol, are cut together; while idea and image of God appear to accord completely in the first statue shown, the two elements move farther apart in each successive image; the idea is always the same but the statues gradually become rougher: a chain of images leads to a symbolization of the nature of all deities. That accounts for the

171

religious significance. The military tendency is symbolized in an editing process that employs the same statues; the editing intercuts shots of the Baroque Christ (apparently exploding in the radiant beams of his halo) with shots of a mask of the Goddess Uzume, completely self-contained: the temporal conflict between the closed egg-form and the seraphic star-form produces the effect of an instantaneous explosion, a bomb. We have seen another symbol when putting together the statues of Napoleon and the statues of the Gods and we could find many other proximities, because the attribute of such an 'opened' symbolization is to lend itself to a varied, indefinite treatment.

The quotes, the symbols, should have been understood by the public for whom the film was meant and an historian might be tempted to count them up. I feel that we cannot hope to understand the symbols merely by looking at a film and noting quotes or symbols, because we never find them in a 'pure' form; they do not exist by themselves and can only be observed in the process through which they receive their specific meaning in the film. In *The Birth of a Nation*, clear, unequivocal symbols help to state the old America precisely; by connecting every object, every photograph to other information, the open, multivalent symbols of *October* prevent the film from describing the past in an oversimple manner; it is important, for our enquiry, to understand that the way in which symbols are integrated in a film reveals to the external investigator some of the historical conceptions of the film.

We have raised many abstract questions, related to intertextuality, history, quotes, symbols, without giving any interpretation, or general view of the film; before trying to go further, it is necessary to demonstrate how time works in *October*. Remember first how it is used in *The Birth of a Nation*; take, for instance, Ben's return home; the scene consists of two shots and the first runs almost a full minute in length, which is extremely long; it begins with the young sister running out to meet her brother; they look at each other for some time; then, she bursts into tears and they embrace; here, narrative time is identical to filmic and 'real' time.

October can be divided into two parts: before 25 October; the day of 25 October. In the very middle of the film, a subtitle tells us that it is 25 October. Before, it was dark but we cannot say whether it was day or night – the long sequence was not obviously set at night or in the daytime but in a sort of darkness lit by artificial light. Now, it is the day on the morning of 25 October. We see a battleship, first in medium shot, then in long shot, with the structure of an iron bridge in the foreground. Here, the way in which the film uses time begins to make itself felt (as a matter of fact, it is used in the same way throughout the film, but we do not perceive it very clearly). At the beginning of the film, we saw the same iron structure; a large crowd, peaceful and happy, was walking in procession through the streets of Petrograd; the government ordered the soldiers to fire on the crowd and to open the bridge; the crowd ran away but was unable to cross the river; many people were killed.

Until now, the metallic structure has been one of the mechanisms on which the government has relied; the long shot with the battleship and the bridge could represent this: the revolutionary machinery (the boat) is fighting against the official machinery. But shortly after that, we see some sailors on the pier; we have not seen them landing from the battleship and there is a break in continuity here: were they on the pier before the subtitle giving the date, which would mean they had been there for some time? Or have they just left the ship?

The sailors lead us back to the same sequence of the crowd in the streets. They are there, listening to a Bolshevik leader's speech; there is considerable use of cross-cutting from the listening sailors to the orator; the men are still and the emphasis is on the motionless link between them and their leader. Only on the morning of 25 October do the sailors keep moving; they rush about on the pier: the bridge, the huge iron structure that the government had ordered to open, once again slowly closes.

We find at least three sorts of time[5] in that sequence:

1. Narrative time. Some sailors run on a pier; the two parts of a moving bridge meet. Those scenes are short narrations, in shortened time (successive moments in what could be a single connected sequence).
2. Editing time. The link between the shots is only created by the logic of editing; for instance, we see a ship, a pier, a bridge; there is a connection between the water and some

man-made building that dominates the water; the editing suggests a logical continuity, which is measured by the time devoted to each image but which is not narrative time.

3. Symbolical time. The film insists on the transformation which occurred on the morning of 25 October. Before this date, the government controlled affairs and people followed its orders; the sailors were quiet. The same sailors who had been enclosed in a sort of perpetual present (I suggest we might read the cross-cutting in that way: the editing allows no possibility of change), jump into the present and are seen as a part of the making of history; the bridge – which had been a grave for many people (and that meant eternity) – is now no more than a bridge carrying pedestrians and tram-ways, in other words it signifies the return to daily life for ordinary people.

The film in its 'context'

I think we should stop at this point and recall what has already been said, in order to avoid any confusion. By comparing *The End of St Petersburg* with *October*, I may have implied that I preferred the latter film to the former. All those who have tried to create a new type of film have always had a tendency to condemn the other forms of cinema and that was the case with Eisenstein, the director of *October*, who considered *The End of St Petersburg* 'as classic in the field of purely metric montage' with the two extremes 'of simplicity and complexity'.[6] In studying *October* and seeing how history is produced in it by the very movement of the film, we see more clearly how *The End of St Petersburg* over-estimates the value of historiography, over-rates the importance of the already constituted and universally accepted historical discourse, in order to reinforce its own political lesson by the use of this discourse. This does not necessarily mean that the political objectives of *October* are clearer; the film claims to expose the manner in which history is built up, but it confuses the audience because of its length and its complexity. The very few studies that have been devoted to it have always tended to confine it to the traditional frames, that is, to find in it a chronological continuity and to compare the details

174

of the film with more recent versions of the events of 1917. In order to avoid such a simplification, it was necessary to break down the mechanisms involved in *October* and show how history is not a given fact to be recognized, but the result of a continuous interaction between the expressive levels, a few aspects of which we have studied.

However, *October*, like *The End of St Petersburg*, is the result of an order. The shooting conditions were quite exceptional in the Soviet Union of 1925. When the Bolsheviks came into power, they were already aware of the importance of the cinema as a means of mass communication. In the very middle of the Civil War, a team of film-makers, led by Vertov and Tisse – who was to be the cameraman on *October* – was provided with the equipment and the means of transport it needed in order to travel to the various battlefronts, film the hostilities and produce newsreels, which were then presented and commented upon by party officials. In the years following, film production was systematically encouraged and, in 1927, the Soviet Union was able to release more than 200 films. But the laboratories were unable to manufacture film stock, all of which had to be purchased from capitalist countries. The state, which could not afford it, had to leave the field open to private initiative.[7] The development of the cinema is a typical, although little-known aspect of the NEP. Regional associations, co-operatives, were set up and negotiated film purchases from Germany as best they could.[8] Although a central body had been created in 1925, the producers retained their independence until around 1930.[9] No censorship, no domination by private capital, constant encouragement from the authorities: no other cinema met with such favourable conditions at that time, and as a result the Soviet Union enjoyed some of the most memorable experiences in the history of the cinema. The film-makers were unanimously in favour of the regime but few were actual members of the party.[10] Most of their films have an essentially moral outlook, either when denouncing the evils of the old regime in the story of an individual or of a family, or when trying to paint a picture of the future. The orders issued in 1925 and 1927 should then be understood as an attempt by the government to give the cinema a new orientation and to create a political cinema. The Bolsheviks were not in a position to exercise total control of the cinema; to do so, they had to control the branches (which had doubled in number between 1924 and 1926), the unions, the administration, the press, and in all these areas they met with strong resistance. The cinema employed relatively few people, and produced a great deal of material. It had remained aloof from the struggle between Stalinists and opponents, and was at that time a privileged area; the film-makers enjoyed an exceptional independence, the unique and very temporary aspects of which they did not fully appreciate. Therefore, the producers of *October* profited from all the advantages that official patronage could offer (shooting facilities, unlimited use of film, help from the people and the army in crowd scenes), without submitting to any external control.

Study of the film material allows us to raise two important questions, which only the film itself can answer:

1. At a time when the leaders of the opposition were being liquidated, but when opponents were still numerous, what margin of freedom remained to those who were not members of the party, when dealing with a subject as important and as controlled as the history of the Revolution?
2. To what extent did the official directives and slogans, widely distributed within the party, reach the non-Bolshevik intellectuals?

1926 was marked, in the Soviet Union, by the official recognition of a change, started long before: the transition to socialism in one country. The revolutionaries of 1917 were convinced that Europe would not resist the shock of the world war and that, in the advanced industrial countries, the proletariat would rise. The Russian bourgeoisie, the 'weakest link' of the capitalist chain, had given way first, but the revolution was only the prelude to a general upheaval. It seemed impossible that a socialist country could exist in isolation in the middle of a capitalist Europe, and the foundation of the Third International marked the intention to continue the offensive. The suppression of the second revolutionary attempt in Germany, the liquidation of the Communist Parties in Balkan Europe, the failure of the British general strike, showed that the capitalists had once again got the upper hand and were far from collapsing. Renouncing the expectations of the eight previous years, Stalin declared that socialism would be founded in one country, without the help of the Western proletariat.

October ignores all that is not Russian. The outside world is mentioned only three times: the fraternization between Russian and German soldiers, the subtitles indicating the help brought to Kerenski by the British, the rotation of the clocks telling the time in the major foreign cities when the Bolsheviks assumed power. The allusion to the British – who were not the only ones to have helped the counter-revolutionaries – is topical: in 1926, the Soviet Union and Great Britain were on the verge of breaking off all diplomatic relations, the press was full of attacks on the British, and the film, in passing, adds an extra sting to it. The fraternization attempts are immediately suppressed; after this sequence, there is hardly any further mention of the battlefront; military events, which have played such an important part in Kerenski's failure, are ignored. As for the rotation of the clocks, it is organized around a clock telling the time in Petrograd; the world does not break in – Soviet time strikes throughout the world.

The concentration of events in a single place is even more striking than these details. Except for the fraternization in the trenches, the film takes place entirely in the capital, and in only a few districts of the city. Where do those who make the revolution come from? Two subtitles suggest that they come from the suburbs. But these subtitles echo words spoken by members of the government; in other subtitles that the film takes into account (that is to say, which do not report some-body's words, but are a commentary 'from the outside'), only the inhabitants of St Petersburg themselves are mentioned. Not a single shot is devoted to the outlying districts; *October* only shows the heart of the capital in an obviously identifiable manner, as an island bordered by the Neva River and one of its tributaries, where the official buildings and bourgeois streets lie. This centre is shown twice only. First, in July: the common people enter the centre, freely and without preparation; they are massacred there. Later, after the mobilization, we see maps of Petrograd, on which a pencil has drawn crosses and circles, then we see photographs of the places thus marked – they are the occupied buildings around the Winter Palace. The assailants

177

move in circles, they surround the Palace, and enter it from below (through the cellars), and from above (over the terraces), through the doors and head towards the heart of the Palace. The revolution is the conquest of a place, first its theoretical delineation on a map, then its occupation; a continuous movement which evolves from the exterior to the interior. 'The revolution is accomplished' when the centre is reached.

This conception of the revolution raises a political problem which we will return to later. Here, I only mention the systematic progression from the outside to the inside. The majority of the shots are filmed indoors by artificial light or at night (plate VI). The predominance of black is striking, even at first sight. When studying it in detail, we discover that the distribution of day and night is important. The main shots in natural light describe two failures, then Kornilov's troops, and finally the flight of Kerenski. All the successes (the arrival of Lenin, the mutiny of Kerenski's troops and the capture of the Palace), take place at night. Lenin only appears at night, or indoors, in artificial light; the mobilization of the proletariat, the occupation of strategic spots in the city, the assault on the Palace, all take place entirely in the dark. It is useless to refer to the historical circumstances: the film has its own particular chronology, different from that of the historians (plate VI). I will demonstrate this in a very simplified manner. We know that the second part of the film is devoted to the day and the night of 25 October, as stated by a subtitle appearing at the end of the mobilization sequence. First, in broad daylight, we see Kerenski's flight and the arrival of the cadets who have come to protect the Palace: the day of 25 October. Then, that night, revolutionary troops surround the Palace: the evening of 25 October. But suddenly we find ourselves in daylight, on the morning of 25 October, in front of the building where delegates to the Congress of Soviets arrive. The alternation of day and night does not reproduce the various stages of a day in conventional sequence; it is like a mark designating each side in turn.

The deepening into night and the progression towards the heart of the enemy coincide. The revolution is not an outburst, a large movement expanding outwards; it is expressed by the crowding around Lenin, in one room of the Palace, of those who have participated in the assault. In *Metropolis*, and in many

178

other contemporary films, we find the opposite movement, the workers emerging from the dark and the inside to occupy the open space. The use of the hidden space has various meanings; we have already talked about its symbolic aspects, and we will return to its political significance. Let us point out out here how close it is to the leading theme of the Bolshevik programme: to stay inside, dealing with Soviet problems only, hoping that the capitalist world will forget about you, leaving you free to work more thoroughly. *October* is not a hymn to the conquering revolution; in it, revolution is concentration, confinement within oneself, in a space beyond the reach of foreign influences.

Another way towards the Revolution

In order to understand the mechanisms in the film which prepare the Revolution and ensure its success, we cannot be satisfied with a description of the various classes involved, as was the case with *The End of St Petersburg*. We will instead begin with a short sequence showing a conflict and a Bolshevik success, in order to define more accurately the stake and the form of the struggle. For our purposes, the sequence of Kornilov's offensive is eminently suitable. I will summarize the sequence numbering each scene:

1. Blasts of factory hooters alternate with captions indicating that Kornilov is attacking;
2. Armed workers coming out of a yard;
3. Statues of various deities; in the middle, the statue of Alexander III reappears, restored to its pedestal;
4. Alternation of Kerenski, Kornilov and statues of Napoleon;
5. Train loaded with Kornilov's soldiers and tanks;
6. The release of the Bolshevik prisoners;
7. Distribution of arms to the workers;
8. After a caption designating Smolny, arms and leaflets;
9. Men blocking a railway;
10. Discussion between Bolsheviks and Asiatic soldiers;
11. Cossack dance.

We notice at once a stressed asymmetry; the defenders of   179 the revolution occupy three-quarters of the sequence and the scenes in which they appear enclose the passages devoted to Kornilov. The alarm, the first reaction of the workers, precedes the entrance of the military. The montage of episodes 3 to 5 is a simple mix of shots which offer a formal resemblance. The presentation of the gods is made up of a line of close-ups of statues, gradually moving from the most sophisticated (a many-armed Indian deity) to the simplest (a coarse idol in wood). The episode of the apprentice dictators begins with two men who are gradually replaced by statues. The last scene consists in alternating crossed movements according to opposite diagonals. The three scenes all aim at an extreme simplification of forms and movements; each of them expresses only one notion: the religious pretext, personal ambitions, the use of agents who do not understand what they are meant to do, either because they come from far away, or because they are foreigners. These scenes re-employ images already known or introduce images which will appear in later sequences. We are presented with a sort of synthesis of power from which we will try to characterize counter-revolution.

Power is shielded behind an immense facade: God and the country. The first sequence clearly establishes the link between Tsardom and Christianity by intercutting shots of the over-thrown statue of Alexander with church domes; the link is hinted at in later episodes. The scene of the gods completes and makes more precise what was rather vague before. From this whole, the clergy are almost absent: they appear in only two shots at the beginning of the film, which reappear, where a priest smiles as he swings a censer. This restraint is important. A few years later, the cinema attacked the priests violently, accusing them of sabotaging the construction of socialism. *October* attacks the deity but leaves the church alone; isolated at the end of the scene, repeating a mechanical gesture, the priest is only a religious profiteer, as ambitious generals are profiteers of the political system. The film distinguishes clearly between the religious idea and the practice, concentrating its criticism on the former and ignoring the latter.[11]

The representations of the deity have human form; when returned to their original shape, all that remains is the raw material. Despite appearances, the profound reality of power is

180

the absence of humanity. We have pointed out the symbolization by stone or metal: power is, in turn, compared with a palace, statues, domestic objects. The governors are always isolated and never act themselves. Kornilov appears alone, against an empty background in scene 4, and he is absent in scene 5 where we see his troops. Kerenski, the ministers isolated in their offices, dictate their orders by telephone to anonymous minions. An impersonal device, the telephone is the essential medium of power; at the other end, there are only machines. Think of the bridges which divide the city in two and enable the July massacre to take place: these bridges seem to function by themselves, they are monstrous iron appliances which, in their very motion, crush the workers. The first phase of the revolutionary offensive is the conquest of the machines by the people: sailors prevent the bridges from being closed a second time, a detachment goes and occupies the post. Once the instruments are subjugated, the government is powerless.

Power is a gigantic construction, the sinews of which are hidden. When you reach the core, you find nothing but a vacuum. The inconsistency of the authority is strongly emphasized. Confronted with Kornilov, Kerenski hides himself: he hides under the covers, neglecting the organization of the counter-attack. During the attack on the Palace, we see repeated shots of the empty armchair, which the leader has deserted. When the revolutionaries arrive in the room where the ministers sit, they find motionless old men and furniture covered with dust-sheets.

In the heart of the building, there is nothing; power is a mere semblance, and those who serve it or use it are insubstantial shadows. The sequence shows the government partisans filing off: old people, fat bourgeois and bigoted women. Only young men and women are left to protect the palace and they disperse as the assailants come closer.

Power has three components: the impressive facades of religion, imperial majesty and patriotism; the blind obedience of mercenaries, who are too young or too foreign to think about their actions, and of sophisticated machines; the vested interests of a few parasites. It is hard to reconcile this conception of authority with Leninism, the official doctrine of the Communist Party, as it was expressed in Stalin's writings, in the press, and

in the courses intended for the militants. Religion is the only
exception: the Bolsheviks too considered the Church and the
monarchy as superstructures, artificial constructions concealing
the real problems, pursuing illusory aims rather than questioning the social order. But the Bolsheviks were not the only ones
to denounce religion and patriotism in that manner. The
criticism of the idea of God, presented as a creation of man, in
which man alienates himself and disregards his own condition,
had been widespread in Russia in the nineteenth century, and
many opponents of the Bolsheviks adhered to it completely. The
difference does not lie in the description of the effects produced
by religion, but in the explanation offered. It would be pointless
to remind you of the general outlines of historical materialism;
I will stress only two points, which bring us back to the film.
Lenin regarded the state as the instrument which the ruling
class used in order to protect itself against the subjugated classes
and to steer the economic development in the direction most
favourable to its own interests. The facade does not hide an
empty centre: it must be destroyed in order to unmask the real
enemy – the bourgeoisie. The adversaries are not impotent
profiteers: they are the ones who control production. Their
domination of the political and economic machinery enables
them to find allies not only among thoughtless young men and
frivolous women, but among the middle classes, who profit
indirectly from the exploitation of the proletariat and have a
vested interest in continuing this exploitation.

Completely alien from Marxist-Leninism, the vision of the
old regime that *October* offers is close to the mainly moral
denunciation which the Socialists developed in Russia before
the spread of Marxism. In 1927, all parties were forbidden and
it was impossible, other than in private conversation, to uphold
a criticism of the bourgeoisie which was not founded on an
analysis of class conflicts. The cinema was undoubtedly the
only place where a non-orthodox position was still possible. In
their statements to the press, the film-makers of *October*
described themselves as historical materialists; their film
contradicts this claim. Ten years after the Revolution, in a
milieu like that of the cinema where the influence was weak,
Marxist-Leninism was not much more than a label. The exclusive
use of written sources has led historians to look on the political

evolution of the Soviet Union in the terms and the vocabulary of newspapers. The cinema shows that in the 1930s, there were at least two different political languages, that of the party, the only one which was officially authorized, and that of the sympathizers.

How did the sympathizers define themselves with regard to the party? We can answer this fairly accurately, thanks to the scenes devoted to the defenders of the Revolution in the Kornilov sequence. The passages dealing with the government have a simple construction, based on the repetition of identical figures or forms. The montage of the scenes devoted to the revolutionaries is extremely varied and changes from one episode to the next. Each scene is centred on a topic but the montage establishes a principle of perpetual rotary motion, with the result that no scene can be isolated. Nothing is definitely built up and the meaning of the whole becomes more precise and changes according to the succession of the shots.

Scene 2 is dominated by a continuous movement of workers coming out of a factory; only the place enables us to identify characters, for we know nothing else about them. The subtitle is vague: 'Everyone out for the defence of Petrograd'. This passage confuses us: a little earlier, the film shows the arrest of the militants and the success of the repression; logically, the workers have no arms left and are in no position to mobilize. In fact, it is an anticipation, which will be justified only much later on, in scene 7, where a subtitle indicates that 'the government has been obliged to open the arsenal'. But before this clarification a procession of armed people reappears in scene 6, this time without any setting. We glimpse flags, we guess that there are soldiers, women – distinguishable by their scarves – but we cannot identify the crowd. The march is interrupted by the opening of the prisons and by the insertion of shots showing hands grabbing arms. These three new developments are given meaning in the following scenes. At the beginning of scene 7, a subtitle announces that 'the proletariat takes charge of the defence of Petrograd'; scene 8 displays a Bolshevik flag, already seen at the arrival of Lenin. We should note, in passing, that the crowd of workers, at first poorly defined, acquires its proletarian identity only when it appears beneath the Bolshevik flag; we should also note that the soldiers are identified by their uniforms, but are not named: there, the army is only an element of the armed proletariat. Scene 8 again shows rows of rifles and guns being passed to workers and packs of leaflets; scene 10 reveals that these leaflets are proclamations destined for the Asiatic soldiers brought by Kornilov. There is no chronology or thematic classification; each scene shows, in a different form, a single event: the arming of the proletariat. Against this permanent background, a series of questions are raised: begun, resumed, gradually explained and enlarged upon. The 'clan' in power were presented as individuals, with particular characters; the proletariat is shown by the constant motion of the masses.

The final scenes are rather different. We will omit scene 11, which contradicts scene 3 by contrasting the immobility of the gods with the ceaseless mobility of the men. Scenes 9 and 10 describe the encounter with Kerenski's troops in a pattern that follows the classical historical narrative: by blocking the railway, the revolutionaries stop the train, and by talking with the soldiers, they convince them to give up their expedition.

The whole sequence provides a scheme of historical explanation. The adversary is motionless, alien to time and none of the scenes where the bourgeoisie appears include action (plate VI). The proletariat acts, with variable results: the third rising, the mobilization against Kornilov, is their first success. The parallel with the previous risings explains why they were finally successful. The initial defeats were due to their lack of arms. Against Kornilov, against the Palace, the revolutionaries organized themselves militarily. However, no fighting took place; the soldiers of Kornilov, the Cossacks of the Palace, listened and were convinced; not a single death occurred during the capture of the Palace. The possession of arms is a preliminary condition, but the instrument of the revolution is the spreading of the word.

This word is the word of Lenin; it is obvious that the leader and the revolutionary discourse are looked upon as one; Lenin appears amidst banners bearing slogans announcing the programme that the revolutionaries will carry out throughout the film. After this initial scene, he appears only occasionally: a few shots in the middle of the film, when the decision to rise is taken; a few shots before the attack, a quick incursion to pronounce the final word in the penultimate shot. Lenin, even though he shows the general line, does not participate in the actual events; he is as a flag, which *October* distinguishes carefully from the party. In July, the Bolsheviks are there, but between the crowd and them, there is no merging; each one demonstrates in its corner, peacefully, and the government has no difficulty in suppressing the movement. On the contrary, faced with Kornilov, the two forces join together. The film indicates neither the origin of the crowd, nor the process which enables the Bolsheviks and the workers to constitute themselves as revolutionary agents. Here again, the discrepancy between the film and the official doctrine is obvious. Only the presentation of Lenin corresponds to some of the party's views. Since his death, Lenin had become the object of a cult. Leninism, at least in the version proposed by Stalin, was held as an absolute truth, the final explanation of the past and a code of action for the future. In this sense, the party accepted, to the same extent, a story showing Lenin omnipresent and attentive to the smallest details, as a version where Lenin's word is the absolute arm, infallible when correctly used. According to the official line, the interpreter of this word is the party. Party and proletariat are the same – the former is only the conscious fraction, the advance guard of the latter. Using Leninist thought, the party put forward the goals of the struggle carried out by the proletariat and defined the strategy necessary to achieve these goals. *October* on the contrary, makes a distinction between the party and the working masses. The working class appears from the beginning of the film, but it has no social coherence, it does not depend on a mode of production any more than the group in power does. On its side, the party only exists through the initiatives of its militants. There is a proletariat only when the two forces have joined in the dynamics of the mobilization. We have already mentioned why the party did not enforce strict controls over the cinema. However, the distance between the historical system developed in the film and the theoretical line of Marxism-Leninism is such that a complementary explanation has to be looked for.

October puts forward the spirit of conquest, the will to win. The proletariat stop the destructive machines; once at the controls, they will be able to transform them into constructive machines. In 1927, the Soviets began to prepare the first

Five-year Plan, which was expected to bring about a huge leap forward. To those who worried about the economic weaknesses of the country and feared too drastic a progression, Stalin answered that the workers' capacity for struggle would overcome all drawbacks. The old Bolshevik guard, faithful to a strictly economic interpretation of Marxism, was liquidated for the benefit of another generation who believed in the virtues of improvisation and of a dialectic answer to the difficulties of the moment.[12]

October is not a propaganda work, even though the film brings into play, in its most original aspect, mechanisms which meet the aims of the party. Written documents only deal with the struggle between the opponents and the majority: they do not reveal any of the preoccupations of the Soviets. The testimony of *October* has therefore no equivalent. The film ignores Stalin and does not overestimate the role of the party: we are far from the cult of the personality which will mark the next decade. This independence from the Bolsheviks goes along with a fundamental agreement with the Stalinist programme. One detects an unfamiliar aspect of Stalinism, which, at the outset, was not a mere police dictatorship. In view of the specific position of the cinema, we would need to study systematically the political orientation of the films, in order to re-evaluate Soviet history of the 1920s: this work remains to be done.

Notes

1. The most important films are: *Fall of the Romanov Dynasty*, *Moscow in October*, *Arsenal*, *The Great Road*. See: Jay Leyda, *Kino. A History of the Russian and Soviet Film*, London, 1960, p. 222; Richard Taylor, 'From October to "October": the Soviet political system in the 1920s and its films' in *Politics and the Media*, edited by M. J. Clark, Oxford–New York, 1979, pp. 31–42; R. Taylor, *The Politics of the Soviet Cinema, 1917–1929*, Cambridge, 1979; R. Taylor, *Film Propaganda. Soviet Russia and Nazi Germany* London – New York, 1979.
2. See above, p. 33.
3. 'Calling-up' or 'Evocation'? 'Evocation' seems more usual since

it implies the use of a mental image of the historical period which is then converted into a physical image – in other words the film itself. On the other hand the term 'Calling-up' is good because it has the implication of 'recall' – the bringing back to consciousness of our idea once current but now disregarded.

4. 'A dialectic approach to film form' in *Film Form*, London, 1963.

5. For the timing in historical films, see above, pp. 55–59.

6. S. Eisenstein, 'Methods of montage', in *Film Form*, p. 73; see also Leyda, *Kino*, p. 234.

7. In every conference and congress, discussions on cinema led to the same conclusions: the party had not been successful in its attempts to utilize the pictures; the reasons given for such a failure were shortage of working capital, lack of material and skilled people, concurrence between private entrepreneurs and societies involved in production and exhibition. See Taylor, *Politics of Soviet Cinema,* pp. 10–11, 104.

8. The Rus Studio was created with the help of the International Workers' Aid, a communist-sponsored international organization with headquarters in Berlin. The Proletkino Studio was organized by a group of Russian trade unions.

9. At the Twelfth Party Congress (1923) the Soviet cinema was accused of becoming 'an instrument for bourgeoise influence and for corruption of the toiling masses'. In June 1923, the Council of People's Commissars established a new governmental organ, the Sovkino, which was to control all film production and distribution in the USSR. Although interested in production and exhibition Sovkino never succeeded in controlling production of the film industry's economic base – raw film, cameras, projectors – and never controlled the whole production and distribution. In January 1929 the Central Committee of the Bolshevik Party still asserted that 'the task of the Party is to strengthen the supervision of the work of the film organizations by every means and to secure the ideological firmness of film productions, decisively struggling against manifestations of the accommodations of the Soviet film to the ideology of non-proletarian elements'. See Taylor, *Politics of Soviet Cinema,* p. 82 ff.

10. The shortage of film stocks led to the closure of production in 1919; most of the producers, artists and technicians emigrated. Filming started again in 1921 but with new men. Pudovkin writes: 'I began my work in the film quite accidentally. Up to 1920 I was a chemical engineer and looked at films with contempt'; in 1920, at the age of twenty seven, he entered the State Film School and, as early as 1925, he directed his first feature film. Born in 1899, Kuleshov made his first film in 1917 and began to teach film theory and practice

187

three years later. Dziga Vertov was twenty two when he became head of the cinema department of the All-Russian Central Executive Committee.

11. The anti-religious propaganda began in 1923 with *Brigade Commander Ivanov;* the film was strongly criticized and no other film followed until the 1930s.

12. Soviet Marxism, for a long time, wavered between mechanical and dialectical materialism. According to the first interpretation, all social changes were related to one another: if the economic bases of society were transformed, the social relations would change; any alteration in economy would result in modifying the society. At the end of the 1920s, the mechanism was violently criticized by the dialecticians; Stalin and his followers saw evolution as a discontinuous course of development involving periods of sudden transformation; an accelerated industrialization would result in restructuring of social relationships. During that period, dialectical materialism became the accepted methodology of science. Eisenstein, who had little interest in dialectic in his early work seems to have discovered it around 1927.

8
The Italian Resistance in the Second World War

The first Russian films dealing with the Revolution were produced several years after 1917 and were necessarily influenced, if only indirectly, by the arguments concerning the origins and consequences of the Revolution. If we want to discover how present history is transposed to film, how events are screened immediately after they happened, we have to find another example. One of the most interesting examples is that of Italy, at the end of the Second World War. In the case of Italy, film production – which never stopped – escaped for a few months from the obligation of serving official propaganda purposes. In the rest of Europe, studios were closed or, in the countries where they were still active, they were used to legitimate the national war effort and to counter the possibility of questioning that role. Italy, after September 1943, was divided in two. The North was under German control.[1] The South, occupied by Allies who did not agree on the conditions of post-war rehabilitation in Italy, administered by politicians whose only preoccupation was to avoid defining the future form of government, was in a strange position. There was less raw material available, but due to the lack of official directives, the film-makers were in a position to deal with the urgent questions of the day. The majority of them did not take the opportunity and kept on shooting melodramas, comedies of manners, private theatricals, as they had been doing for many years. At the same time, a few men tried to produce films dealing with the country and people of Italy in 1944–5.

Obviously, filming wrecked villages and towns, starving children and women was contentious: Italians wanted to persuade the Allies that they had been treated as enemies by the Germans and that they had paid for the mistakes of the fascist era with their suffering. To what extent were they successful? We must admit that Italian films dealing with the war and the Resistance were much admired in the United States.[2] Did these films influence opinion in favour of the Peninsula? Some writers described the films as 'realist' – a misleading word often used to describe the Italian cinema in the 1950s. The films describing post-war Italy are no more 'real' than films dealing with the Risorgimento: they take their material from daily life, but by choosing, cutting, editing, they insert it into a subjective presentation of Italy. The war was still going on or had just come to an end, and film-makers were already using it as a source of material; in doing so, they acted as the first 'chroniclers' of Italy at war, they set a pattern that historians tend to ignore but that, at the time, people in Italy and elsewhere were involved in. Italian cinema provides us with the rare opportunity of studying a fragment of historiography in the making.

Who was guilty?

Defining the period is not difficult. Fourteen films dealing with the war were shot between 1944 and the beginning of 1946: there was then a gap of more than ten years, as if showing the war was considered improper;[3] thus we shall restrict our enquiry to the war itself and the immediate post-war period. But we cannot seriously discuss every film produced in that period: interesting though they are, I suggest that we eliminate those films which use the war as a backdrop for individual destinies or which add only certain battle sequences to an essentially fictional narrative.[4] We will consider only four films, two of which – *Aldo's Saying* and *Days of Glory* – are virtually unknown, at least outside of Italy.

The first was shot on a modest budget in Piedmont,[5] the second was produced in Rome under the control and with the help of the National Association of Italian Partisans, who gave the film-makers every assistance. Both films use the same kind of material: some footage taken by the partisans, numerous stills, sequences shot in the ruins and in devastated cities, some re-enacted scenes.[6] We are not given any new information in these films: the stills, which had been published in newspapers and magazines, were and are available in libraries, the commentaries, given in voice-over, consist of generalities about German atrocities and the valour of the partisans. However, the films are first-class items of evidence, for they show how Italians saw themselves, how they wanted the world to see them.

Aldo's Saying opens with Turin in ruins, showing photographs of executed hostages; we then go back in time, joining the partisans during the war. The sequence is reversed in *Days of Glory*, but we find the same elements: we are with the partisans; they are thinking of their friends and families, and we witness an arrest, we see houses on fire and dead bodies. The similarities between the two films are not limited to the opening sequences: in both films we travel through the mountains, designated by various signs, particularly by snow; we see leaves and we discover the partisans concealed by the foliage; partisans march past with military precision; montages of several political newspapers inform us that all political parties were active in the resistance. I will not continue with the parallels: I have said enough to make it clear that the two films use the same scenes, the same visual tricks, the same signs.

War crimes are frequently illustrated with stills, sometimes with filmed documentaries. Three sequences in *Days of Glory* dealing with the slaughter of the 'Fosse Ardeatine'[7] mix, in a pathetic manner, the opening of graves, the bodies, the relatives trying to identify clothing, photographs of some of the victims. There is an attempt to personalize the horror, to link the general descriptions of execution and torture with particular, easily identifiable individuals: this body, whose hands are still unbound, this crying woman, this mother who lingers in front of her son's coffin and slowly leaves, these young victims whose photographs are pinned on the wall. Why did Italy suffer so much tragedy? Germans are accused of arresting and executing many people, but the accusation is only made in voice-over, and the pictures themselves, backed by other texts, charge the Italian fascists with the crime. The punishment of fascists is re-enacted in both films: In *Days of Glory*, a well dressed man

191

THE HISTORY OF YESTERDAY

wearing hat and jacket is assassinated by a man in shirt-
sleeves; in *Aldo's Saying*, a fascist is court-martialled by partisans
in the courtyard of a farm and a volley of shots tells us that
there is no pity for the enemy. A long sequence in *Days of
Glory* recalls the fate of the former chief commissioner of Rome,
Caruso, who had been a mere tool in the hands of the Nazis
and was sentenced to death after the Liberation. The fascists are
guilty – so too are the women convicted of sexual intercourse
with the Germans; both films dwell on the closely-cropped
women's hair and *Days of Glory* adds (without pictures) that
'the beautiful ladies of Italy' welcome the Allies.[8] These
anomalies are puzzling. Why are Germans comparatively less
guilty than the fascists? Does the insistence on legal punishment
tend to prove that Italians mercilessly prosecuted the traitors?
Or does it make a distinction between the few people who supported the Germans and the majority of the Italian people who
resisted the occupying forces? And what about the women? Why
do both films stress their humiliation? And, if the films are
meant to demonstrate something, who is to be convinced? The
Italians themselves? The Allies? By studying two feature films,
we should be able to answer some of these questions – but we
must realize that our analysis exceeds certain limits; something
tells the viewer that he sees more on screen than he could put
into words.

Long live the Allies! Turin – liberated by the partisans –
welcomes the American troops. Both films clearly distinguish
between the liberation of the town, carried out by the Italians,
and the later arrival of the Allied troops. In an interesting slip
of the tongue, the commentator in *Days of Glory* announces
'the Allies' when we see, on screen, Italian 'bersaglieri' –
followed by American tanks. There is no manifest tendency to
reduce the Allied offensive to the minimum, but in practice we
chiefly witness the actions of the partisans.[9] Who are the partisans? Italians, from all walks of life. Most of the re-enacted
scenes are devoted to the partisans. In *Aldo's Saying*, a long
reconstructed sequence shows the meeting of the partisans for
the final assault to liberate Turin. It is a glorious spring morning.
Wearing jackets over their work clothes, people hurry along the
road; later we will also see country people – but first we stop at
the headquarters: a huge villa, surrounded by a park, with a

192

drawing room where a man plays the piano to pass the time before the attack. This sequence as a whole could be dismissed as a clumsy attempt to stage a situation and illuminate the social characteristics of the Italian resistance movement, but it does suggest another possible interpretation. We have said that the fascists – the leaders, the men who are court-martialled and shot – were 'bourgeois'. We might assume that the films place the bourgeoisie in conflict with the workers and the peasants, or at least, oppose a section of the middle class to the rest of Italy; but we are unequivocally informed that the resistance was led by the bourgeoisie. The working classes instinctively took the 'right' side – and on both sides of the conflict, the middle class assumed a leading role, as of right. This is no more than an assumption. If it is incorrect, it remains to be seen why the final meeting of the partisans was shot and edited in such an unexpected manner. I must add another comment, which slightly contradicts the earlier analysis: the clergy play a prominent part in the resistance, and not only in the various religious ceremonies, in which the armed partisans surround the priests, or in the commemoration prayers. A priest also appears heading a column of partisans through the snow, and we see a bishop cycling towards the German headquarters to negotiate the German surrender. Priests, like the middle classes, are often portrayed as natural leaders.

Finale: the recovery of Italy. The two films differ in the conclusions they draw. In *Aldo's Saying*, the partisans return to the mountains for a final visit; they bid farewell to the dead and part company. *Days of Glory* ends with tools, engines, motors – the rebuilding of Italy. In both cases, the films suggest the end of a nightmare, the resumption of normal life and the activities of peace-time. These films have often been criticized for their artificial, rhetorical style.[10] Certainly, the re-enacted scenes often look ludicrous, the dialogue sounds grandiloquent – but this in itself is revealing. The excesses and the falsehoods together beg puzzling questions – questions that remain unanswered but that cannot be ignored. At the same time, the films develop a clear, general line: Italy suffered martyrdom; Italian partisans rose and drove the enemy away; horror in the past, hope for the future, unity of the majority of the Italian people.

193

We now turn to the fictional films, but we will not contrast them with the two films we have just been discussing. The two films we are now going to study were produced at exactly the same time as the two others, with the same difficulties, the same shortage of film stock[11] – and one of them, *The Sun Rises Again*, was commissioned by the National Association of Italian Partisans.[12] Apart from these superficial likenesses, many episodes are similar in style to the films on the partisans; we might assume that the directors of the fictional films imitated the 'ingenuous' style of the non-fiction films, but we would be wrong, for two reasons: first, they had not seen the partisan films; and secondly, the films we have analyzed above are clumsy, but not ingenuous. The fictional films were produced by professional technicians and actors; the amateur film-makers involved in producing the partisan films achieved exactly the same results. The specificity of the fictional films, of course, lies in the story, which focuses on a few characters from start to finish. We will try to allow for this specificity, while considering how far these fictional films overlap with the non-fiction films.

Rome: Open City

Instead of giving a straightforward account of the films, I would like to get the reader to feel the 'variations' in intensity, the 'tempo' which makes certain moments look different from others.

1. Rome by night. The Germans encircle a block of flats: a man escapes by the terrace. The Germans, who are looking for the engineer Manfredi, search a flat. In his office, Major Bergman, head of Gestapo, is told that Manfredi has escaped.
2. The following day. Popular streets of Rome. Cold, weak light, demolished buildings. Women sack a bakery.[13] A pregnant woman, Pina, comes home with stolen bread; she meets Manfredi, who wants to be hidden and asks for Don Pietro, the parish priest. Marcello, Pina's son, fetches Don Pietro. Manfredi entrusts Don Pietro with meeting the partisans. Don Pietro goes to an underground press and gets money for the partisans (plate VIII) Digression: Marina, Manfredi's mistress, is surprised not to receive news from

him; she is visited by a troublesome German friend, Ingrid, who supplies her with drugs. We return to the popular district. Don Pietro speaks with Pina: she is a widow and she is going to marry Francesco, the man who has made her pregnant. Both leave. Don Pietro brings the partisans the money.

3. The same night. People in their flats. Explosion. People look through their windows. Children run in the twilight – they return home after blowing up a train. Major Bergman, in his study, congratulates the Italian chief commissioner for having identified Manfredi, who is head of the Committee of National Liberation.

4. The following day. Germans surround the block of flats where Pina and Francesco live. Manfredi escapes. Women and children are gathered together in front of the building. The Germans take Francesco away; Pina runs after them; she is shot dead. The partisans lie in ambush; the lorries carrying away Francesco and other resisters are stopped by the partisans; the prisoners escape. Manfredi and Francesco meet Marina in a restaurant; they go to Marina's home. Manfredi upbraids Marina for her drug habit. Marina angrily calls Ingrid.

5. The following day. Manfredi and Francesco meet Don Pietro, who will take them to shelter. While Francesco is waiting to say farewell to Marcello, his friends leave; two black cars stop at the pavement; the Germans force Manfredi and Don Pietro into the cars. The two men are questioned by Major Bergman. Marina is in the next room: after denouncing Manfredi, she was arrested to stop her from telling the partisans. Manfredi is tortured; he dies without speaking.

6. The following morning. Don Pietro is executed; after witnessing the execution, Marcello and his comrades go back to Rome (plate VIII).

The sun rises again

Milan. Megaphones announce that 'a disloyal king' has signed the armistice;[14] a young Italian soldier, Cesare, enters a brothel to dress in plain clothes; Germans encircle the house but Cesare escapes.

Autumn. Cesare comes back to his village. His father, who is the bailiff of the landlord and very satisfied with his position, would like his son to work at the brickworks. Refugees, whose houses have been destroyed, arrive in the village; American bombers fly over the country. Cesare becomes acquainted with a young working woman, Laura, whose father, foreman in the brickworks, is a leader of the local Resistance.

One day, Cesare and the parish priest, Don Camillo, while collecting firewood, catch Matelda, the landlord's woman, flirting with a young man. Cesare becomes acquainted with the landlady.

Later, Cesare has become the landlord's companion: he spends his days with his new friends, who fear being called up by the Germans and get ready to flee to Switzerland; he sometimes sees his brother Mario, a black marketeer, and Laura. Many workers rejoin the partisans. Laura persuades Cesare to join them but, as he is leaving, Matelda makes him stay.

Partisans stop the vehicles. One night, they seize a lorry that Mario has filled with flour and they distribute the sacks to the villagers. Cesare is displeased with their conduct.

Winter. The Germans occupy the village. Snow, cold, fear: the roads are empty. The Germans commandeer cattle, the partisans get ready for a rising. One evening, Mario is pursued and nearly killed by the villagers. As he has seen some partisans meeting in the church, he tells the Germans. The partisans escape and the Germans capture only Don Camillo; they also arrest Cesare who is in the street. Both men are chained to a stake and, by torch-light, the German commander gallops madly round them. The partisans attack, Cesare is rescued but a young partisan is caught. The Germans force all the villagers to get out and to fall into line; they drag Don Camillo and the young man between the lines of loudly praying villagers and then kill them.

Spring. Cesare is now with the partisans. Everybody speaks of the coming Liberation. Matelda tells Laura the Germans want to take the villagers as hostage whilst her husband tries to persuade Laura's father he has always been a partisan. The partisans settle in the village; the Germans attack but the partisans set the cattle at them. While fleeing the Germans shoot. Matelda, who is looking through the window, is killed.

People celebrate the Liberation. Cesare and Laura meet again.

Matelda is buried and the villagers say: 'The landlords also were hard hit by the war'.

Class war in the village?

The two films look very different. *Rome: Open City* begins and ends with approximately the same pictures: the town taken from outside, in long shot; many things have happened, many people have been tortured and killed but the city is still the same – the nightmare continues (plate VIII). *The Sun Rises Again* opens in a town overwhelmed with fear – but it ends in a village where the inhabitants take on a new lease of life. Is such an opposition very significant? Is it enough to distinguish one film from the other? If we study them thoroughly we very soon realize they are alike in many ways.

Both stories start with the arrival of a foreigner or stranger. Cesare has been abroad for a few years and has lost touch with the villagers; Manfredi, a Communist leader who has to keep constantly on the move, is at home nowhere. Notice that the stranger, who takes a fresh view of the things and who endangers the people who receive him, is a commonplace in Italian resistance films of 1944–6.[15] The strangers enter a disturbed society where rules and traditional habits are no longer effective. The first sequence in *The Sun Rises Again*, often dismissed as irrelevant, is on the contrary, a rather good introduction. A young soldier goes to the brothel and gets undressed not to make love but to escape; the whole of the Italian army seems to have found shelter there and the prostitutes, by delaying the Germans, protect the Italian men. The first daytime sequence in *Rome: Open City* starts with women and children sacking a bakery in front of a policeman; a passer-by asks the policeman: 'What are you doing' (by implication: 'Why are you not stopping them?') and the policeman replies: 'Unfortunately I am wearing my uniform' ('Thus I cannot take bread'); the policeman helps Pina to carry the stolen bread home and accepts two loaves in return. Looking around them, the outsiders see only the disturbance, which enables them to observe 'the seamy side' of society.

197

The films provide us with what we might call a 'social cross-section' of Italy at war (plate VIII), and both particularly insist upon the lower classes. Cesare first meets Laura when she is asking for someone to help her mend her heating; he enters the house and stops in amazement at the sight: 'Is this a private house or a dormitory?' The large family is crowded into one small gloomy room; the camera, panning slowly, picking out a few rudimentary objects – a table, a stove, a wash-bowl, some beds – contrasts the dark impersonal room and the few utilitarian objects. Cesare returns one night and finds exhausted people sleeping all round the room. In the building where Pina and Francesco live, we see the same promiscuity, with overcrowded flats, crying children, exhausted women. The poor are particularly affected by the war: many of them have lost their jobs,[16] prices are constantly rising, workers and countrymen can no longer afford food or coal. Other Italians do not suffer too much. Both films single out people with modest incomes, but they do so in different ways. *Rome: Open City* hints at it: men and women who are in league with the Germans, black marketeers – in other words, people at the margin of the social mainstream – lead a pleasant life. *The Sun Rises Again* looks at Italy with a more critical eye: the upper class lives as it did before the war; the film systematically contrasts the darkness of Laura's home with the comforts of Matelda's estate. The conflict is not only suggested – it is emphatically underlined. Cesare is divided between two couples, corresponding to the two worlds; his father and Matelda offer him a pleasant life, beyond war and suffering; Laura and her father urge him to fight for liberty. The first pair are deliberately associated with well-being and land ownership, the latter with factory work. Fleeing from bombed towns, refugees arrive at Matelda's and Laura's houses: at Matelda's, they enjoy the opportunity to rest in the countryside; at Laura's, they endure cold and hunger.[17] Here, a second difference between the two films is evident. In *Rome: Open City*, nearly all Italians are resistance fighters, at least in spirit; most of the time we are with the poor, but when Don Pietro is entrusted with meeting the partisans, he visits a rich tradesman and well-to-do craftsmen; Manfredi gets help from a middle-class man (the restaurant owner) as well as from workers. The poor people in *The Sun Rises Again* spontaneously resist, for their lives are in danger: the Germans enlist the men, and requisition food and tools; in the cold of their workshop, the brickworkers agree that they must fight 'to maintain our work and our future'; together they join the resistance. The landlord and his friends, on the other hand, ignore the situation or, when they are menaced, fend for themselves.

From this, we might conclude that the films give conflicting views of Italy, and that the second stages class war in a small Lombardy village, but this would only render an account of one aspect of the films. Effective though it is, the difference is balanced by similarities. First, those on the margin – the small group of outcast men and women – appear in both films; if we include in this category those policemen who assist the Germans, while never taking the initiative in repressing the partisans,[18] the main members of the groups are people like Mario, Cesare's brother, Marina, Manfredi's mistress, Lauretta, Pina's sister. The few traitors are very close to these characters and society reacts by banishing them. We have seen how Mario is treated by the villagers: let us add that Lauretta leaves her home and family, that Marina is discredited because she is a drug addict and a lesbian and that, at the end of the film, we gather there is no hope for her. Treachery looks like a shameful family disease and the marginals, who are not criminals, do not deserve to be punished.[19] The partisan, non-fiction films we analyzed earlier held members of the middle class responsible for the horrors of war and insisted upon the arraignment of traitors; in the fictional films, nobody is brought to trial. We cannot explain this discrepancy. It is well known that some leaders of the resistance, especially the Socialists and the members of the Action Party, called for a ruthless purge,[20] that the members of the Christian Democratic Party and the Communists[21] mitigated the purge and that many people who had supported the Germans managed to clear their names. Can we suggest that the two films anticipated the coming amnesty and pleaded not guilty for the whole of Italian society?

Whatever the answer may be, it is clear that the landlord in *The Sun Rises Again*, his wife, his friends are not traitors; they only show selfishness and irresponsibility. The first time Laura meets Matelda she tries to make her understand: she does not hate her or her riches, she simply wishes to end injustice. It is too early: Matelda does not listen to her, and shortly after that, Matelda, driving her cart, knocks Laura down. The women are now enemies, but they soon make it up. Two incidents tell us that they have become friends: when the Germans conduct a search in the village, Laura finds shelter with Matelda and the women sympathize; later, Matelda, learning of the German plans, tells Laura of them. What has happened? With the arrival of the Germans, the rich are in danger: the landlord is afraid of losing his wealth, Matelda is humiliated by the German officers, who treat her as a prostitute. Both rally to the resistance cause without being asked to prove their sincerity or to atone for their previous apathy. Italians are now united against the foreigner and the final sentence of the film, pronounced by the villagers, makes it clear that the rich will not be called to account. Resistance takes the same form in *Rome: Open City* and in *The Sun Rises Again*. In both films, we find workers as privates (Francesco in *Rome*, the brickworkers in *The Sun*), the railway employees as liaison officers, the foremen as non-commissioned officers (when Don Pietro goes to the underground press, he is welcomed by Francesco, but it is the foreman who gives him money and instructions); the priests act as a support system, helping the partisans and encouraging the people.[22] Whereas the fictional and non-fiction films differ in determining the liability for the martyrdom of Italy, they are consistent in describing the organization of the resistance and the hierarchy of responsibilities.

What does this secret army do? We witness two operations in each of the two films: all of them can only be described as miraculous. Remember the children led by a disabled boy, blowing up the train, and the partisans stopping German lorries in the middle of the town and rescuing the prisoners. The partisans attack the Germans in the village and free Cesare; later, although without proper weapons, they defeat the Germans by using cattle as a decoy. We discern an element of irrationality which can only be described as a miracle: actions, descriptions, which are supposed to be deeply rooted in contemporary experience are altered by the use of improbable, wonderful interventions. Miracles, it is true, have a fail-safe guarantee: at the end of *The Sun Rises Again*, there is a miraculous 'last ditch' rescue, but it is not by chance that this trite device is connected with providence,[23] for the religious involvement in these films is deep and potent. Insisting upon the function of the priests is not enough: it would be easy to object that film-makers were simply recounting actual experience. In a country divided between four political powers (fascist and royal governments, the Germans and the Allies) the Church was the only universally respected authority. The point is that the Catholic faith – Catholic sensibility might be better – is the best common denominator of the Italian people. Manfredi, who is a Communist, never speaks of his party or of his platform, whereas Don Pietro does not stop referring to Christian charity; if the two men understand one another, only the second speaks of his belief. It has often been noted that the distressing shots of tortured Manfredi picture him as a Christ – at least as one crucified – and we might add that the dying resister is blessed by the priest: 'You wanted to kill his soul,' the priest says to the Germans, 'You merely killed his body'. The Christian mark is even stronger in *The Sun Rises Again* where the execution of the priest turns into an outburst of mysticism; when the villagers are gathered by the Germans to witness the shooting, the camera first takes them in motion and in close-up: it is like a living wave which crosses the screen; they then come to a stop and the camera, now taking them in long medium-shot and in artificial light, with exaggerated darkness in certain parts and strong illumination in others, makes them look like statues; the priest starts intoning litanies, which the motionless crowd echoes; prayers make the viewer feel a 'spiritual wind' and he is confirmed in this feeling when he sees the Germans helplessly shouting and gesticulating around the still ardent villagers.

It is difficult not to interpret the execution as a collective offering, the two martyrs being two other Christs – and this leads us to wonder who are the victims in our films. Three Italians die in every picture: possibly an accident. But look: they are, every time, a priest, a resister (Manfredi and the young partisan), a woman (Pina, Matelda). The partisan deaths are unremarkable, for they too are soldiers. But what about the women? Pina, running after the lorry, has no chance of catching it; who shoots at her and why? The Germans are in flight, the nightmare is over when Matelda is killed. There is no narrative

201

necessity for the two women to be shot. Look at them, lying on the ground: both are photographed from above, with the feet in foreground, the head in the background, the skirt tucked up, the thighs conspicuous. The shots were carefully arranged, and chance played no part in the exposure of two half-naked women. In both films, Pina and Matelda were guilty of sexual transgression, Pina for being pregnant without being married, Matelda for having lovers. Let us draw a parallel with the non-fictional films: hair and sex, women and guilt. The series of victims is well arranged, in ascending order: war = fighting-men have to die. Why is there a war? Because somewhere there is guilt.[24] Offence: sex; punishment: the death of the 'bad women'.[25] If this were not enough, a sacred offering, the death of a priest is also necessary.[26]

Historiography again

The films we have been discussing can be seen as descriptive social films, as 'fictional documentaries': a social community, homogeneous, or apparently divided, facing the war. If we go deeper into the analysis, we realize that this dimension, which is important and should not be underestimated, is paralleled by another, less manifest dimension, the presentation of war as a religious ordeal. In this respect, the films are very similar, but can they be described as equivalent? Of course not. Their conclusions are completely different, with the ordeal continuing in one case, ending in another. Yet, the finales should not be isolated from the rest of the film. The films portray the same people, the same society, the same circumstances. The difference lies in the way these elements are brought into play – in other words, in the style of historiography.

We shall illustrate this by using two parameters we have already resorted to – time and point of view.[27] *Rome: Open City* is shot in full-length time as I have tried to make clear in my account of the story: we follow the characters in their daily life; there are no breaks – or, if there are, they coincide with periods in which nothing happens. The whole of the story occurs in less than three days – from the end of one night to a morning about fifty years later. Thus, we are always in the present, we have no difficulty in identifying the moment of the day or in situating one character with regard to another, according to the hour. There are many characters whose point of view we adopt in turn. This multiplication of points of view makes us feel distressed with Marina, worried with Manfredi, hopeless with Francesco: but, simultaneously, we are outside the fiction, for we know too many things; we are immediately informed when the Germans establish the identity of Manfredi, when Marina betrays him. We are not in the story – and the story is not in history, since there is no evolution – Italy has been placed in a motionless present. No wonder that Don Pietro's sacrifice is useless: Rome in out of time, beyond salvation.

The Sun Rises Again makes use of undetermined time, together with breaks. At first, we suppose there is a precise chronology, with the succession of autumn, winter, spring, summer. But we must remember that the armistice was signed in September 1943 and the North liberated in April 1945. Seven seasons instead of three – the filmic time does not correspond with the main stages of the war. If the succession of various sequences, interrupted by breaks, gives the idea of constant change, the film clearly indicates a basic division into two parts: before and after the Germans. We emphasized one aspect of this partition when we spoke of the apparent class struggle and of the subsequent unity of the Italians, but that was only a minor point compared with the modification which occurs in the filming process. With the arrival of the Germans, the style, which had thus far been 'realistic' (the word seems rather vague: I mean by it, no use of visual tricks, neutral light, the camera moving according to the motions of the characters or to the changes occurring in the story) becomes suddenly 'expressionist' with a systematic use of long shots, a rough opposition between long-shots and close-up, a sophisticated use of black and white, darkness and lightness, a clever distribution of shadow. We have entered another space – the world of the devils, the world of evil and, if we take into account the sexual implications, the world of the unconscious. I wonder if the reader has noticed that we see the film from the point of view of a character who is by no means a 'hero'. Cesare is constantly exposed to various, contradictory influences: having no precise idea of the situation,

203

offering no resistance, he eventually escapes uninjured. Thus, the evolution, the constant motion of history – a history that never stops – is doubly staged: the ordeal has been endured, the life of ordinary people resumes.

Two conceptions of history, two modes of writing – of staging it. The same view of Italian society produces two conflicting models of historiography, for differences in historiographical traditions and patterns do not reside in the choice of elements but in the way of distributing (of editing) them.

Notes

1. Mussolini was overthrown and arrested in July 1943; he was then rescued by the Germans and he established the 'Social Republic of Italy', commonly known as 'Republic of Salo'.

2. *Rome: Open City* (titled *Open City*) was shown in New York on 25 February 1946 and made a big hit; it ran for more than one year in New York and is said to have brought in about $500,000; it had a very good press; reviewers agreed that the fiction sounded like a documentary (see *New York Times*, 26 February; *New Yorker*, 2 March; *Life*, 4 March); Agee, although criticizing the story, was enthusiastic (*The Nation*, 4 March). From Mussolini's overthrow onwards, Americans were always less hard on the Italians than the English, because of the numerous Italian families living in the USA. Did films like *Rome: Open City* influence American opinion? Or did they make a hit because Americans were well disposed towards Italians?

3. It may be interesting to give more precise information about the number of produced films dealing with the war: 1945: 5; 1946: 9; 1947: 1; 1948: 2; 1951: 1; 1953: 1; 1955: 1; 1959: 3; 1960: 6; 1961: 14. Eight films from 1947 to 1957 makes less than one film every year. 1959 is marked by a revival, with a maximum in 1961 and a good score in the following years. At the end of the 1950s, the Cold War had moderated and screening the fascism or the Resistance was no longer considered as adopting a definite position regarding the Communists and their place in Italian political life. On the other hand, the neo-fascist Italian Social Movement was growing stronger and some politicians favoured a right-wing government supported by the fascists; the large protest against the 'opening to the right' included meetings, rallies and production of films upon the end of the fascism.

4. Three of the ten eliminated films of 1944–5 are very interesting, they are: *A Day of Life, To Live in Peace, Païsa*. The first is a timeless psychological story which would not be anachronistic during the Risorgimento or even during the American Civil War; the second is a comedy of manners with the war as a tragic background. *Païsa* is, on the contrary, entirely centred on the war and the sufferings of Italy, from spring 1943 to winter 1944; it has been excluded only because it is less known than *Rome: Open City* and because discussing five films would have taken too much space.

5. It is said to have been shot by a cameraman who, shortly before that, used to work for the Republic of Salo; this is typical of the political confusion of post-war Italy.

6. For the detecting of the fakes, see W. Hughes, 'The evaluation of film as evidence', in *The Historian and Film*, especially pp. 58–9.

7. On 23 March 1944, a partisan attack killed 32 German soldiers in Rome; as a reprisal, Germans arrested and killed 335 Italians in 'Fosse Ardeatine', caves situated in the suburbs of Rome.

8. Does this suggest that the women who made love with Germans were ugly? Or that they had their hair cropped to become ugly and to be expelled from the ranks of the 'beautiful ladies of Italy'?

9. For a general view of Resistance in cinema, see A. Fleming, 'The cinema and the second world war: the Resistance,' *University Vision*, 1972, 8, p. 37 and Roger Manvell, *Films and the Second World War*, London, 1975. It has often been noticed that, during the Cold War, the Italian resistance was denigrated and the partisans called brigands and murderers. But that was not yet true in 1944 – and especially in the north; thus, it is difficult to pretend that our films only aimed at picturing the partisans as good, disciplined soldiers. One might suppose that the movies anticipated the disparaging of Resistance – but it is no more than an hypothesis.

10. See the text quoted by Guido Fink in 'Flashback; films and history', *Cultures*, II, 1, 1974, pp. 138–9.

11. The film-makers of *Rome* had so little film stock that they intended to make a short. The shooting began in August 1944, two months after the liberation of Rome.

12. Ordered in October 1945 the film was shot between December 1945 and March 1946.

14. It might be interesting to study 'intertextuality' (see p. 162) in this scene: had the queue for food and the women's claim for bread pictured in *The End of St Petersburg* and *October* influenced the film-makers? They influenced in turn other film-makers who adapted their screening in other films on war.

14. The armistice was announced on 8 September 1943. In the north

Germans arrested and often killed Italian officers; they tacitly allowed soldiers to go back home; in June 1944, they tried to enlist Italians, many of whom joined with the partisans.

15. Five of the six sketches of *Païsa* are built upon the disturbances brought about by the foreigners; in *One Day of Life* a nunnery is upset by the arrival of partisans; in *To Live in Peace* the calm of a village is interrupted when American soldiers ask to be hidden from Germans.

16. Pina: 'I used to work at the textile factory. They sacked me. The Germans carry everything away.'

17. The film is filled with simple, short indications which, all together, make a large panorama. For instance, we catch a glimpse of a miserable funeral procession, shot in long-distance; the deceased was a poor man who died of starvation – but we do not know anything of him; he has no importance and the shot only tends to create a sensation.

18. The chief commissioner of *Rome* would like to have Manfredi arrested by his men but the Germans forbid him to do it; the Italian soldiers assigned to Don Pietro's execution do not shoot at him and he is killed by a German; the policemen of *The Sun* protect Mario, keep the partisans from getting food but do not fight with Germans.

19. Mario is killed during the Liberation but he is never charged with having helped the Germans nor brought to trial which differentiates him from the men sentenced in the non-fictional movies.

20. Action Party: a small party of intellectual resisters who were to disappear shortly after the war.

21. The amnesty for fascists was promoted by the Communist leader Togliatti while he was Minister of Justice.

22. While collecting firewood, Don Camillo confesses to having become a priest without religious belief; he does not want to renounce since he is in a position to help people.

23. Compare with the function of chance in *The Birth of a Nation*, above, pp. 94–95.

24. Don Pietro to Pina: 'Are we sure not to have only got our deserts?' War as a punishment . . .

25. Another direct binding between sex and punishment: Manfredi is caught and tortured because of his mistress.

26. We have characterized Don Camillo's execution as 'collective offering'; we might use the same words for Don Pietro since he is escorted by the children he used to take care of.

27. See above, p. 50 and p. 55.

Conclusion

Before I finish I should like to draw together the issues dealt with in this book. I have tried to discuss two subjects at the same time – history and the cinema – and perhaps it has been too much. Although it has a certain superficiality, our study may help us to understand what 'history' means for historians as well as for 'ordinary' people and to predict in which direction historians should begin to explore film messages.

It is always difficult, for a research worker, to consider the social significance of his own research. We historians are fully aware of our individual techniques but remain puzzled when asked: 'Why are there historians? Why does society give them the right (which means, at the same time, the money) to impose an "historical" view on "reality"?' Using a Weberian expression, I would say: 'Why are we legitimated? What do people who do not practise history look to us for?'

Our research on historical films begins to answer this question. The majority of the films we looked at were made without any help from historians. Nowadays, it is common to hire one or maybe several 'historical experts' but, before the 1960s, directors and screen-writers thought they could do without any external assistance; nevertheless, they were perfectly sure they filmed 'good', 'true' history.

Most of the films have revealed rather poor material – dates, portraits, conventional scenes, events – and we have realized that specialists and non-specialists have very different notions of history; details which are, from our point of view, rather minor (clothes, furniture, room settings) become, in pictures, a proof of 'historical value'; a few names of men, battles, countries, learned in school books, rediscovered from the names of squares or streets or from historical films are the whole of history for many people. And they are convinced that historical events

207

happened – because scholars are paid to study them and teach them in school. In short, by studying the past, by writing books that nobody but themselves will read, historians prove that there is 'history'.

As professionals, we would like to criticize the ideas, the stereotypes, the simplifications in the films, but we must resist this temptation, accept the view of history that we are given for what it is and try to explore the historical knowledge of the film-makers. It is admitted, today, that the history of a society is not only the description of its social and economic structures but, at the same time, the description of its intellectual and cultural background – and historiography is one of the frameworks in which people situate their present and their future.

By looking at historical films, we are able to describe the 'basic historical knowledge' of a society. Novels and plays would help us, but in a different way, by descriptions and by various sets of names. Remember Napoleon in *October:* he is named once only, and rather late in the film, as 'Bonaparte'; we have studied all the connections made between Napoleon, Bonaparte, the Old Russia, the British intervention and so on and I think it worth remarking that, for the film-makers, Russian audiences were obviously able to recognize Napoleon or to distinguish Bonaparte from Napoleon. Were they right? That is another question we are not able to answer – but we might get a better view of the United States in 1914, or Soviet Russia in 1917 by describing the historical prejudices of film-makers, as revealed in their films.

Now we face another question: why do people who are not interested in 'scientific' investigation think they are concerned with history? What did the film-makers or their audiences expect from a return to the past? We have noticed that in the films we discussed, history is a mere framework, serving as a basis or a counterpoint for a political thesis. History is no more than a useful device to speak of the present time, but it does that in various ways.

Finishing and showing a film cannot be compared to publishing a book; many books are published every year whereas, during certain periods, there are very few films. During the 1950s in the United States, films were not exactly rare but in 1915, or in Soviet Russia in 1927 a new film was an important and acclaimed event. Wilson is said to have asked for a private showing of *The Birth of a Nation* in the White House and many influential Americans found it necessary to see the film and to express their opinion; *October* had been ordered by the Council of People's Commissars but was completed without direct government control: the 'official' if 'heretical' view of the Revolution had a limited but unquestionable importance in the first years of the Stalinist period.

Before the television era – that is, before the middle of the century – there were very few films directly concerned with questions of the day. It would be helpful to know the reasons for this lack of interest in the present, but that is not our problem here. Of course, politics reappeared in other contexts, for instance in satirical films or in historical films; as we saw in the course of studying certain historical films, present-day concerns were fully involved in films ostensibly dealing with the past. The main advantage of history is that it allows people to describe the present time in a free, imaginary way. If it is easy to discover the references to contemporary politics, it is more difficult to locate the ideal world dreamed of by the film-makers; we could say: 'These men remade, transformed society so as to show it as they would have liked it to be', but the films discussed prove that things are more complicated; *The Birth of a Nation* and *La Grande Illusion* stage two dreams whose functions and relations to the present time are totally different.

La Grande Illusion is an answer to the difficulties of French political life. France in 1937 was strongly divided between right and left, Communists and Nationalists: a civil war seemed imminent, especially as Spain was already a battlefield between fascists and the popular front. In that context, a return to the First World War was a means of rediscovering the days when the French were united. France was also surrounded by hostile countries and threatened by the possible outbreak of the Second World War, a prospect that many Frenchmen wanted to avoid. If France were neutral, uninvolved in a new international conflict, what would it be like? As we said after looking at the film, the most interesting theme is the prophetic vision included in the film: France seen as a prison camp, kept out of the battle; here, the dream is more than the mere denial of reality: it is an anticipation, a rehearsal of the future.

209

The Birth of a Nation is more a phantasm than a dream. By presenting much evidence, it makes the audience think it wants to look back on the past but, as we saw, it reduces history to a series of events, modified by chance or by human action, which seem to have no cause – as North and South, which looked at first rather different, eventually prove to be almost identical. The film, which is entirely devoted to the black problem, carefully separates the Civil War from the racial question; it then paints an horrific picture of black domination and, as a counter-point to that fanciful description gives us an idealized portrait of the old endogamous white American family. In that case we cannot isolate clear-cut connections between the content of the dream and the reality of contemporary political or social life. Is it always necessary to demonstrate that a myth, a fantasy are deeply rooted in the surrounding 'concrete', 'real' world? I know that many historians think so, but I believe that the question is worth considering a little more thoroughly. Films like *The Birth of a Nation* convince me that, occasionally, film-makers conceive or perhaps rediscover purely 'artificial' myths.

Are there only two types of dreams, either connected to present life or completely separated from it, in historical films? I cannot give a considered opinion here, but I am convinced that a more detailed study would reveal many other types of dreams or phantasms.

We all know of important, well-paid, busy men who claim they spend their few moments of leisure in reading history books and, we can be sure they do not do that to let themselves drift into dreaming. History is considered as a serious topic; it is taught at school because it is a discourse, defining a stretch of logically linked sentences, giving an explanatory model for studying societies, suggesting a set of rules, a series of categories which allow people to classify men and events. We historians do not pay enough attention to the common patterns of causality, used by people who are not interested in historical research. Is their discourse planned around a very simple model, such as: 'A caused B which caused C . . .' or is it more elaborate? In the Risorgimento series of the 1950s, in films like *The Horse Soldiers* or *Long Live Italy*, history is no more than an attempt to locate some events against a backdrop and to arrange them in order.

We would find the same standards, the same rules of explanation in the majority of the films. We are so familiar with this type of direct, linear causality that we might think it is a characteristic of all films and fail to investigate systematically the historical mechanisms used in the films. Only when we are confronted with an irregular usage of time and causality are we obliged to realize that time and causality are two basic components of any historical discourse; by looking at *October* and *Napoleon Bonaparte*, by comparing them with other films on the same period, I wanted to make it clear that some films – which are, I must admit, exceptions – can challenge the conventional conception of historical time.

This is not a privilege of the cinema: historical books and articles, novels and plays would no doubt lead to similar conclusions. But what is peculiar to the cinema is the simultaneous use of several systems of expression. When the makers of a film meet to prepare it, they choose a subject and they write at least the outline of a text which has its own logic, sometimes a moral, and which tends to show one or more things. The story and the combination of pictures may or may not have the same meaning. The Risorgimento series of the 1950s, although it includes a great many films, is homogeneous with respect to narration, shooting, editing process. On the contrary, the films dealing with the French Revolution, the Russian Revolution, the Italian Resistance, which stage the same events, differ in the way they order these events – thus they stage different conceptions of historiography. In *The Sun Rises Again* the apparent class struggle developed in the story can be explained only if we take into account what the pictures suggest about the final unification of all Italians. In *Rome: Open City* the story stresses heroism in the face of an ordeal, and the picture treatment emphasizes the unavoidable continuance of the ordeal. I am of course summarizing far too much here and more subtle shades of meaning are needed. All I have done is to point out a direction for research. Allow me to repeat this as a conclusion. I think that one of the tasks of an historian is to find out how the people of a period in the past felt, understood and perhaps expressed the problems of their time. The records most commonly used are in written form; they tell us how people expressed their questions, but they do

211

not necessarily express *what* they felt, and we must also consider other sources which escape the formalization implied in writing. The cinema forms a specific documentation, which has no equivalent in any other period; up to now it has been rarely and wrongly used. I have tried to give you examples of what can be expected from it, but I am sure that if any of you take this path you will go further than I have done.

Index of Films

213

ITALY

Aldo's Saying   1945

Production: Turin Partisans, with the help of A.N.P.I.
(National Association of Italian Partisans).
Production team unknown. Photography: Fernando Cerchio.
Cast: Piedmont Partisans.

The Brigand of the Wolf Cave   1952

Production: Cines–Lux Film.
Director: Pietro Germi. Screenplay: Tullio Pinelli, Fausto
Tozzi, Pietro Germi. Photography: Leonida Barboni. Music:
Carlo Rusticelli. Editor: Rolando Benedetti.
Cast: Amedeo Nazzari (Captain Giordani), Saro Urzi
(police superintendent), Fausto Tozzi.

Days of Glory   1945

Production: Titanus–A.N.P.I.
Directors: Mario Serandrei, Giuseppe de Santis, Marcello
Pagliero, Luchino Visconti. Photography: Massimo Terzano,
Giovanni Pucci.

1860   1933

Production: Cines.
Director: Alessandro Blasetti. Screenplay: Alessandro
Blasetti, Gino Mazzucchi. Photography: Anchise Brizzi,
Giulio de Luce. Editor: Ignazio Ferronetti, Allesandro
Blasetti.
Cast: Non-professional players.

The Leopard   1962

Production: Titanus–Pathé Cinéma–S.G.C.
Director: Luchino Visconti. Screenplay: Suso Cecchi
d'Amico, Pasquale Festa Campanile, Enrico Medioli,

Massino Franciosa, Luchino Visconti. Photography: Nino Cristiani, Enrico Gignitti, Giuseppe Macari. Music: Nino Rota. Editor: Mario Serandrei.

Cast: Burt Lancaster (Prince Salina), Alain Delon (Tancredo), Paolo Stoppa (Don Calogero), Claudia Cardinale (Angelica).

Long Live Italy   1960

Production: Cineriz–Tempo Film–Galatea–Francinex.
Director: Roberto Rossellini. Screenplay: Sergio Amidei, Diego Fabri, Roberto Rossellini. Photography: Luciano Trasatti. Music: Renzo Rossellini. Editor: Roberto Cinquini.

Cast: Renzo Ricci (Garibaldi), Paolo Stoppa (Nino Bixio), Franco Interlenghi.

The Lost Patrol   1953

Production: Vides Film–Diana Cinematografica.
Director: Piero Nelli. Screenplay: Piero Nelli, Franco Cristaldi. Photography: Alfieri Caneparo. Music: G. Petrassi. Editor: Enzo Alfonsi.

Cast: Non-professional players.

The Red Shirts   1952

Production: G. Prandi.
Directors: Goffredo Alessandrini, Franco Rosi. Screenplay: Enzo Biagi, Renzo Renzi. Photography: Leonida Barboni, Mario Scarpelli. Music: Enzo Masetti.

Cast: Raf Vallone (Garibaldi), Anna Magnani (Anita Garibaldi), S. Reggiani, Carlo Ninchi.

Rome: Open City   1945

Production: Excelsa Film.
Director: Roberto Rossellini. Screenplay: Sergio Amidei, Federico Fellini, Roberto Rossellini. Photography: Ubaldo Arata. Music: Renzo Rossellini. Editor: Eraldo da Roma.   215

Cast: Aldo Fabrizi (Don Pietro), Marcello Pagliero (Manfredi), Anna Magnani (Pina), Maria Michi (Marina).

The Sun Rises Again   1946

Production: C.V.L.
Director: Aldo Vergano. Screenplay: G. Aristarco, Giuseppe de Santis, Carlo Lizzani, Aldo Vergano. Photography: Aldo Tonti. Music: Giuseppe Rosati. Editor: Gabriele Varriale.
Cast: Vittorio Duse (Cesare), Elli Parvo, Massimo Serato, Lea Padovani.

The Wanton Countess (Italian title: *Senso*)   1954

Production: Lux Film.
Director: Luchino Visconti. Screenplay: Luchino Visconti, Suso Cecchi d'Amico, Giorgio Prosperi, Carlo Alianello, Giorgio Bassani. Photography: G. R. Aldo, Robert Krasker. Music: Anton Bruckner's VIIth Symphony. Editor: Mario Serandrei.
Cast: Alida Vali (Livia Serpieri), Farley Granger, Massimo Girotti.

SOVIET RUSSIA

The End of St Petersburg   1927

Production: Mejrabpom Russ.
Director: Vsevolod Pudovkin. Screenplay: Nathan Zarki. Photography: Anatol Golovnya.
Cast: A. Tchistyakov, Ivan Tchuvelyov, V. Obolensky, Vera Baranovskïa.

October   1928

Production: Sovkino.
Director: S. M. Eisenstein. Screenplay; S. M. Eisenstein, G. Alexandrov. Photography: Eduard Tisse.
Cast: A. Nikandrov (Lenin), N. Popov (Kerenski) and non-professional players.

UNITED STATES OF AMERICA

The Birth of a Nation   1914

Production: D. W. Griffith–Epoch Producing Corporation. Director: D. W. Griffith. Screenplay: D. W. Griffith, Frank Woods. Photography: George Willy Bitzer, Karl Brown. Music (for the sound version): J. Carl Breil, D. W. Griffith. Cast: Henry B. Walthall (Ben Cameron), Ralph Lewis (Austen Stoneman), George Siegman (Sylas Lynch), Lilian Gish (Elsie Stoneman), Mae Marsh (Flora Cameron).

Gone with the Wind   1939

Production: Selznick International Pictures. Director: Victor Fleming. Screenplay: Sidney Howard. Photography: Ernest Haller, Ray Rennahan, Wilfrid M. Cline. Music: Max Steiner. Editor: Hal C. Kern. Cast: Vivien Leigh (Scarlett O'Hara), Clark Gable (Rhett Butler), Leslie Howard (Ashley Wilkes), Olivia de Havilland.

The Horse-Soldiers   1959

Production: John Lee Mahin. Director: John Ford. Screenplay: John Lee Mahin, Martin Rackin. Photography: William Clothier. Music: David Buttolph. Editor: Jack Murray. Cast: John Wayne (Colonel John Marlowe), William Holden (Major Kendall), Constance Towers (Hannah Hunter).

Bibliography

Theories of Film

ARNHEIM, R. *Art and Visual Perception* (Berkeley, 1966).
ARNHEIM, R. *Film as Art* (London, 1958).
BALAZS, B. *Theory of the Film: Character and Growth of a New Art* (London, 1952).
EISENSTEIN, S. M. *Film Essays and a Lecture* (New York, 1970).
EISENSTEIN, S. M. *Film Form* (New York & London, 1963).
EISENSTEIN, S. M. *The Film Sense* (London, 1970).
EISENSTEIN, S. M. *Notes of a Film Director* (New York, 1970).
GESSNER, R. *The Moving Image* (New York, 1968).
KRACAUER, S. *Nature of Film: The Redemption of Physical Reality* (London, 1961), reprinted as *Theory of Film* (London, Oxford & New York, 1965).
KULESHOV, L. *Kuleshov on Film* (Berkeley, 1974).
PUDOVKIN, V. S. *Film Technique and Film Acting* (New York, 1970).

Film Language

BAUDRY, J. L. 'Ideological effects of the basic cinematographic apparatus' (*Film Quarterly*, Winter 1974–75).
BELLOUR, R. 'To analyze, to segment' (*Quarterly Review of Film Studies*, 1976, 3).
DAYAN, D. 'The tutor code of classical cinema' (*Film Quarterly*, Fall 1974).
ECO, U. *A Theory of Semiotics* (London, 1976).
FLEDELIUS, K. 'Considerations about content analysis in audio-visuals' (*Untersuchungen zur Syntax des Films*, 1979, 1).
FLEDELIUS, K. 'Film analysis: the structural approach' (in M. J. Clark, ed., *Politics and the Media*, Oxford & New York, 1979).

FLEDELIUS, K. 'Syntagmatic film analysis with special reference to historical research' (*Untersuchungen zur Syntax des Films*, 1979, 1).

KRAMPEN, M. 'Iconic signs, supersigns and models' (*Versus*, 1973, 3).

METZ, Ch. *Film Language: A Semiotics of the Cinema* (Oxford, 1974).

METZ, Ch. 'Methodological propositions for the analysis of the film' (*Screen*, 1972, 14).

PANOFSKY, E. 'Style and medium in the moving pictures' (in D. Talbot, ed., *Film: An Anthology*, Berkeley, 1967).

PRYLUCK, C. 'Structural analysis of the motion picture as a symbol system' (*Audiovisual Communication Review*, 1968, 4).

RUSSEL, L. 'Cinema, code and image' (*New Left Review*, 1968, 49).

WOLLEN, P. *Signs and Meaning in the Cinema* (London, 1972).

WORTH, S. 'Cognitive aspects of sequence in visual communication' (*Audiovisual Communication Review*, 1968, 2).

WORTH, S. 'The development of a semiotic of film' (*Semiotica*, 1969, 3).

Film and Mass Communication

BENJAMIN, W. 'The work of art in the age of mechanical reproduction' (in *Illuminations*, New York, 1969).

ISAKSSON, F. & L. FURHAMMAR, *Politics and Film* (London, 1971).

JARVIE, I. C. *Movies and Society* (New York, 1970).

KRACAUER, S. *From Caligari to Hitler. A Psychological History of the German Film* (Princeton, 1971).

McQUAIL, D. (ed.) *The Sociology of Mass Communication* (Penguin, 1972).

PETERSON, R. C. & L. L. THURSTONE, *Motion Pictures and Social Attitudes* (London, 1933).

SCHRAMM, W. (ed.) *Mass Communications* (Urbana, 1960).

SCHRAMM, W. & D. F. ROBERTS, *Process and Effects of Mass Communication* (Urbana, 1971).

SEYMOUR-URE, C. *The Political Impact of Mass Communication* (London, 1974).

TAYLOR, R. *Film Propaganda, Soviet Russia and Nazi Germany* (London & New York, 1979).
TUDOR, A. *Image and Influence: Studies in the Sociology of Film* (London, 1974).
TUNSTALL, J. (ed.) *Media Sociology: A Reader* (London, 1970).
WOLLEN, P. (ed.) *Working Papers on the Cinema: Sociology and Semiology* (London, 1969).

The Film as Historical Evidence

ALDGATE, A. *Cinema and History: British Newsreels and the Spanish Civil War* (London, 1979).
BARSAM, R. M. *Nonfiction Films: A Critical History* (London, 1974).
BURNS, E. B. 'Conceptualizing the use of film to study history: a bibliofilmography' (*Film and History*, 1974, 4).
BAWDEN, L. A. 'Film and the historian' (*University Vision*, 1968, 2).
BUSCOMBE, E. 'America on screen? Hollywood feature film as social and political evidence' (in M. J. Clark, ed., *Politics and the Media*, Oxford & New York, 1979).
DAVIES, PH. J. 'Film as a teaching resource' (ibid.).
ELTON, A. 'The film as source material for history' (*Aslib Proceedings*, 1955, 7).
FERRO, M. '1917: history and the cinema' (*Journal of Contemporary History*, 1968, 4).
FIELDING, R. *The American Newsreels, 1911-1967* (Norman, Oklahoma, 1972).
FIELDING, R. 'Archives of the motion picture: a general view' (*Journal of the Society of Archivists*, 1966, 4).
GRENVILLE, J. A. S. *Film as History. The Nature of Film Evidence* (Birmingham, 1971).
GRIFFIN, P. 'Film, document and the historian' (*Film and History*, 1972, 2).
HOUSTON, P. 'The nature of the evidence' (*Sight and Sound*, 1967, 2).
ISENBERG, M. T. 'Historians and film' (*The History Teacher*, 1974, 7).
LOVELL, A. & J. HILLIER, *Studies in Documentary* (London, 1972).

MARWICK, A. 'Archive film as source material' (The Open University, *War and Society* course, Milton Keynes, 1973).

O'CONNOR, J. E. 'Historians and films: some problems and prospects' (*The History Teacher*, 1973, 6).

PONTECORVO, L. 'Aspects of documentary and newsreel research' (The Open University, *War and Society* course, Milton Keynes, 1973).

PRONAY, N. 'British newsreels in the 1930s' (*History*, 1971, 56 & 1972, 57).

PRONAY, N., B. SMITH & T. HASTIE, *The Use of Film in History Teaching* (London, 1972).

ROADS, C. H. *Film and the Historian* (London, 1969).

ROADS, C. H. 'Film as historical evidence' (*Journal of the Society of Archivists*, 1966, 4).

SMITH, P. (ed.) *The Historian and Film* (Cambridge, London & New York, 1976).

SMITH, P. 'Political style on film: Neville Chamberlain' (in M. J. Clark, ed., *Politics and the Media*, Oxford & New York, 1979).

STREBEL, E. G. 'French social cinema and the popular front' (*Journal of Contemporary History*, 1977, 12).

TAYLOR, R. 'From October to *October*: the Soviet political system in the 1920s and its films' (in M. J. Clark, ed., *Politics and the Media* Oxford & New York, 1979).

TAYLOR, R. *The Politics of the Soviet Cinema, 1917–1929* (Cambridge, London & New York, 1979).

Index

The more important page references are printed in bold type

INDEX

Open University, 10, 35 nn. 4, 14, 36 n.
17
Our American Cousin, 114 n. 11

Paisa, 205 n. 4, 206 n. 15
Palermo, 57, 62, 66 n. 11, 118, 134,
135, 136, 137
panning, 11, 155
Papal States, 133
parallel montage, 85, 90
Paramount, 35 n. 8, 36 n. 15
Paris, 15, 67, 68, 159
Pathé, 10, 11, 12, 35 n. 8
Petersburg, battle of, 84, 86, 87, 90, 96,
103, 128, 161
Petrograd, 28, 159, 171, 173, 177, 183
pieces of evidence in films, **61–64**,
169–170
Piedmont, 127, 128, 133, 190
Pinchot, A., 64 n. 2
Pines, J., 114 n. 15
point of view, **52–55**, 57, 65 nn. 9,
10, 125, 126, 202, 203
Poland, 48
Popolo d'Italia, 138 n. 2
Popular Front, 67
Poulsen, J., 37 n. 25
Proletkino Studio, 187 n. 8
Pronay, N., 11, 35 nn. 6, 7, 10, 11, 13
propaganda in films, 159, 186
Provence, 70
Prussia, 68, 127
Pudovkin, V., x, 163, 187 n. 10
punctuation in films, 85

readiness, 44, 49
Reconstruction, in American history,
32, 83, 110
The Red Shirts, 51, **127–133**, 137, 215

Reed, J., 23
referent, 9
Renoir, J., 28
Ricordi, G., 127
Roads, C. H., 9, 34 n. 2
Robespierre, M., 51, 76, 78
Roman Empire, 116
Rome, 64 n. 4, 116, 127, 130, 133, 138
n. 3, 139 n. 10, 190, 194, 195, 203,
205 nn. 7, 11
Rome: Open City, **194–195**, **197–206**,
211, 215
Rouget de Lisle, C. J., 48, 68, 69, 77,
80 n. 6
Russia, 11, 17, 23, 159, 163, 208
Russian Civil War, 175
Russian Communist Party, 181
Russian middle-class, 160

Russian Revolution, 19, 144, **159–188**,
189, 209, 211, 216
Rus Studio, 187 n. 8

St Petersburg, 163, 165, 168, 177
Savoy, House of, 45, 46, 55, 128, 135,
140 n. 16
Segestum, 135
Senso, see *The Wanton Countess*
sequence, 8
The Servant, 24
1788, 80 n. 9
Shakespeare, W., 41
Sherman, W. T., 60, 93
shortened time, 57, 168
shot, 7, 8, 33, 85
Sicily, 55, 56, 57, 62, 117, 118, 119, 121,
127, 134, 135, 136, 137, 161
signs, **160–166**, 168
Slade Film History Register, 4, 7, 34 n.
1
Slavery, 94, 105
Smith, P., vii
Social Republic of Italy (Republic of
Salo), 204 n. 1, 205 n. 5
Somme, 81 n. 9
sound-track, 8
Soviet, 178, 179, 185, 186
Soviet Russia, 18, 162, 166, 208, 216
Soviet Union, 175, 176, 177, 183
Sovkino, 187 n. 9
Spain, 45, 209
Spanish Civil War, 19
The Spanish Civil War, 10
Stagecoach, 26
Stalin, J. V., 17, 181, 185, 186
starting point, 59, 60
Stendhal, 75, 81 nn. 15, 16
Stevens, Th., 32, 33
Strebel, E. G., 81 n. 10
Stroheim, E. von, 147
structural analysis, 33
subtitles in silent films, 86, 88, 97
Sumner, Ch., 32, 33, 88, 114 n. 10
The Sun Rises Again, **195–206**, 211, 216
symbolical time, 60, 75, 78, 126, 174
symbols, 160, 166, 167, 171, 172

Talleyrand, Ch. M. de, 80 n. 1
Taylor, R., 186 n. 1, 187 nn. 7, 9
Ten Days that Shook the World, 23
Terror, 47, 83
Third International, 176
Third Republic in France, 48
The Thousand, Garibaldi's followers,
50, 117, 118, 119, 126
The Times, 8
Tisse, E., 175

225